BOB CHICKEN

A PASSION FOR THE BIKE

Graeme Fife

BOB CHICKEN
A PASSION FOR THE BIKE
By Graeme Fife

Copyright © Graeme Fife, 2005

Published by Robert J Chicken Snr

First Published 2005

ISBN 0-9551225-0-3

www.bobchicken.co.uk

Set in 12pt /14pt Times New Roman
Typesetting and Design by Prime Secretarial Services, London, England

Printed and Bound by Butler and Tanner Ltd, Frome, Somerset

CONTENTS

To Penny

In proud memory of her Father she never met,
Lieutenant Colonel Cedric William ('Bill') Chicken,
Adjutant to General Rees,
Commander of the 14th Indian Division ('the dagger division')
killed on active service in Burma December 1943,
eldest brother of *Bob Chicken*

AUTHOR'S NOTE

For help in the writing of and research for this book I am most grateful to a number of people who were exceedingly generous with time, reminiscence and expertise: Sid Barras, Keith Bingham, Alan Cater, Cedric Chicken, Christine Chicken, Robert Chicken, Peter Crabtree, Philip Darnton, David Duffield, Luke Evans, Richard Hallett, Keith Lambert, Pat Liggett, Phil Liggett, Carlton Reid, Yvonne Rix, Chas Roberts, Brian Robinson, Bill Squance, Dave Yates, Monty Young.

Andrew Maxwell-Hyslop was a superb editor, a rare bird, indeed – intelligent, sharp and extremely courteous at every stage. For the final shaping, streamlining and vast improvement of the book, Mark Tassell of Prime Secretarial Services is largely responsible and his services are much appreciated.

Bob and Christina Chicken have not only been of huge encouragement and support to me in this, and other, undertakings, their hospitality has been wonderfully generous.

Graeme Fife
Sevenoaks, July 2005

FOREWORD

By Phil Liggett

Throughout his adult life, Bob Chicken has fought his own battle in supporting the cause of cycling and has never taken 'No' for an answer in his championship of the British and European Bicycle Manufacturing Industry.

Bob has the mentality and application of a top-flight cyclist, which he never was. As any competitor will tell you, the hardest of athletes to beat in any race is the one who believes in himself, can see his goal and goes for it full out.

As recently as this decade, Bob – in the face of opposition from the Bicycle Association, of which he is a member – put his own money on the table in a bid to establish an international bicycle exhibition in the centre of his beloved City of London. He is not only a Freeman of the City, a matter of great pride to him, but he also belongs to the Worshipful Company of Marketers, an ancient City Guild. When those who were less committed to the idea of the exhibition saw this tall, determined figure marching towards them, you could see them shrinking into doorways: they knew they would have no argument with his intention to win through and the only response must be to go along with him.

The concept was taken on board by Jack Morris, Chairman of the Business Design Centre, a venue named by *The Times* as 'London's Jewel in the Crown', and, in September 2001, a truly magnificent and, in the event, very successful, cycle show was staged there. It is now more popular than ever. This was the triumphant result of a long and often lonely battle waged by Bob, one that would have been conceded years past by many lesser mortals.

I first met Bob – it is a shock to think of it – some thirty-three years ago, when, as a rookie journalist, I was asked to visit his home and interview his son Cedric who, thanks to his connection with the Peugeot company in France, had initiated and was now managing the import of their bicycles to the UK. I had noted the address, a prestigious road in north London, special street lighting etc. Not the sort of place, I told my editor, that someone from a bed-sit in Muswell Hill should be strolling down.

Bob invited me in and plied me with questions about my job with *Cycling* magazine; it was some time before I got round to talking to Cedric. Naturally inquisitive, Bob was clearly very keen to find out where I fitted into the cycling scene but it was equally obvious that he wanted above all to promote cycling, as a sport and a pastime, in Britain as well as to see his company thrive.

In 1971, I became race director of The Milk Race, sponsored by the Milk Marketing Board and the National Dairy Council. I knew that Bob had already put money into several of the race competitions and, in 1973, the R.J. Chicken company also began providing a fully-equipped service car. Bob's lavish support and generosity, including marvellous hospitality for visitors to the race, made a huge difference to the two-week stage race, famous world-wide.

Bob's love of Tottenham Hotspur F.C. – he has been a paid-up supporter for 77 years – should not be held against him. On alternative Saturdays in the 1980s, you'd find him entertaining customers and friends in the West Stand box. In more recent years, Bob undertook Executive Membership of the Tottenham Team Sponsors, under the name of R.J.Chicken and Sons, and he has been match sponsor of a number of games since. Surely Bob's determination to succeed must eventually rub off on the Spurs.

When Bob told me, in 1973, that his sons Cedric and Robert were returning to the fold to join the family company, I saw the delighted twinkle, the deep satisfaction, in his eyes.

Today, R.J.Chicken and Sons, under the joint direction of Cedric and Robert, with a long-serving staff, enjoys prosperous times and a promising future in a highly competitive market, fully backed by many of Europe's leading manufacturers of components who have, like RJC, weathered and survived big upheavals.

Perhaps, in the years ahead, my friend and fellow cyclist, author Graeme Fife, will write a second book bringing the story fully up-to-date. But, such a book would not have been possible without Bob Chicken, doyen of the bicycle industry, an industry he has loved and to which he has been devoted all his adult life.

Phil Liggett MBE
Hertfordshire 2005

SYNOPSIS

This is an account of the life and work of Bob Chicken, a man who has been at the forefront of the bicycle industry in the UK since the end of the Second World War. The story draws in a wider social history both of Britain since the War and of the decline in its manufacturing base, in particular that of the cycle industry. The loss of so many famous brand names and marques is a sad reflection of wasted expertise, lost opportunity, muddled vision. The onslaught of competition from the Far East cannot be minimised, but neither can the stolid failure of so many once-powerful companies to adapt and change in a fluctuating market.

The book gathers in many threads linking the making of the machine to its use for sport, leisure and as a practical mode of transport. The story is as much a celebration of the bicycle as of Bob Chicken's involvement both in the cycle industry and in championship of the cause of the bicycle and cyclists in the UK…the wheel's spin and the wind's song.

MEETING MR. BOB CHICKEN

Audere est facere
'To dare is to do', motto Tottenham Hotspur F.C.

As the author of this book, I should declare an interest. This is not a ghostwritten account of Bob Chicken's life. I have limited the story here to an account of his role as a central figure and moving spirit in the British bicycle industry since the end of the War. As an animating and generative force in both the industry and cycle sport he occupies a unique position. Put simply, he has devoted much of his life and work to the furtherance of the cause of the bicycle in Britain. It is that aspect of his deeds and being which I have hoped to convey here.

Bob Chicken has exerted such an influence in the cycle industry since the end of the Second World War, and for that alone I admire him. This is hardly a controversial statement. I don't know anyone remotely connected with bikes and cycling who does not admire him. He stands for much that we all espouse: independence of spirit, as typified in the emancipation the bicycle brought to men and women in the early days. He stands for strength of mind and purpose in his elected aims, traits central to anyone who has ridden through sleeting rain onto the lower slopes of the Galibier, 'the Giant of the Alps', for instance (as I have) and on into swirling snow and so over the col. He stands for good humour, conviviality, friendship and comradeship which are at the heart of the cycling fraternity. Above all he stands for the pledge of his word, the honour of an undertaking agreed, even if not signed; in short, he does what he says he will do, and such loyalty – to bond and faith - is rare in the commercial world, in any world. It is what I value especially highly in him, as indeed in anyone.

I have told the story as accurately as I possibly can whilst accepting that I do have a bias: I am passionate about bicycles and cycling and count as valued friends many people in the world of cycling, whether ex-pro riders, journalists, men of the industry, or the pals with whom I have shared miles of road and hours of conversation on and about the two-wheeled machine which is so much a part of our lives.

We met at a Wednesday lunchtime meeting of the Pedal Club in January, 2000, when he was President and I was guest speaker. It was the start of a friendship and association which has strengthened over the past five years. I soon realised that, clearly, the fabric of his life's work has been remarkable, not least because the work is still unfolding, his energy, at 83 years old, blasting away at the inevitable decelerations and depletions of age with rumbustious impatience. Then, one afternoon at the first Cycle Show in Islington, 2001, he asked me if I would consider writing the story. He knew that I had done a similar thing for George Francis, the great boxing trainer. Indeed, Bob's son Cedric had told his father that he really should get the story told; because I had written about cycling, because we had become friends, Bob put the idea to me. At the time I was occupied with other things and soon to be embroiled in the writing of a big history of the French revolutionary Terror. The account of less bloody revolutions would have to wait but, in the late summer of 2004, I began.

This is not a conventional biography, apart from a pretty full account of the years Bob spent in the Royal Navy during the War. I call him Bob throughout, largely because it seemed to be needlessly coy to deny our friendship by the more customary neutral distancing of 'Chicken'.

Bob's commercial interests have been many and various but the driving impetus of his work has been involvement in the bicycle industry and on that I have concentrated. There was another, I hope equally compelling, reason for this: the demise of the British cycle industry, in lugubrious parallel with that of motorcycles and cars, since the end of the War, owing to a number of factors, is a melancholy symbol for the general diminution of Britain's standing in the world. Caught between loss of Empire and search for a new role, between the 'special relationship' with America and almost innate suspicion of Europe, we straddle a bizarre No Man's Land, like a shell-shocked lone survivor stumbling about a battlefield, trumpet in hand, sounding Reveille to the emptiness, the silence, the wafting, acrid smoke, the desolation.

 Thus, in tune with Bob's own sense of opportunities missed or cast away, I have made the book an elegy to a loss of identity, a loss of purpose, a loss of stature, threading through the more factual narrative of the disappearance, one by one, like disillusioned players in a game of Musical Chairs to an accompaniment of Rule Britannia, of bicycle manufacturers, frame builders, component manufacturers, some with names which once resonated across the globe. For even today, as 'Hoover' is universally a vacuum cleaner, 'Thermos' a vacuum flask and 'Biro' a ballpoint pen, 'Raleigh' is generic for 'bicycle' in Africa,

Since Bob spent some time in the Lebanon after gruelling duty on the Malta convoys, I have also included a brief account of the background to the prevailing state of affairs in the Middle East, following the First World War, as well as a summary of the progress of the Second World War in Greece and the Balkans, leading up to the Battle of Sirte, in March 1942, in which Bob was involved.

And, because I was writing an account of how the bicycle very nearly disappeared, it also seemed to me important to explain where the bicycle came from in the first place. This draws in the social context and the historical milieu in which the velocipede came to being, established itself, became hugely popular and then succumbed, inexorably, to the advent of the racier, speedier, noisier motorcar. Noisier ? Let no one overestimate the importance of noise in the matter of invention; vis à vis technology, noise is crucial. For example: the entire military arsenal has, for centuries, been loaded with decibels as well as ammunition. Decades if not centuries after the invention of the primitive firearm - arquebus, hackbut, matchlock, wheel-lock, flintlock and blunderbuss, the longbow of Agincourt and Crècy delivered the clothyard arrow, a deadlier missile than the lead bullet, with greater accuracy at higher velocity, greater range and vastly superior rate of fire.

Why, then, did the longbow cede place ? In part because it didn't go 'bang'. So, the archer's skill was lost and the boys got their toys. If noise doesn't count for anything, why else are our ears today constantly assailed by a barrage of electronically-processed squeaks, bleeps, notespreads and barps to signal that a vehicle is reversing, a computer is cobbling programme settings, a car's seat belt is not fastened, a single mobile phone is ringing to alert an entire railway carriage of passengers - sorry 'customers' - that the owner is about to announce to the world and his wife that he/she is on a train ? Noise, noisome noise.

The first three chapters of the book, therefore, sketch the story of the bicycle, in its various epiphanies as a transport of delight and sport, of usefulness and affordable purchase, from its invention to the eve of the Second World War. Because so much of the history of the bicycle has to do with technological brilliance and invention, I have devoted a chapter to two of the seminal figures in the development of components, in particular to the man whose name has always been synonymous with excellence and the best in the *European* tradition, that is, after all, the root tradition of the bicycle: Tullio Campagnolo. There is racing, too, and the dogged shying away of the British authorities from the highest attraction in cycle sport, road racing, one of the greatest free shows on earth, available in Europe but hardly at all in Britain.

Bob Chicken has always supported that root European tradition. Not for sentimental reasons, but rather as a natural evolution for Great Britain, gradually divested of her colonies in the aftermath of the War, as a partner in Europe rather than some fading superpower in a world that was so rapidly changing. But Britain has consistently and to her great loss, resisted the advances of Europe, like jilted Miss Haversham, grieving for the groom who, in changing circumstances, thought better of what she had to offer.
 But, it is not all solemn. The forays into Europe had their lighter side.
June 1994. Morning. The coach park in South Mimms Service Station, close by Bignell's Corner on the A1, formerly a famous meeting place for cyclists and start point for stage

races. In a coach hired by RJ Chicken and Sons sits a group of twenty-six prominent members of the cycle trade and five journalists invited by Bob and his sons, Cedric and Robert, on a spree to Holland, to visit the Vredestein tyre factory at Doetinchem near Arnhem. The mission ? To look round the Vredestein headquarters, take notes, report on the Vredestein operation and the Chicken involvement with the Dutch outfit and have a bit of a beano, not necessarily in that order of priority.

The coach doors shut, the driver pulls out onto the motorway and the charabanc party heads for Harwich and the ferry to Hoek van Holland. The traffic is light, the day is young, the ambiance is jovial. Half an hour into the journey someone says: 'Where's Bob ?' Cedric looks round. Robert looks round. Everyone looks round. No Bob ? Ah. No Bob. Head of the event. Bit of a problem. Must have left him behind.

What to do ? Stop ? Wait ? Go back ? Bit late for that. Cedric ?

'He's got his car. He'll follow on. He'll catch us up. We left in plenty of time.'

'You sure ?'

'Probably.'

'Possibly.'

'He'll catch us up. Press on.'

Harwich, later that same day.

The coach waits in the entrance to the ferry terminal. Bob parks his car in the car park, walks up to the coach and taps on the door. The door opens to admit him. What followed next, namely the exchanges between Bob and his two sons, had best be left unrecorded in detail. A clinical summary will do. Suffice it to say that Bob, having given vent to a certain weight of spleen and remonstration in the matter of going into the South Mimms Services to pay a bill having first told Cedric specifically to wait for him, only to emerge and find that he had, inexplicably, been abandoned, *sans* means of contacting the fugitive coach, the company proceeded through customs and on board the ferry without further ado.

Tempers cooled.

Varsseveld. Evening. The journalists depart from the hotel mob-handed, bound for a local bar. They drink as much beer as they can, a joyous task prematurely scuppered by the barman announcing that the bar had run out of beer. The intrepid hacks move on to another bar. Curiously, the same thing happens there: different barman, same announcement. In Dutch. The small town boasts, alas, only one more bar and when the journalists have squeezed it dry, too, drained its capacity to the very lees, they return, beerily but now beerless, to the hotel where Bob and the others, oenophiles all, have been doing their own best to rattle the wine racks. In the words of one of the journalists, Richard Hallett, 'they were so pissed they didn't recognise us'. In my view this is surely a calumny. A partial calumny at the very least. It is undoubtedly true that Bob and company may have been, by this stage of proceedings, in highly convivial spirits, full of bonhomie and a cheery disposition not to care too much about anything much, not least due to a generous consumption of the best that Holland has to offer in the way of red wine, (not great) and this may have induced a certain impairment, if not of vision then, frankly, of any interest in whoever it was blocking the view across the hotel bar in such an unruly fashion. Blurred shapes. Blurred shapes moving in strange patterns of motion. Leaning over. Lurching. Shuffling. Swaying about as if tossed in a wind, except that there was no wind. It is, however, also undoubtedly true, that a gaggle of journalists who have just rendered the entire beer provision of Varsseveld null and void are not going to be best placed to adjudge of the level of clarity in anything at all, whether it be someone else's optical powers or the distance between one bar stool and the next.

Morning.

The Vredestein courtesy coach is due at 8.30 outside the hotel. The party of invited passengers duly assembles and boards, The coach drives off, once more with a single absentee yet to be identified. Bob has claimed his place early. Once bitten…The roll is called. The missing guest finds a name. Richard Hallett, still asleep, has missed the bus. He will, of course, subsequently claim that his tardiness was deliberate. 'Have you ever *been* round a tyre factory ?' he said to me. 'I've had less boring experiences in Asda.'

When he does finally surface, up through the fathoms of hangover, Hallett phones the factory and apologises profusely for his dereliction.

Bad mistake.

The Vredestein people are graciousness itself; they will send a car instanter to collect him, he will be hardly delayed at all. He will, they assure him, despite misplacing the official transport, nonetheless still enjoy full benefit of the guided visit to the tyre factory. He puts the phone down and groans. However, luck is on his side. Does he deserve luck to be on his side ? Probably not, but then, I have never been treated to a tread by tread tour of a tyre factory.

The car arrives driven by one of the Vredestein employees, gathers up Hallett and they drive off, up the motorway, sailing haplessly past the exit to Doetinchem. This blunder entails a round trip of some 80 miles to the next available exit and back to the exit giving ingress to Doetinchem and the Vredestein HQ, almost too late for any but a whistlestop curtailed tour of the factory.

That evening…

There's more to that part of the story, but I think I had better get on, for it is a big story and Bob's part in it a large one.

Graeme Fife

Sevenoaks- February 2005

STEEL WHEELS
AND DIAMOND FRAME

A little over a hundred years before the steel guns of the Second World War fell silent, an English engineer, Henry Bessemer, was conducting experiments to find stronger materials for the manufacture of gun barrels. In 1856, the year the Crimean War ended, he read a paper to the British Association, in Cheltenham, describing what became known as the Bessemer process for the decarbonisation of iron and the manufacture of high-grade steel.

Steel, which is tougher, more malleable and more durable than iron and takes a finer edge, had been known for aeons. To produce the basic metal, raw iron ore is melted and cast in moulds known originally as 'sows', for the main channel into which the molten metal ran, and 'pigs' for the smaller offshoot moulds. Hence 'pig [properly sow] or cast iron' which can be made quite hard although the harder it is the more brittle it becomes. In early manufacture, the best iron, known as 'wrought [ie malleable, workable] iron', contained very little slag – refuse matter separated from the metal by smelting - and was highly resistant to shock but comparatively soft. Steel, being almost devoid of impurity, combines hardness with elasticity. The intrinsic impurities in pig iron can be eliminated by oxidisation and, in all the old refining processes, iron oxide, in the form of ore, mill scale or iron silicate slag (basis cinder), acts as the vehicle for introducing oxygen into the pig iron.

The first mention of the metal recorded by the Oxford English Dictionary refers to a line in the Anglo-Saxon poem *Beowulf*. The root of the Teutonic word from which it is derived is the same as that of 'stay' meaning 'firm, rigid' and an early manufacturing process, known as blister steel (because the resulting metal had a blistered surface), was probably discovered by accident in old forges. A stone box filled with charcoal into which are packed bars of wrought iron is heated for several days at full red. The iron absorbs enough of the oxygen content of the charcoal's carbon to become steel. The carbon content imparts hardness, wear, resistance and strength. However, it also renders the metal infusible, ie impossible to melt.

It occurred to Bessemer that the necessary oxidisation for purifying the ore could be taken directly from the atmosphere if a blast of air were blown onto or through melted pig iron. By experiment he discovered that the stream of air not only purified the iron but, quite against expectation, neither cooled nor froze the liquid ore. The metal stayed hot enough to remain molten, even when the carbon had been evacuated. What remained after cooling was pure iron which, until then, could *not* be melted because of the carbon content. The whole reaction required only a few minutes; at the end, an ingot of mild steel could be cast ready for the forge or rolling mill.

It took some years of trial and error before the process became a commercial success, but Bessemer's method for producing cheap steel revolutionised the engineering industry. In 1868, 110,000 tons of Bessemer steel were produced in the UK and, by 1888, production peaked at 1,700,000 tons. Also in 1868, another engineer, William Siemens, born in Germany but naturalised as a British citizen in 1859, had hit upon a method of producing mild steel of exceptionally trustworty quality. A good grade of pig iron is melted on an open hearth; to this is added some selected wrought iron scrap which alloys with the pig iron. More wrought is added until the carbon content is reduced to the desired percentage, mainly by dilution. Large-scale factory production of high-grade steel coincided kindly with advances in the development of the bicycle and its manufacture for a mass market.

The precise history of the bicycle's invention is notoriously difficult to pin down. There is the famous sketch – probably bogus - by one of Leonardo da Vinci's pupils, Giacomo Caprotti, c.1493, of what might be a prototype, a scribble attributed to a mediaeval monk perhaps nodding at the contemporary belief that cherubim and seraphim scooted about the ether on wheels, but these are fanciful ideas, merely, not solid artefacts. In a stained glass window in the Stoke Poges church near Windsor, dated 1642, there is an image of a contraption similar to a Celeripede which appeared in France in 1791.

In that year, responding with élan to the revolutionary temper of the time, a Monsieur de Sivrac reputedly demonstrated what he called a *Célérifère*, 'Swift Bearer', in the gardens of the former Palais Royal in Paris, which, in good republican form, had been renamed Palais Egalité. By means of rigid vertical forks, de Sivrac mounted two large wheels on a horizontal wooden bar to which he fastened a padded saddle. A rider could sit astride this *Célérifère* and walk it forward at some speed.(1) Perversely, the English called it Celeripede, 'Swift foot'.(2) Within a few years, the egalitarian Revolution having succumbed to the single-minded political will of Napoleon Bonaparte, the *Célérifère* reemerged as the *Vélocifère*, 'Speedy Bearer', and a club of dandies ran races on it along the Champs Elysées. The Tour de France belatedly followed suit in 1975 and the advent of the hi-tech scooter for use by besuited executives and lecture-bound students in the Paris traffic recalls the simplest of means to faster locomotion: wheels combined with feet, as, too, another contemporary Parisian fad, roller blades. Indeed, the Oxford English Dictionary actually defines the early velocipede as 'a kind of roller skate'.

The immediate disadvantage of de Sivrac's crude conveyance was that the fixed front wheel made steering cumbersome if not hazardous. In 1817, the agriculturalist Baron von Drais de Sauerbrun of Mannheim refined the original French design. He made the front wheel of the *Vélocifère* manoeuverable by passing the fork through a socket in the wooden bar and, as Master of the Woods and Forests to the Duke of Baden, scooted across country, through woodland, over hill and dale on his 'dandy-horse' as an Englishman called it. The first bicycling gamekeeper, forsooth.

Keeping tabs on legal ownership for profit was, at the time, haphazard. Eager exploiters of a good wheeze were quick to pounce. For instance, an article *Evolution of Cycle*, in the *Strand Magazine* of 1892 states that: 'Mr Dennis Johnson…a coachmaker at 75 Long-acre [in Covent Garden, London] took out a patent for this dandy or hobby-horse in 1818.' Keen, therefore, to capitalise on his ingenuity and pre-empt plagiarists, von Drais brought his brainchild to Paris, the cultural hub of continental Europe, where the French, ever eager to Gallicise, called it a *Draisienne*.

1. Some writers dismiss the de Sivrac episode as spurious, a yarn spun by the historian Baudry de Saunier in 1891.

2. Carlton Reid, editor of *Bicycle Business* bought a modern version, also in wood, of de Sivrac's paddler for his children and reckons that, starting on it, any child can learn to master bike-riding in a morning.

A sleeker model followed - six-spoked equi-sized wooden wheels with iron tyres, light-flanged wrought iron front and rear forks, a curved frame bar with carved horse's head as a finial, a long, quilted saddle and handy steering piece – which clearly prefigures the modern machine. In a long letter to his brother and sister in America, begun on Valentine's Day, 1819, the poet John Keats writes:

> *The nothing [ie worthless novelty] of the day is a Machine called the Velocipede.*
> *It is a wheel-carriage to ride cock horse upon, sitting astride and pushing it along with the toes, a rudder wheel in hand – they will go seven miles an hour.*
> *A handsome gelding will come to eight guineas, however they will soon be cheaper, unless the army takes to them.*

That very month, the city of London Magistrates of Police banned the Velocipede 'on account of the crowded state of the metropolis'. However, bucking the law, Regency bucks roared about Brighton and the roads leading to the capital on the dandy horse, periodically in uproarious company with the massively corpulent Prince Regent, and the machine enjoyed wide popularity in Germany, England and the USA during the 1820's and 30's. The English model had a curved thin metal steering rod which extended over the front wheel and, bent to horizontal, was then attached to the hub. In front of the saddle sat a raised rest for the forearms. There were even three-wheeled versions with a small wooden platform mounted at the rear to accommodate a chair upon which could sit the fashionable lady whom the perspiring beau velocipedist wished to impress with promenades in the park. Being seen was the thing. Fashion, novelty, *le dernier cri*. The military *didn't* adopt the dandy or hobby-horse, however. Perhaps the gay blades, the exquisites and swells of the frivolous post-Waterloo 20s who careered about on it with reckless abandon lent the toy too fey an image, too effete for sterner, more manly functions, initiating an early prejudice against the two-wheeler. Had the strategists in the Army Office in Horse Guards' seen a use for it, the objective of achieving superiority in warfare at all costs being a prime spur to inventive ingenuity, who knows how much sooner the bicycle would have taken shape. A *Punch* cartoon of 1874 shows a squadron of Light Dragoons mounted on high bicycles, with the caption: MORE ECONOMY. A hint to 'Government' – a cheap remount for Light Dragoons. Another, in 1887, depicts 'Scouts [on bicycles] chased by cavalry…a Sociable towing a stretcher mounted on four wheels, The Ambulance…Rudge'sWar Cycle – a quintuple with rear-mounted Gatling gun…a bike-propelled shed with rifles poking out of loopholes, The Armour-Plated Cycle…a lone army cyclist pointing a revolver at a Zulu brandishing his assegai: "Surrender".'

The intrinsic problem was transmission, a means of translating the muscle power of the legs directly to the motive power of the wheels. In 1839 or 1840, (the date is disputed) a Scottish blacksmith, Kirkpatrick Macmillan, devised a mechanism which replicated that of early textile spinning wheels. He constructed a velocipede with vari-sized wheels; to the hub of the larger front wheel he connected treadles by way of rods and cranks. These treadles, similar to those used to drive early sewing machines – and more of them later – converted reciprocal leg movements into the rotary motion required to make the wheel turn. For the first time, the rider could lift his feet off the ground during motion and in 1842, having proved his machine's worth over the 14 miles from his home in Courthill to Dumfries, Macmillan embarked on an epic 140 mile trip to Glasgow. The story that Gorbals police fined him five shillings for mounting the pavement and injuring a child is almost certainly apocryphal and evidence of more early prejudice. On his journey, Macmillan bowled along stretches of roads once described by a compatriot John Loudon McAdam as 'loose, rough, perishable, expensive, tedious and dangerous to travel on' but now boasting a much better surface. For, in 1823, the redoubtable road trustee of Ayrshire brought to fruition experiments in what became known as 'macadamisation', roads constructed of small, broken stones and raised above the level of the adjoining land for better drainage. This system had been pioneered and perfected by Roman military engineers two millenia earlier, to expedite the rapid advance of their all-conquering legions.

Macmillan did not patent his invention – he probably could not afford to - and in 1845 another Scot, Gavin Dalzell, a Lanarkshire cooper, produced a similar machine with the treadles driving the rear wheel. (Almost there but not quite.) On this pedal cycle, Dalzell claimed to have raced and beaten the Royal Mail coach, which was bound by statute to cover a minimum ten miles every hour.

In 1861, Pierre Michaux, a manufacturer of perambulators in Paris was asked to repair an old wooden Draisienne. Whether the idea came in a flash or as the result of long brooding isn't known, but Michaux decided it must be possible to improve the antiquated steed by fixing levers directly to the hub of the front wheel. (The more immediately force can be applied to the hub around which the wheel turns, the more efficiently that pressure is translated into motion. The slacker the linkage, the more wasteful of energy.) His son Ernest suggested a crank 'like that of a grindstone' to which could be attached rotating pedals and the two of them converted a *Vélocifère* belonging to M. Brunel, a Parisian hatter, into what the English called a boneshaker, from the bruising effect of negotiating cobbles on solid tyres. Michaux's machine, like many prototypes, was a limited success. The awkward posture of the rider, feet stretched out towards the larger front wheel, (36 inches, the rear at 30 inches) was inefficient: turning the pedals imposed considerable strain on the hips and pelvis while steering involved twisting the whole upper body. Nevertheless, the advent of pedals brought the solution closer and Michaux Père et Fils made (and sold) 142 vélocipèdes weighing 59 lbs in 1862 at their tiny factory on the Champs Elysées. Two brothers, the Oliviers, both engineers, seeing the commercial potential, first of all injected a huge financial investment into the Michaux concern, then expanded it and finally took it over as the Compagnie Parisienne des Vélocipèdes. By early 1870, the 500 factory hands operating 57 forges at the huge works near the Arc de Triomphe, were producing 200 machines daily. The wheel hubs were fitted with ball-bearings, invented by Jules Suriray, Superintendent of Prisoners' Workshops, in 1869 the year that the word 'pedal' as part of a bicycle first appears in English. This simple but brilliant contrivance greatly reduced friction on axle bearings and contributed much to the increased efficiency, and speed, of the bicycle.

When the Michaux exhibited their *vélocipède* at the Paris Exhibition in 1867, the Paris agent of the Coventry Sewing Machine Company, Rowley Turner, took one back to Coventry and persuaded his firm to manufacture a large batch of the machines to supply the demand the Michaux operation could not, at the time, satisfy. Turner's foresight was timely. The ruinous Franco-Prussian War of 1870-1, (Paris was besieged and fell to von Moltke's invading Germans in January; the Commune rose shortly afterwards) put not only the Olivier firm out of business - Michaux had taken a pay-off and left - but also around sixty other manufacturers of vélocipèdes in Paris. Accordingly, the renamed Coventry Machinists Company Ltd went into full production to supply the demand the Parisians could no longer meet. (3)

The word 'bicycle' made its first appearance in a report in the *Daily News* dated 7 September 1868 referring to 'Bisycles and trisycles [sic] which we saw in the Champs Elysées and Bois de Boulogne this summer'. The journalist was no scholar. The Classical Greek is kuklos, anglicised to cuclos or cyclos – as in Cyclops 'Round Eye'. The bi- for 'double' is actually Latin, from Greek di-. The French who, for the moment, were having to buy their machines from across the Channel, picked up the English word but, typically, gave it their own flavour in an affectionate diminutive and spoke of a *bicyclette*, 'a wee bicycle'.

---

3 Another sewing machine manufacturer, Newton, Wilson and Company of London and Birmingham also diversified into the making of velocipedes. The first patent on a sewing machine was granted to Elias Howe of Massachussetts in 1846. Several imitations of his invention which infringed his patent followed, notably that of Isaac Merritt Singer, whose commercial instinct and nose for publicity attached his name indelibly to the housewives' friend rather than the now largely forgotten name of its true begetter.

In February 1869, one John Mayall had ridden the 53 miles from London to Brighton on a Coventry Machinists' velocipede in about 15 hours. Cancelling out the publicity boost this feat delivered it, the company suffered a considerable blow soon afterwards when their brilliant works foreman, James Starley, a design genius, quit to set up his own company at the St Agnes Works in Coventry. From there in the following year, as the garrison of the mighty French fortress of Sedan, the entire French army and their commander, the Emperor Napoleon III, surrendered to the encircling Prussians, Starley launched his radical rethink of the Michaux solution to the problem of transmission: the Ariel bicycle, 'Fitted with Lever Tension Wheels, India Rubber Tyres, Improved Rudder, Registered Cliptail Sliding Spring &c'. With a front wheel over twice the size of the rear wheel and the saddle fitted to a sprung scrolled frame rod almost perpendicularly over the front hub, the rider's legs could develop a natural pumping motion, as in treading water, and transmit near full power direct to the revolution of the wheel.(4) The Ariel was fitted with a centre steering head to replace the old boneshaker's socket type, which had a tendency to swing round and trap the rider's leg against the frame. Starley devised other innovations in the quest of a lighter machine which could deliver a smooth ride: rubber-covered oblong wooden pedals, instead of heavy cast brass and triangular shaped, so as always to present a face to the rider's foot; footrests on

stays for freewheeling; a light, open-work steering handle made of gunmetal, an alloy of copper and tin or zinc; a mounting step. Rubber tyres replaced iron. British colonial possessions in the Far East had provided a ready supply of rubber, eagerly exploited by the rubber manufacturer Thomas Hancock, who founded the trade in india rubber.(9) In 1843, he discovered vulcanisation, the use of sulphur to harden rubber at a high temperature.

---

4 The size of the front wheel actually varied because it had to match the inside leg measurement of the rider, crotch to instep, as with trousers.

The suspension steel wheels and the first round rubber tyres, hard on the tread, spongy on the inside, made for a smooth enough ride but the wooden spokes were, inevitably, very rigid and, in 1874, Starley, who had also just launched his 'Europa' sewing machine, introduced tensioned wire spokes, set tangentially to the hub to resist the torque of pedalling and give a truer run to the wheel. A *Punch* cartoon of the time has a country yokel peering in disbelief at the sight of a man aboard this tall, wispish Ariel, named after Shakespeare's 'airy spirit' in *The Tempest,* floating along at anything up to 20 mph, and exclaiming that here approached 'a man a-riding upon nawthin'. Starley's inventive brilliance cost him dear. He carried out much of his experimenting at home and one day, needing to do some soldering, he bought a bottle of dilute hydrochloric acid to which he added zinc. His youngest son Joseph, presumably mistaking the fizzy liquid for ginger beer, later took a fatal swig from the bottle.

The first recorded bicycle race in England was held at the Welsh Harp, near Hendon, north London, on Whit Monday 1868 for the prize of a silver cup, won by Arthur Markham.(6) More significantly for the future of bike racing, the day before, at Saint Cloud, (across the Seine from where the office of the Tour de France organisation now stands), an Englishman resident in Paris, James Moore, won a race over 1,200 metres. In November the following year, Moore won the first long-distance bicycle race, completing the 83 miles from Paris to Rouen in 10h 25m. Four years later, riding a Starley 'Ariel', he set the world's first hour record: 14 miles 440 yards. The machine weighed 51 ½ lbs, the front wheel had a diameter of 48 inches, (thus the length of the machine's gearing), the rear 22 inches.

---

5 Born in 1786, he died in 1825 and is also known for his asociation with Charles Macintosh, the inventor of waterproof fabrics. The macintosh coat gives us 'mackintosh'.

6 The Welsh Harp is so-called because in the 1890s the reservoir was rented by the landlord of 'The Old Welsh Harp' tavern in Kingsbury and reserved exclusively for fishing.

Before long, front wheels as tall as their rider and tiny rear wheels were the form, making what was known as the 'high bicycle', in popular parlance 'penny farthing'. (7) Once rolling, the high bicycle, in French La Grande Bi[cyclette], gathers a fine speed and momentum but, because of its high gearing, was hard work when going uphill and a potential menace on the downhill, as the rider, unable to keep his feet on the accelerating pedals, had to let them spin unchecked as the big wheels rolled free. The brake, a spoon-shaped tongue of metal lowered onto the big wheel, was rudimentary at best and, when the machine was in full career, near useless. Headlong tumbles – croppers, (originally a hunting term), headers, imperial crowners or purlers - were frequent. On 10 June, 1899, the 44 year-old French composer Ernest Chausson was out riding with his daughter near his summer retreat at Mantes, west of Paris. When he dropped behind and did not reappear she went back to see what had delayed him and found him lying dead in the road. He had run into a wall.

Humber & Co. Limited, founded by Thomas Humber in Nottingham, advertised their No. 3 Racer [high] Bicycle of 1889 – 'Holds the World's Record ONE MILE 2 min. 31 4/5ths Sec.' Made in Beeston, near Nottingham, it boasted 'an 18 inch back wheel with special racing spokes and patent hollow rims 9/16 inch [deep] and ½ inch [wide] best grey racing rubbers; improved double row balls to front wheel [56 inches], also patent ball bearings to steering head and pedals; framework of best weldless steel tube throughout, beautifully enamelled plain black.' As a result 'weight is saved in every way without detracting from strength and rigidity, and the wonderful successes achieved by racing men on this Machine prove its quality better than any words possibly could.' At its most extreme, the high bicycle required its rider to adopt a virtual upright posture, using the saddle as little more than a rest, holding the narrow bars at mid-thigh height so that the action of pedalling on very short cranks resembled the leg action of a modern gymnasium fanatic on a treadmill.

---

7 In pre-decimal coinage, the farthing was a quarter ('fourthing') of the size and value of the bronze penny and stamped with a wren, the smallest British bird.

Chain-driven transmission had been in use in heavy industry since the 1840's, but it took nearly 40 years for the technology to be applied to the bicycle. Rousseau of Marseille produced a system of cranks attached to chainwheels positioned on extensions of the fork in around 1878; Harry J. Lawson's Bicyclette of 1879 also used a chain transmission but both machines were overshadowed by the Kangaroo built by the firm of Hillman, Herbert and Cooper in Coventry, which was fast becoming the cycle manufacturing capital of Europe,. The chain drive, clumsy as the first effort was, nonetheless permitted a smaller front wheel, and in 1885, John Kemp Starley, nephew of James, made the crucial breakthrough. His Rover Safety Bicycle which 'set the fashion to the world' had almost equal wheels, a curved diamond frame, half-hoop handlebars, forks as straight as many ultra-light modern carbon forks, a sprung saddle and a *chain* drive to the *rear* wheel. The choice of the name Safety was an astute marketing ploy. Six years later, the London depot of the Starley firm were advertising an improved model as 'The First Machine to accomplish over 21 miles [c. 33.6km] in the Hour, Bordeaux, August 1888'.(8) The new Rover had 30 inch wheels geared to 54 inches, 'unless otherwise ordered' which shows how closely manufacturers were monitoring the needs of pernickety athletes. Although die-hard enthusiasts, races and idlers alike, continued to favour the lofty, long-view perch of the imperious penny farthing, the Safety soon caught on and, as if to signal its victory, the old-fangled machine became known as an Ordinary. An 1898 issue of *Cycling* reports that 'Osmond [a prominent racer], at his best on the Ordinary, was riding when the rear-driver began to establish itself as a racing cycle.' The big wheel of the high bicycle floated over potholes and, the intermittent hazard of large stones and, the impossibility of making an emergency stop apart, delivered a smoother ride than the more gainly smaller wheels could offer.

But, it was too large to be easily stored, tricky for any but an expert to ride and the advent

---

8 It was in Bordeaux, a little over a hundred years later, that Chris Boardman set his first world hour record of 52.270km.

of the more manageable machine meant that the salad days of Osmond and his ilk were numbered. The bicycle had effectively achieved what has remained its essential diamond-frame shape to this day. The French, risqué as ever, dubbed the Safety bicycle *La Petite Reine*, likening its equi-size wheels to a woman's breasts, the hubs as nipples. In 1888, when British factories were producing six times as many Safeties as high bicycles, another Scotsman, a veterinary surgeon working in Belfast, John Boyd Dunlop, made a significant contribution to the development of the bicycle. Dunlop fitted his young son's tricycle with pneumatic tyres as a trial run. The experiment worked and

Dunlop set up production, though the tyres had to be glued to the wheels in the factory and puncture repair was, therefore, a major operation. Derided as 'bladder wheels', 'pudding tyres' and 'windbags', Dunlop's pneumatics hit a worse set-back. A patent for pneumatic tyres (for coaches) already existed. However, Dunlop refined his design, for the bicycle, fixing the tyres tight round the rim by means of wire and holding nuts, to facilitate their removal; the first 'wired on' tyre. Alas for poor Dunlop, in 1891 a similar detachable tyre appeared on the French market, manufactured by Edouard Michelin, and the mammoth Paris-Brest-Paris race that autumn was won on a bike fitted with Michelins.

RACING AND SOCIAL CHANGE

Long-distance racing on bicycles had become quite a fad, as much to advertise the machines as to parade the endurance of their riders. In March 1891, the first major long-distance road race on diamond-framed, small wheel 'safety' bicycles, Bordeaux-Paris, 572km, was won by the Liverpudlian George Pilkington Mills, member of the celebrated Anfield Bicycle Club and works manager at the Humber bicycle factory in Beeston in Nottinghamshire.(9)   Mills beat several rivals mounted on Ordinaries and his victory spelled the final demise of the high machine and a new era in cycle sport.

 Mills was already famous for smashing the old Land's End - John O'Groats record. High machines had lowered it from a fortnight to 11 days; safeties had cut that by half, but Mills turned in 5 days, 1h 45m riding a tricycle. After his victory in the Bordeaux-Paris, the strictly amateur National Cyclist's Union, formed in 1883, a querulous bunch of stiff-collared wet blankets who exercised Draconian control of racing rules, even across the Channel in France, passed a resolution that Mills 'be asked whether he had payed [sic] the whole of his expenses in the above-mentioned race.' The Union Vélocipédique de France may well have allowed *their* amateurs to compete for prizes up to 2,000fr - about 16 months pay for a manual worker – but the po-faced NCU, on the stuffy Victorian principle that no *gentleman* would *ever* compete in sport for pecuniary reward, had insisted that Bordeaux-Paris should be contested by pure amateurs. Accordingly, the French 'professionals' were barred, though one of them, Charles Terront, was retained by the Brits as a pacer. *Le fair-play* is an indelibly Anglo-Saxon attribute, there was no trusting Johnny foreigner, 'sporstmanlike' means honourable, and wasn't Waterloo said to have been won on the playing fields of Eton ?

At the first control in Angoulême, the local officials, confident that no rider could cover 127km without needing several hours rest, had prepared a lavish reception: slap-up meal,

---

9 Polite society of the day used the term 'bicycle'. The abbreviation 'bike' was considered vulgar.

hot baths and showers, clean beds. Mills and his principal rival Holbein arrived, but while Holbein tore into the food, Mills slipped out through a side door and rode off to pick up his next pacer, Lewin Stroud, lurking on the outskirts of town. Despite a furious chase Holbein came in 1h 16m down on Mills who won in 26h 34m 52s, at an average of 21.518kph. He was cheered in by an estimated crowd of 7,000 who had been walking the cobbled streets by the Porte Maillot on the western outskirts of the city since early morning. Among them was a young lawyer, Henri Desgrange, destined to break the world hour record, unpaced, on the Buffalo velodrome, two years later; he watched in admiration as Mills, mud-caked and gaunt, rode in at the end of his epic ride.

The newspapers took note of the staggering popular success of the race which had lured an eager public away from the stadia onto the streets, and the chief reporter of the *Petit Journal*, Pierre Giffard, was the first to capitalise on it. He had already promoted an 80 mile race from Paris to Rouen and back for motor cars in 1885, won by Comte de Dion in a steam-drawn landau.[10] Now Giffard organised an even grander-scale race for bicycles later that same year: Paris to Brest and back, an epic. Paris, the capital, byword for urbane culture and Brest, rainiest city in France, perched on the very lip of Finisterre, 'Land's End', a wild region of Celtic mist, Atlantic storms and old Roman cart tracks. A crazy notion ? Maybe, but for Giffard it promised at least 3 days racing, heroic write-ups, exclusive reports, quotes from riders, *sales*.

Among the 575 riders who applied there was not one Brit. They'd proved their mettle - first three into Paris from Bordeaux - and scoffed at this latest French folly. 1,200km on broken up country roads ? Don't need it, old boy. Of the 207 riders who did take the start on Sunday 6 September 1891, the two favourites were French: Jiel-Laval, fifth in the Bordeaux-Paris, sponsored by Clément, the bike manufacturer, and the pacer Terront. He had raced frequently in England where he was known as 'Froggy' - how drole - and he entrusted the organisation of his pacemakers to an English friend, a noted bike rider,

---

10 De Dion, industrialist and manufacturer of cars and bicycles, was later instrumental in the inauguration of the Tour de France.

Herbert Osbaldeston Duncan who, by a quirk of the rules of the day, in the grip of the NCU, was himself a former Champion of *France* over 10km. Jiel-Laval's soigneur-manager was a Frenchman born in England, Frédéric de Civry, a descendant of the Dukes of Brunswick. De Civry, him being of noble family and all, had scandalised the gentry by mixing it with frightful oiks in bike races, even if they were *British* oiks. For sure King Edward VII might ride out on a bicycle with the royal family and other nobs follow his lead, but racing on a bicycle was beneath a fellow of blood. A contemporary cartoon has an Athlete asking an Aesthete: ' Don't *you* bicycle ? ' to which the Aesthete replies: 'Er, no. It develops the calves of the legs so. Makes them stick out, you know. So coarse. Positive deformity.'

In 1889, *Punch* carried a cartoon of a human skeleton exhibited in a glass case: the femur and tibia are massively oversized, the pelvic girdle grossly displaced and the posture of spine, rib cage, neck and shoulders hunched as if from some terrible deformity, the arms braced like those of a monkey picking at a nut. The case, purporting to be housed in the British Museum, is inscribed:

'RESTORATION of BRITISH CYCLIST 20th CENTURY'

while the cartoon bears the caption: 'A WARNING TO ENTHUSIASTS.'

The inaugural Paris-Brest-Paris field included ten tricycles, two tandems and what must be the only Ordinary ever to complete the course - ridden by an antiquarian, M. Duval.

Terront, an independent from Bayonne, had done much of his preparatory training in the Pyrenees, with the occasional 240km round trip to Pamplona for a race. He arrived in Paris a month before the start and made long forays deep into Picardy, then to Brittany, where he'd done his military service (at St Brieuc) for the topping up. Also riding was Dubois, who'd set a new record for Paris-Rouen-Paris, 260km in 11h 43m on a warm-up ride 10 days earlier. Neither he nor Jiel-Laval had a particularly quick turn of speed, whereas Terront, aside from his long-distance exploits, was a handy track rider with a string of sprint championships, 6-day wins and 10km titles in his *palmarès*.

From the false [neutral] start outside the offices of the Petit Journal, near the Opéra, cheered by a huge crowd, 207 riders set off in small groups through the city traffic to the real start in the Bois de Boulogne. Paris was not yet ready to shut down for a mere bike race. Terront, wearing no. 5, (he'd applied early) was in the leading bunch - his rivals had been caught up among the lesser riders - and, picking up his first pacer, he let rip. The pace man soon tired; Terront shelled him out and cracked on through Versailles, the roads lined with spectators, including women who had tumbled out of bed indecently early to gasp huskily as the lean-muscled two-wheeled centaurs sped by.

Further on, the road ran parallel to a railway line, and from the carriage windows of a passing train Giffard and several of Terront's pacers waved handkerchiefs, cheering him on. He covered the 50km to the first checkpoint in 1h 50m and paused only long enough to sign. He cast off weary pacers one by one; champed and fretted behind a closed level crossing in Dreux, but the pursuit didn't materialise and he was off again. After a brief stop to wolf down a bowl of soup, another bevy of pacers relayed him to the second check in Mortagne. He had, by now, been 7 hours in the saddle and was increasingly anxious about his rivals - of whom he had no news - and punctures. He called his Michelin pneumatic tyres, held in place on the outside of the rims with short rods fastened by screws, 'air puddings'. The machine itself, a Humber custom-built in the Beeston factory, weighed 21.5kg (double the weight of a track machine or an Ordinary), was fitted with a Carter chain-guard and oil bath, high-reach forks (slightly-raked) and headset, cross-tube sloping at about 23°, horn attached on the underside, shallow drops handlebars with repair kitbag slung from the stem, single 'bean' front brake, unequal sized wheels and minimal pedal clips which hooked over the toe of his walking shoes. Every replaceable part of the bike had been marked with a lead seal, to ensure that the rider came in on the same bike on which he'd started. Jiel-Laval rode a Clément bike, naturally, fitted with Dunlop pneumatics glued to the rims with canvas strips.

Terront's first puncture – in the rear tyre - came after nightfall, at around 8.15pm, caused by a brand new hobnail of the type used to strengthen *sabots*, (clogs, favoured by textile workers for lobbing into the looms that put them out of work to jam them.) Sabotage ? Terront believed so. He rumbled the few kilometres on a flat rim into the next check at Laval where, luckily, the Michelin man was on hand to effect the change of tyres. Terront's man fumbled and fussed for 40 minutes (the early Dunlops had taken anything up to 4 hours to replace) and, suddenly, a small knot of cyclists emerged from the blackness, Jiel-Laval amongst them. He signed, remounted and rode off, leaving Terront to his frustration. After a frantic chase, Terront caught up and they rode into Rennes side by side.

Terront asked Jiel-Laval where he was going to sleep.

' I don't know ' he said ' they haven't told me.'

In Rennes Terront bolted two bowls of soup while Jiel-Laval took a short rest. By the fourth check at 2.15am, Terront had reestablished a lead and was anxious to press on. But the *commissaire* was asleep; Terront hammered on the shutters but it took 10 minutes to rouse the slug-a-bed, by which time Jiel-Laval had arrived, though clearly in a poor state from lack of sleep. Terront reached the next check at 6.56am, with an advance of 20 minutes then punctured again, on another bright new nail. He punctured five times in all, lost and regained his lead each time but, chasing into Brest, was mortified to see his rival heading towards him from the turn.

At 2am the following morning, Terront picked up another pacer at the control in Guingamp and learnt that Jiel-Laval was in bed, asleep. He slipped off into the night unobserved and, when Jiel-Laval eventually woke up, three hours later, his manager de Civry told him that Terront hadn't been through yet. Meanwhile, Terront, periodically boosted by washes and rub downs, milk from the pail, buttered pastries, soup and dripping slices, soldiered on despite a violent nose-bleed and reached Alençon at 7.10pm to be told that Jiel-Laval was 21/2 h down. Barring accidents Terront had the race won but, as he was setting off, a telegram arrived: Jiel-Laval at 10mins. It was bogus, but spurred the ex-postal courier who'd ridden his first races on hired wooden machines to another furious burst of energy. No rest stops now.

In the dark, he rode into a fallen bough. The bike tipped heavily onto the crank and broke it. He snapped, too, and burst into tears. However, the emotional release somehow bucked him up and he remounted and rode one-legged into the next village where, by good luck, he found a blacksmith. Although his hands were trembling with fatigue, he managed to get the broken crank off while the smith removed a replacement from a pacer's bike. In Dreux, Terront took a reviving drink of champagne and by 5.30am, dawn breaking, he reached Versailles along a road crowded with cyclists gathered to escort the first man home. Terront, filthy with mud and gore from his nose, didn't dare stop to clean himself up before the finish: the ever-present spectre of Jiel-Laval whispered in his ear constantly. Ten thousand people cheered the ragamuffin into the velodrome. It was 6.12am: he had ridden without sleep for 71h 35m, averaging 16.140kph. He washed, rubbed down with eau de cologne and, unable to sleep, tucked into a large bowl of chocolate, soup with grated cheese, two eggs, steak and a bottle of good claret. Jiel-Laval eventually tottered in at 3.40pm and of the original 207, only 99 made it, some after several days on the road interspersed with overnight stops.

It was a singular triumph for Terront himself - money, reserved seat at the Opéra, banquets in his honour, his picture in every paper in France - but for the safety bicycle, too. Road racing had arrived. The heroes who had thrilled fans in the packed vélodromes were now riding the roads of France, in easy view of people who had never even been to Paris, and close enough to touch. Bike shops were selling the machines favoured by the top riders and the newspapers reporting their astonishing feats of endurance sold by the bushel.

The social impact of the new two-wheeled machine was staggering. Like that other demotic invention and boon of the age, the sewing machine, the bicycle was at once enormously popular, a force for liberation, and the butt of savage obloquy. Pi and pompous starched masculine opinion that put the little woman firmly in her place, especially the maids of all work, frowned on the sewing machine, calling it a diabolical contrivance expressly designed to make mischief. The devil found work for idle hands which is precisely what the sewing machine did with hands more properly occupied in the plying of needle and thread: it rendered them idle. Why, the denizens of old Alexandria had banned the introduction of hydraulic power precisely because it would make the slaves *lazy*. Censure of the bicycle, that it both encouraged and ennabled reckless, hectic speed and wanton careering about the highways, emanated from stiffnecks on both sides of the Channel. A French journalist wrote: 'Velocipedists are imbeciles on wheels' and a contemporary cartoon shows an inert pedestrian being carried away as a velocipedist in a striped jersey explains to an *agent de police*: 'See, mister policeman, it was 'is fault, he should've kept 'is eyes open.'[11] Drawing on this undercurrent of hostility, in 1868 Daumier produced a cartoon of The Grim Reaper, in flowing black hooded robe with scythe, astride the two-wheeled marvel of the age, cycling past the latest crop of gravestones – among them, Gioacchino Rossini, composer and chef, surely far too corpulent ever to have contemplated mounting the new-fangled contraption.

However, Paraclèse Bellencontre, official doctor of the Véloce-Club de Rouen championed the healthy and *decent* mode de vie born of the bicycle. When women dance, he said:

> *Their shoulders, which are generally naked, become bathed in perspiration and are therefore utterly exposed to infections of the lungs and to catarrh. The waist is so tightly squeezed by the fabric of the dress and bodice that a reduced intake of oxygen is insufficient to supply the body with blood, not to mention the candle-fumes from the chandeliers and bodily excretions...on a vélocipède, however skittish it may be, our mothers, sisters and daughters would never wear such flimsy diaphanous*

---

11 I myself observed a man walk into the road outside the National Portrait Gallery straight into the path of an oncoming woman cyclist. He decked her and then screamed at her for getting in his way. She cursed him and rode off. I went over to suggest he might have apologised and got a mouthful for my pains. *She* had hit *him*.

dresses...designed to lure the eyes of their dancing partners downwards.

Englishmen seemed to be more on the side of the dancers, lambasting the saucy womens' fashions that the bicycle endorsed and encouraged. Capacious skirts and underskirts, tightly-boned corsets and high laced boots were not conducive to ease of mounting or propelling the Safety and there was a steady move, among the racier of the female cyclists, to so-called 'Rational dress', as pioneered by the American womens' rights campaigner, Amelia Jenks Bloomer. In 1849, following the original lead of a Mrs Elizabeth Miller, she had taken to wearing a short skirt with loose trousers gathered round the ankles, the prototype of a fashion of divided skirts worn by women horse-riders, in particular, and affectionately christened 'bloomers'. The effect of this flighty garment on impressionable males unused to flagrant visible evidence that women actually had legs underneath the dense draperies was intoxicating, indeed.

At sight of Miss Courtenay in a Bloomer he was ravished.

The Course of True Love never did run smooth Charles Reade.

And:

Deborah looke very piquante in a bloomer dress of dark blue.

The Hawaiian archipelago: six months among the palm groves of...the Sandwich Islands Miss Arabella Bird.

Another item of clothing favoured by the sporty woman, knickerbockers, loose-fitting breeches gathered in at the knee, took their name from the pretended author of Washington Irving's *History of New York*. Cruikshank's illustrations for the book showed a number of Dutchmen in close-fitting knee breeches of the type we call plus twos, and 'knickerbocker' entered the language. In June 1894 *The Pall Mall Gazette* reports an 'assumption that the knickerbocker ladies [cyclists] were doing something confessedly unseemly'. To the imbecility of riding the machine in the first place is added the charge of dressing like a tart to do so. A writer in *Woman* damned the whole exercise:

Few will contend that the lady cyclist is a thing of beauty. The pedal action is too like the rhythmic swing of a carpet beater, and the

addition of dust to a heated face and shapeless garments in no way
suggests personal cleanliness.

In 1893 *Cycling* reported that Tessie Reynolds cycled from London to Brighton and back in 8 ½ hours, paced by her males friends, clad in baggy knee breeches (almost plus fours) waisted jacket with a skirt to the knee, boater-style hat and high necked cotton blouse. The scandalous 'Brighton Female Scorcher' as she became known, caused 'real pain, not unmixed with disgust'. Across the Channel, the aesthetic line if not high was at least practical and provoked no outrage among the French: another 16-year old, Hélène Dutrieu, boldly raced her track bicycle clad in long-sleeved pullover, knee breeches, black stockings and soft, buttoned pumps, a costume which, snarled the English fashion writers, 'makes her look, if like anything else on earth, like an ugly, badly-made man'. They made no reference to the significant technical point that Dutrieu's mount had a crossbar – Reynolds' didn't.

The staid unbicycled generation might sniff and snort about the depravity engendered by the bicycle, whilst young people seized the chance it offered to get out and about. Ownership of a bicycle meant an entirely novel independence. The bicycle was faster, more convenient, cheaper to run than a horse and was even, for a time, promoted as 'the horse which eats no hay' and 'the camel of the occident'. Courting couples could spin out not far beyond the confines of town and city, with abandon, with ease, with delight, on unchaperoned trysts into the country. An early advertisement for Gladiator cycles has the French Park Keeper in a fore-and aft official hat glowering in triumph at the furtive young man and woman trespassing in the woodland of his domain, their bicycles leaning against a tree, he himself leaning against his own as he writes in a notebook. 'This time I've caught you' he crows 'because now I, too, have a Gladiator.'

In 1892 Harry Dacre wrote the song which encapsulates the romantic notion of lovers sealing their affection aboard the companionable two wheeler, 'Daisy Bell'. The story goes that Dacre arrived in America with his bicycle and, to his chagrin, was charged import tax. Someone remarked that if he'd tried to bring in a bicycle built for two he'd have been charged double. Hence:

But you'll look sweet, on the seat of a bicycle built for two.

The Bois de Boulogne, venue for musical rides by society ladies, also housed a Chalet du Cycle offering refreshment and a parking area for bicycles. If the weather was inclement, the city's indoor vélodromes offered a snug and sociable alternative.

In England, clubs, both social and sporting, proliferated, up and down the country, from Liverpool to Lowesoft, Carlisle to Canterbury, Truro to Tynemouth, and Paisley to the oldest of them all, the Pickwick in London, 'The Pilgrim Fathers of Cycling' founded in June 1870.

The bicycle undoubtedly contributed greatly to a more general social mobility, to a widening of horizons formerly cut off by lack of opportunity to stray far, if at all, beyond the parish boundary. A popular catchphrase demystifying the difficulty of mastering gyroscopic motion sums up the new spirit of liberty the two wheels ushered in: 'Straddle a saddle then paddle and skedaddle.' (12)

In a study of the pattern of matrimony in rural Dorset, (published in 1969) the social scientist P.J Perry found that marriages within parishes dropped from 77% before 1887 to 41% between 1907 and 1916 and the number of marriage partners who lived between 6 and 12 miles apart increased from 3% to 9%.

The author John Galsworthy later claimed that the bicycle had 'been responsible for more movement in manners and morals than anything since Charles II'. Although the widespread use of bicycles for delivery of all manner of goods and services came later, the Post Office experimented with carrier tricyles in the 1880s and here is a picture of messengers for the Reuters news agency with bicycles and tricycles, in 1896. Clad in distinctive long military tunics and pillbox caps with shoulder-slung despatch pouches, these Reuters boys are the forerunners of contemporary urban cycle messengers, a cheerful crew of two-wheeled privateers taking on the clash and fumes of the heavy

---

12 Skedaddle, US military slang, had been introduced in the Civil War, 1861-5, probably by a professor at Harvard, from classical Greek *skedanumi*, 'to disperse in confusion'.

motorised traffic brigades.(13)

T.H.Escott's 1897 evocation of the happy-go-lucky meeting of pedalling enthusiasts must surely have been duplicated up and down the country:

> A favourite rendezvous in the neighbourhood of London is Bushey Park [near Hampton, Middlesex], and there, when the weather is fine as many as a thousand bicyclists congregate. During the summer, too, in the heart of the city, when the business traffic of the day is done and the streets are clear, an active scene may often be witnessed by gaslight. Under the shadow of the Bank and the Exchange, the asphalt thoroughfare is covered with a host of bicycle riders, performing a series of intricate evolutions on their iron steeds.

And when, at the beginning of Jerome K. Jerome's *Three Men on the Bummel* (1900), Harris, hero of his *Three Men in a Boat* about a skiff trip up the Thames, says, 'What we want is a change' what he proposed, after the others balk at a sailing venture, the change, the complete change, was a cycling holiday.

> The bicycle bounded over the road like a thing of life; farmhouses and churches, dogs and chickens came to him and passed. Old folks stood an gazed at him, the children cheered him.

In 1908, Kenneth Grahame's *The Wind in the Willows* bears witness to another craze developing alongside that of the bicycle and destined, eventually, to throttle it. Sitting at the side of the road, by the wreckage of Rat and Mole's canary-coloured cart, Toad stares raptly at the cloud of dust kicked up by the speeding motor which has just ploughed into and past them:

> "Glorious, stirring sight' murmured Toad, never offering to move.
> 'The poetry of motion. The *real* way to travel. The *only* way to travel.

---

13 Reuters took its name from Paul Julius Reuter who, in 1849, began using carrier pigeons to relay news of stock prices rapidly between his home town of Aachen and Brussels.

Here today – in next week tomorrow. Villages skipped, towns and cities jumped – always somebody else's horizon. O bliss. O poop-poop. O my. O my." (14)

In 1894, the first motorcars could move no quicker than a horse. Yet, nine years later, stripped down touring cars, expertly tuned, routinely achieved speeds in excess of 80mph and even as fast as 100mph. The enthusiasm for sheer motor-driven speed, careless of the damage it caused, was endorsed by other literary men. In the back seat of the Lanchester which 'sang like a six-inch shell across the Sussex Downs' sat Rudyard Kipling who applauded the fact that the arrival of the car had, finally, introduced a major blood sport to England. Another incurious speed merchant, the poet John Masefield, hurtled across the same hills in an Overland which let forth 'soul-animating strains' while George Bernard Shaw wrote a letter to the motoring papers urging drivers who had caused an accident not to stop if they had a lady passenger on board.

The price of the average bicycle offered by British manufacturers at the end of the century was about £20, at a time when 83 per cent of the population received a weekly wage of about one pound.(15) But, in an early play of what has bedevilled UK industry time and again, the advent of cheap imports from America jolted the complacent home manufacturers. In July 1897 Rudge-Whitworth cut the price of a standard machine to 12 guineas; within 4 years the price was £9 and, by 1909, £4. That still meant that the lower paid had to buy on the never-never but the precious advantage the bicycle offered was lure enough.

Just as small arms manufacturers and gunsmiths in the early days had converted to the production of bicycles – BSA (Birmingham Small Arms) was the most celebrated – so, too, bicycle manufacturers - Humber, Lea Francis, Rover, Singer, Sunbeam, Swift, Star,

---

14 Of course the portrait of Toad owes much to the disgraced Oscar Wilde and 'cars' is nudge-nudge for 'boys'.

15 At a current minimum wage of around £240 per week, the comparative cost of a bicycle today would be around £4,800.

Triumph, Morris in Britain and Peugeot in France, were producing cars. In 1903, some 62,000 cars were being produced, worldwide, approximately half of that number in France alone. In December 1903, two brothers who ran a bicycle repair and manufacturing business in Dayton, Ohio, Wilbur and Orville Wright, became the first men to achieve sustained and controlled powered flight over the sand flats near Kitty Hawk, North Caroline. Their plane, *Flyer 1* travelled 37 metres at a maximum of 3 metres above the ground in just 12 seconds. That same year saw the first edition of the Tour de France, a race which, because of the passions it aroused, its founder Henri Desgrange declared to have been killed by its own success.(16)

In spite of the sometimes ugly and violent behaviour of vehemently partisan cycling fans, official atitudes to bike racing in France were lenient. Perhaps the sheer momentum of the sport's popularity round the quite thinly populated hexagon proved impossible to counter. Certainly, bicycles could not mete out a fraction of the grief scattered by cars careering madly down public highways in excess of 90 mph. Moreover, by the 1880's, *The Cyclist,* a weekly magazine which cost one old penny (therefore 240 copies for £1), announced that France had 'gone boldly over to professionalism' and cycle competition on the continent thrived whereas in England, the strict amateur code persisted (and has only lately been challenged) even as local police and magistrates were clamping down energetically on road racing. In its 'Racing Gossip' column of 12 September 1883, *The Cyclist* reports:

> *Besides the interference of the police with the 50 miles road*
> *competition in London, they have, we learn, given notice that they*
> *intend to stop the road race for the Clifton B.C. championship, whilst it*
> *is most probable that the Bristol Cycling Club event will also be*

---

16 Another great race, for automobiles, was also announced, between Paris and Madrid. The advent of long-distance racing provided added incentive although, after a series of terrible accidents on badly guarded main roads lined with dense crowds, the French government halted the Paris-Madrid race at Bordeaux. Three hundred cars entered, six of the drivers were killed on the road and some twelve gravely hurt. Ill-piloted cars ploughed into lines of spectators, injuring and maiming, along the route.

opposed by them. This shows the feeling against these rides is general with the authorities and not the result of the officiousness of a single individual.

In the next edition, under 'Notes of the Week', there appears a copy of a police notice:

Persons using bicycles, including tricycles, are hereby cautioned that such vehicles are carriages within the meaning of the Highway and Metropolitan Police Acts.
[Based on a precedent cited Taylor v Goodwin, decided by the judges, 25 March 1879, verdict: 'Furious driving'.] The Metropolitan Police impose a penalty on any person who shall ride or drive furiously, or so as to endanger the life or limb of any person, or to the common danger of the passengers in any thoroughfare...(17)

In a supplement to the issue for 24 January of that year, the magazine offered 'A short biographical sketch of the life and inventions of the late JAMES STARLEY', elegantly illustrated with line drawings of details of his velocipede with suspension wheels.
Starley was only 50 years old. He'd run away from the impoverished family farm outside Brighton at the age of sixteen fired by a dream of making mechanical things. The impetus his work gave to establishing bicycle manufacture as a major industry in Britain, based principally in Nottinghamshire and round Coventry, cannot be overstated. Alongside his company's name stand the others which resonated for so long, though not exclusively as

---

17 This is by no means the only reference to hardening official attitudes to cyclists recorded by the magazine – distributed in Coventry and London, provincial editor Henry Sturmey, co-inventor of the famous gear - whose pages carried reports on races, amateur and professional, notes on the scene in France, USA, and the Antipodes, notice of social events, news from clubs round the country, letters, trade advertisements, (bicycles, tricycles, clothing and home trainers) small ads, occasional pieces – 'Cycling in Russia'...'The Amsterdam Exhibition'...and the regular column 'La Belle France'.

cycle-makers: Hillman, (named after an ex-foreman at the Coventry Sewing Machinist's Company where Starley had worked) Rudge, Humber, Singer, (another former Coventry worker friend of Starley's), Triumph, Rover, and the company which took its name from the road in which the original works, run by Messrs Woodhead, Angois and Ellis produced their safeties, Raleigh Street in Nottingham.

As the price of bicycles fell and the new automobile craze caught the attention of the moneyed classes, even those who had at first so eagerly taken to two wheels, the English cyclist was more and more identified with the poorer classes. The bicycle, once enormously popular with all classes, became the favoured transport of the people because it was a luxury they could *just* afford. Other factors combined to reinforce a deep-seated prejudice, not least the animosity of early legislators, more of them wealthy motorists than men resorting to the far cheaper bicycle, as well as the refusal by the administrators of cycle sport in Britain, backed by the police and magistrates, to allow road racing.

For example, the Red Flag Act of 1865 restricted the speed of machine-powered vehicles on the roads of Britain to 4 mph, reducible, 'in special circumstances', on the whim of local magistrates and police, to 2 mph. But, a powerful lobby of industrialists, organised by Sir David Saloman, a keen motorist, and backed by colleagues in the House of Commons, finally succeeded in revision of the law. On Emancipation Day, 14 November 1896, heralded by a gathering of motor cars and motorbikes in the Agricultural Hall in Islington, north London, (in which the first ever six-day Long Distance [cycling] Championship of the World had been held in 1878) the speed limit was increased to 14 mph. Eight years earlier, a similar parliamentary lobby by the Cycle Touring Club had succeeded in passing a measure in favour of the bicycle – the legal status of the bicycle was established and the punitive by-laws up and down the country which so restricted cyclists were overruled. Since then, the lobby has been largely toothless.

In France, from earliest times, the glamour attached to the great men of road racing, 'the giants of the route', ensured that the bicycle would always hold a high status in public esteem. From the very outset, young working class boys, farmboys in even the most remote settlements in the country's vast rural outback who watched the Tour de France go through, seized on cycling as a means of escaping poverty. English amateurism, the vaunted Corinthian spirit, overrode any notion that *sport* had any other decent purpose than playing up and playing up and playing the game. Lucre was filthy. Who played games for money ? Footballers, in Shakespeare's term still 'base footballers', and other odoriferous riff-raff grubbing for cash prizes.

Having dominated cycle sport on the continent in the early years, British riders retreated to the enclosed world of club runs, clandestine races and time trials. In the period leading up to the Second World War and beyond, when the wearing of a hat in public was deemed to be requisite, the majority of cyclists wore cloth caps, marking them out as indefeasibly working class, unable to afford the motors that the upper crust owned and to which, after the war, the middle class increasingly aspired.

Henry Ford in the USA pioneered the mass marketing of cars with the model T which he imported to Britain in 1911. The Morris works at Cowley began production in 1914, whence issued the famous Morris Minor in 1928, the same decade in which the Austin Seven made its debut. The German Volkswagen, 'people's car', known as the Beetle, designed in the 1930s by Dr Ferry Porsche, outlived them all.

The First World War claimed most of the cars in England and bicycle despatch riders and regiments of cycling infantry had a limited influence and little cachet. Whilst General Haig, a cavalry man through and through, could, after the war in which infantrymen had been mown down in their thousands by automatic weapons, nevertheless declare the machine gun 'a much overrated weapon', mechanisation, in war as in civilian life, had arrived. Motor buses plied local routes and charabancs took day-trippers out of town to countryside and seaside. The petrol shortages of the Second World War briefly reprieved cycling – and cycle manufacturing. But advances in technology which the war brought in its inevitable train made the manufacture of cheaper and cheaper family motor vehicles ever more viable. Thus, once again, as cars multiplied on the roads of England, the bicycle yielded place.

The Automobile Association, founded in 1905, consisted of volunteer cyclists, wearing identifiable armbands, who patrolled the roads to alert approaching motorists to the presence of hidden police speed traps ahead. Alas, any friendly cooperation between cyclist and motorist,even the possibility of rapprochement, seems to have died with the disappearance of those freewheeling good scouts, as, sadly, any cyclist negotiating the maelstrom of city traffic today will confirm.

CHAPTER TWO
BIANCHI AND CAMPAGNOLO

Like so many generations of other two-wheel enthusiasts, when my pals and I first came to the bike - not just riding it but drooling over the best of its finery – we loitered in specialist bike shops, those Aladdin's caves of sleek racing machines way beyond our pocket money but already a potent living part of our imagination, yearning for the partnership of speed those dashing lightweight marvels of man's inventive and technical genius offered. Intoxicated with the whiff of enamel, silk tyres, Brookes' leather, the zing of Reynolds steel tubing, the heady fragrance of high-grade lube, staring in wonder at the dense mesh of spokes in a line of alloy racing wheels suspended from the ceiling, rims and hubs winking in the sunlight, we swapped the tech talk with the boyish swagger that comes with doing a hard ride in good company. In truth, we knew little of either the hard ride or the precise meaning of the tech talk, but we had the élitist vocabulary off pat. And, just as we spoke in awe of the heroically aloof men who rode the rest off their wheel – Coppi, Anquetil, Merckx – so we could reel off the names of men whose names graced the downtubes and the glittering hand-tooled components, and they conjured an almost shaman-like echo. Alan Shorter, who made the frame I keep in France…Colnago, one of whose scarlet frames I did eventually get to ride, loaned to me by an Adelaide bike shop, which I rode with such pleasure in Australia during the 2001 Tour Down Under…Claude Butler in whose workshop a school friend learnt to build wheels…the master at school who, improbably (he was decidedly a tourer not a racer) rode a Bianchi….Charlie Roberts, maker of the machine owned by the father of another pal…the big brother of a friend at school who had a friend who had a Freddy Grubb…Cinelli stems, handlebars, extensions, Sedis chains, Brookes' saddles, Weinmann, ah, Weinmann, *the* brakes to yearn for and, what joy when, finally, you'd saved up enough to be able to go into the shop, put the money on the counter and ask for the box of precious side-pulls to upgrade the old (very old) Coventry Eagle, gift of an uncle, though long past its (overstated) best and sadly wanting in class. But the name which had something of the Grail about it – and still does - was Campagnolo, Campag to the aficionado, and we were certainly that. It was the way the Campag rear mech, apparently made of goblin silver, was so compact, instantly recognisable from the ubiquitous Huret, and the elegant tongue-shaped levers, speckle-edged with tiny embossed detail, shimmering with the kind of classy superfluity that whispered excellence. The lustrous Campag chainwheels had the filigree refinement of a piece by the great Renaissance craftsman Benvenuto Cellini. Even the specialised Campagnolo tool kit, costing at least a junior prince's ransom, had the glitter and finesse of a casket of jewels. When it came to adding components to the Shorter frame (secondhand), I badly wanted something Campag on it, anything Campag on it, but had not the money. From the very start, the stuff was expensive, three or four times the price of the alternatives. For, Campagnolo had used only ever the best steel and alloys and where other early chainwheels, pedal cranks held in with cotter pins, rarely held true, the cotterless Campag item always ran straight. And the cantilever of his rear mech could withstand rough handling; where a Simplex gear buckled if the bike fell over, the Campag parallelogram absorbed the impact and sprang back into position. So, reluctantly, I sank to Simplex, grubbed for secondhand wheels, rejoiced in Stronglight, for sure, demurred on Weinmann yet again, and, aching for the out-of-price Campag, had an idea: the bolt that holds the seat pin in the frame. Campag made one, twice if not three times the price of a common-or-garden bolt, but I shelled out and Shorter got the holy touch, albeit small: the blessing of Campagnolo. That's how profound was, and is, the effect of the name. Now there is a pantheon of other names, to be sure, each deserving of a place. But, let the few speak for the many in recording the genius of all who have devoted themselves to the perfection of the beautiful machine.

Edoardo Bianchi and Tullio Campagnolo typify the breed of men who, like Bob Chicken himself, adore the whole world of bikes, cycling and cyclists way beyond the dictates and strictures of the commercial world in which they also move. So it seems entirely appropriate that eventually Campagnolo, an organisation noted for its single-minded pursuit of perfection, would eventually be distributed by Bob Chicken's company, Chicken and Son, in the UK.

Edoardo Bianchi, oldest and most celebrated of a cluster of egregious Italian bicycle frame manufacturers, started making bikes in 1885, at the age of 20, in a tiny factory on the Via Nirone in Milan where he had hitherto been making medical

Edoardo Bianchi, oldest and most celebrated of a cluster of egregious Italian bicycle frame manufacturers, started making bikes in 1885, at the age of 20, in a tiny factory on the Via Nirone in Milan where he had hitherto been making medical instruments. He applied the skill and expertise he'd acquired in the finicky work of shaping and honing precision tools for the surgery to the particular design and construction problems of the bicycle. The *piccolo fabbro* then moved to the Via Bertani where Bianchi was one of the first manufacturers to fit a bike with Dunlop's pneumatic tyres. Bianchi also claimed to have been the first cycle-maker to make the front wheel smaller than the rear, thus bringing the pedals closer to the ground and lowering the machine's centre of gravity to allow for a more stable ride. This development also anticipated a chain transmission – John Starley's breakthrough – and simply shows, perhaps, that Bianchi's inventive imagination was no less fertile. From earliest days, victory in competition was an essential to the commercial success of cycle manufacturers and Bianchi bikes have won more races in thei long history than those of any other marque. It began with Giovanni Tomaselli's win in the prestigious international track race, the Paris Grand Prix of 1899, (inaugurated in 1894). His bike was a thing of passing beauty: black-painted frame of slender tubing, the forks - a white-metal crown shaped snugly round the head of each - slim and tapering to a graceful swan's neck shallow rake at the tip. The solid-tyre wheels seem impossibly narrow for so early a date and the sensual sweep of the handlebars, in the shape of ox horns, conjures the very image of speed and streamlining. Here is the embodiment of the Italian gift to cycle manufacture: elegance and technical perfection, the precision, indeed, of the fine, shining steel of those surgical instruments on which Bianchi learned his trade and first gave issue to his design brilliance. The badge on the head of the frame bears the Bianchi logo, a red-crowned gold imperial eagle with wings spread, an adaptation of the former Italian royal crest. The black enamal was eventually superceded by the famous Bianchi *celeste* (close to Cambridge blue) to match the eyes of the Princess Margherita, born in 1901, eldest daughter of king Victor Emmanuel III of Italy and Princess Elena of Montenegro, for whom Bianchi made the first ever custom-built woman's bicycle.

In 1913 Bianchi introduced the first front brake mechanism and by the following year, his factory was producing 45,000 bicycles per year, as well as 1,500 motorcycles and 1,000 automobiles.

In May 1915, Italy declared war on Austria - its twenty-fourth such declaration, all told - and its armies went onto the offensive on the northern frontier, along the line of the Dolomite mountains and the eastern end of the Julian Alps. Several areas of the region had long been disputed territory; even today in a town like Bolzano, (Bosen), in the Trentino (Südtirol) in the Italian Alps, you will hear more German spoken than Italian. The fighting, in the harsh conditions of the snowbound high mountains, was particularly arduous and savage. Bitter old scores, fearsome new weapons. That same year, Bianchi turned his inventive genius to the design of a *Bicicletta Militare*, a sturdy machine with beefy tyres, suspension on both wheels and a folding frame. This was issued to the Bersaglieri (Sharpshooters) of the Royal Italian Army for on and off-road use in the two main theatres of Italian conflict, the Libyan desert and the Alps. It was, in effect, the first mountain bike.

Also in 1915, the great *campionissimo* Costante Girardengo won the Italian national championship for the third time, holding it unbeaten until 1925 [1]. He was the first of many outstanding Italian champions to endorse the Bianchi frame and its international reputation for superb finish, reliability and sheer style.

In that same year, the 14 year-old Tullio Campagnolo was attending the School of Arts and Trades in Vicenza where his father owned two hardware shops that stocked a variety

---

1 His lustrous palmarès include victory in two Giro d'Italia (1919, 1923), six Milan-Sanremo (1918/21/23/25/26/28) and two Giro di Lombardia (1919, 1921).

of metal goods to supply the local farming community - cattle chains, plough-shares, spades and scythes. (Coincidentally, the name Campagnolo means 'countryman'.) Along one wall ran a wooden bench to which were fixed two cast-iron vices and, arranged in racks, a selection of metalworking tools. It was at this bench that young Tullio discovered the great passion of his life allied to an early taste for cycle racing, from the age of 17, with the Veloce Club Vicenza.   Called up after the war, at the age of 20, he was detailed to join the Open Heavy Field Artillery battery in Modena. It's unlikely that acquaintance with cumbrous steel guns did much for his technical expertise, but his natural enthusiasm for life, work and people won him rapid promotion.

 Discharged from the army, he was soon racing in the Cicli Aliprandi colours, financing himself by selling scrap metal – the wooden handcart with 'T. Campagnolo Ferraccio' painted on the side is kept as a sort of sacred relic on the landing at the top of the stairs in the Campagnolo HQ. On 4 November 1924, riding as an independent, he competed in the Gran Premio della Vittoria, from Padua up into the Dolomites of the Belluno region, north of Venice.

His bike, standard for the era, had two freewheels, on either side of the rear hub, one large for the flat, one small, for the gradients. Approaching a climb, the rider dismounted and swapped the rear wheel round. Precious time could be lost, especially since the wheel axle rested in what is known as track ends, that is the slots cut into the end of each rear fork to receive the axle (the 'drop outs') that face backwards. Thus, to take the wheel out necessitated pushing the axle forwards in the slots as far as it would go in order to slacken the chain, demounting the chain from the cogs and pulling the wheel back and out. Putting the wheel back in reversed the process but it was not always easy – with fumbling hands, in a sweat of hurry – to remount the chain without jamming the whole assemblage and then reposition the axle.[2]

---

2 Some riders who knew the roads well would slyly pretend to change gear to bamboozle riders unfamiliar with the terrain and then ride off hard, turning the same big flat-country gear, leaving the dupes to twiddle. Many riders opted for fixed flatland sprockets on one side and freewheels, for the climbs, on the other. Some aces went for freewheels on both sides.

Eugène Christophe, who rode nine Tours de France between 1906 and 1922, brilliantly hit on the idea of making the switch of the wheel altogether easier by making the drop outs face *forwards*.

Demounting and relocating the chain became much more staightforward.[3]

The route of the Gran Premio della Vittoria crossed the Croce d'Aune pass, described nowadays as being open generally from late spring to autumn. November is hardly autumn and although the weather that day was fine down in the valleys, up in the mountains the air was bitterly cold and damp, the roads already deep in old snow and the riders forced to ride through thick flurries of new snow along the slippery furrows left by car tyres. Those spectators who had braved the conditions to stand by the roadside soon drifted away.

 Campagnolo, with tubular tyres tied to the handlebars and under the saddle, another in a figure of eight round his shoulders, bread, salami and cheese stuffed into the back pockets of his jersey, one bottle of water and another of coffee, fixed to the down tubes of the frame, two more in aluminium cages attached to the bars kept up with the leaders in what was proving to be a very lively race and stopped with them to change the wheel at the foot of the 7km climb. None of them had gloves or sweaters and what clothes they had on were already sopping wet with both sweat and precipitation. Campagnolo's fingers were so chilled and numb that he simply could not undo the butterfly wingnuts on the rear axle. As the others rode off on the lower gear. Campagnolo realised he had a bleak choice: either persist in trying to undo the recalcitrant wingnuts and lose more time or ride the climb on the leg-breaking higher gear and hope, somehow, to stay at least in contact with the others.

He opted to ride on and, straining to turn the big gear on slopes of a 6% average gradient,

---

3 In the 1913 Tour, Christophe's front forks broke on the descent of the Tourmalet and he famously not only shouldered the bike and ran 8km down the mountain to a blacksmith's forge in the village of Sainte Marie de Campan at its foot, but then fashioned a replacemen pair of forks out of two lengths of piping. He was, quite clearly, a man of great resource (as well as determination) but also possessed of no little technical skill. He made and perfected a design of toe clips which he then patented and sold the clips (and straps) commercially.

the worst at 11%, the surface skiddy with slush, his heart pounding, he cursed and uttered the words that launched the Campagnolo legend: '*Bisogna cambiá qualcossa de drio*' something *had* to be done about that rear wheel.

At the end of that epic ride, he took fourth place in a class field, caught the train home, and set to work on the problem at the bench, at the same time pursuing his racing career. A sepia photograph signed by him shows a leading bunch of five riders, three following cars and a motorcycle, passing through a small town somewhere north of Vicenza; bright sun, midday shadows, dusty unmetalled road. Campagnolo has written: 'Coppa del Re (King's Cup) 1927. Campagnolo leads the group with 7 minutes advance on the pursuers.' Another picture shows the riders riding through the Valli di Pasubio.[4]

The conundrum of the back wheel nagging at him always, Campagnolo signed for the Nicolò Biondi team based in Carpi, just north of Modena for no better pay than a machine and subsistence, what the French call riding *à la musette*. He raced in two great classics for the team, Giro di Lombardia and Milan-Sanremo, riding Bianchi bikes. Two of the greatest names in Italian cycling dominated the field. However, the great Girardengo was being hustled off the podium by the new man Alfredo Binda.[5] along with another ace, Learco Guerra [6] who also went north across the Alps to come second in the 1930 Tour de France.

He won two mountain stages and it was rumoured that he was paid not to ride too hard against the eventual winner, Henri Desgrange's favourite, André Leduc, in the yellow jersey. Full of praise for the ex-bricklayer from Mantova who had ridden as domestique to

---

4 In the rocky wasteland of the gaunt massif of Monte Pasubio, high above them, thousands of sappers of the Italian 5th Regiment worked for 11 months during 1917 to construct a criss-cross maze of strategic trails and roads, tiny paths cut into the sides of the mountain, a labyrinth of fifty-two tunnels blasted and hacked out of its very heart, 2,280 metres all told, the Strada delle Gallerie for the movement of men and matériel against the Austrian Alpenjaeger.

5 Milan-Sanremo 1929, 1931, Giro di Lombardia 1925/7/ 31, Giro d'Italia 1925/7/8/9/33, national champion 1926-29, World Road Race 1927/30/32.

6 National champion 1930-34, Giro di Lombardia 1934, Giro d'Italia 1934, World Champion 1931.

Girardengo, Desgrange nicknamed Guerra *La Locomotiva,* his esteem for this *passista,* (what the Italians call a high-tempo stayer,) heightened when he learnt that Guerra suffered from blennorrhea, heavy discharge of mucus from the nose.

By 1929, Campagnolo had begun appearing at the start of races in a suit but we can say that it was emphatically on 8 February 1930 when he took the decisive step away from scratching a living as a minor pro cyclist to embark on an outstanding career as a maker of the finest equipment available to the men of the peloton. He took out a patent, the first of no fewer than 135, on his quick-release hub. There would be no more struggling with wing nuts in the biting cold. Later that year, Binda was paid not to ride the Giro – he was crushing the life out of the race – and Campagnolo went into production with two engineers from Brescia, I Fratelli [The Brothers] Brivio working on his design.

The germs of the design of his first rod-controlled derailleur are there in the quick-release hub. The central problem of changing gear is the maintaining of tension in the chain while keeping the wheel stable and Campagnolo's design addressed both with simple efficiency.

His genius was to produce a mechanism which maintained chain tension without adopting a tensioning arm and wheel, as Simplex had done. Moreover, the simplicity of his method reduced the friction and thus the wear imposed on the chain.

He fitted two freewheels to the rear wheel hub. Fixed to the down tube on the chain side were two rods: one released the hub, the second, to the tip of which was attached a curved tang, shifted the chain from one freewheel cog to the other. The rear drop-outs were elongated to allow for significant differences in cog size, and the U-shaped slot was fitted with a toothed rack. This engaged with a matching pinion on the axle to keep the wheel stable and aligned when the outer locking-nut was released. With the first of two rods attached to the right-hand rear stay the wheel could be loosened. Given the forward momentum of the bicycle, the immediate effect of loosening the wheel was to make the axle ride back along the toothed rack of the drop out. A slight thrust of the pedals would bring the axle forward, thus slackening the chain enough for the second rod to flip it onto the adjacent, larger cog. By not pedalling during this operation, the rider allowed natural momentum to take the axle back again to tighten the chain, at which point he fastened the hub locking-nut. The patent for the gear came on 4 May 1933. Working the gear in the saddle, on the move, required no little bike-handling skill: reaching down to work the two rods - first to loosen the clamp on the back wheel axle, then to flip the chain with the second rod, thirdly to clamp the wheel tight once more with the first rod. For the rider who had the poise to manage the delicate operation Campagnolo's prototype derailleur offered a huge advantage: while other riders had to stop to change gear, the Campagnolo men kept moving and made their shift with much greater speed.

Richard Hallett, technical editor of *Cycling Weekly* and *Cycle Sport* rode the 200km Gran Fondo l'Eorica in Tuscany, October 2004, on a 1930s Raleigh which he restored himself. The event recreates the spirit, if not the full technical verity, of the heroic era of bike racing but Richard, being something of a purist, decided that he would go for as close to authentic pre-derailleur conditions as achievable. He fitted his rear wheel with two geared cogs but, since he had only one (poor) front brake – common UK practice at the time though continentals were using two brakes and freewheels as early as 1905 – he used fixed rather than free wheels. This rendered some of the climbs impossible and not a few of the descents a considerable trial, as well. He couldn't get out of the saddle, either because the restored Raleigh had the shallow-sweep Marsh handlebars favoured by British riders in the 1930s which kept him firmly rooted to the saddle, another factor which militated against his climbing all through that long, long day (12 hours) under the Italian sun.

Why this design of bars ? British racing cyclists thought that 'honking' - lifting the posterior out of the saddle in order to achieve more speed - was utterly infra dig, vulgar for scallywags and cheats. Any bona fide sporting fellow should deplore such exhibitionism. The proper posture was seated. There was one permissible occasion for honking and one occasion only: in a hill climb, on *very* steep gradients. Marcel Bidot, a stalwart of the French Tour de France team in the 1930s, later manager, said of Eddy Merckx that what marked him as a true 'all-outer' was the fact that 'he knows how to lift his arse out of the saddle' and he *did* use the word 'arse'.

Hallett also realised that, even allowing for his being an adept mechanic, he was not used to swapping wheels around at speed under pressure as would early racers have been. Thus there was a conclusion to be drawn vis à vis the impact of the newly-introduced derailleur gear.[7] Henri Desgrange first permitted its use in the 1937 Tour de France and Bartali won in 1938 using one of Campagnolo's new gears. The overall average speed of the Tours until then had increased by relatively small increments which could be attributed to slight improvements in machines, increased fitness of riders and marginally better road surfaces. The derailleur, however, made a significant difference because even if the rider employing one had to slow down to effect the change and thus markedly reduce momentum, especially on a climb, he did not have to dismount and swap the wheel round. Say that the change took around 45 seconds to a minute and he would make perhaps an average of six changes per day over 21 stages, that adds up to a significant saving overall throughout the race of between 1hr 35 ½ mins and 2hrs 1 minute.

Campagnolo's fertile brain was working on other ideas too: a frame-building jig, brazing with oxy-hydrogen, a shapely new pedal. These he offered to another former Carpi rider, Corrado Paratella, now owner of a bike-shop in Torino. Paratella argued about the price. Campagnolo lost patience, stomped out of the shop into the courtyard. It was pouring with rain. Having stood awhile in the wet, he reentered the shop and glared at Paratella. 'You want to know why I went out in the rain ? Because this hat is such good quality that it keeps the rain out. You want to know how much I paid for it ? Twice as much as the so-called best on offer.

Same as my pedal, you stubborn mule.' Paratella was persuaded: he ordered the frame-building jig, the pedals, the Campagnolo derailleur, the bottom bracket. Campagnolo was also working on a new hub but, needing to take out a patent, he hadn't the money. Too busy at the workbench to keep abreast of the finances and chase up defaulters. Crisis. A

---

7 In a 1932 edition of the weekly magazine *Cycling* I found an advertisement for a three-speed derailleur made by the Triumph company sold as 'Trivelox', Latin for 'three-speedy'.

frenzy of work in frustration and racking of brains he finally did what any home-loving, Catholic Italian would do: he picked up the hub from the bench, waved it in the air and called on the Madonna in her local incarnation – she'd appeared in a vision to a peasant woman in a village nearby during a visitation of the Black Death. Suddenly, a ring on the doorbell: the postman with a registered letter from the Banco Popolare about payment by a Belgian client of a long overdue invoice at their branch in Liège. He took out the patent

In the summer of 1936, Campagnolo took one of the new derailleur gears to see Binda, now director of Legnano, bicycle manufacturer since 1902, for whom he had ridden, at his home in Cittiglio near Lake Maggiore. Binda had won his fifth Giro d'Italia in 1933 and intended to ride it again but he'd been involved in a big pile-up of riders sprinting down the Via Sanremo in the '36 edition of the Primavera, 'the Spring race' Milan-SanRemo, and broken his femur. The crash ended his career. He was 33 years old and, though he started training for that year's 'Race of the Falling Leaves', the Giro di Lombardia, 'at the last minute' as he put it 'an irresistible impulse made me change my mind'. The thought of not being able to return to competition at the highest level, enforced reflection on the toll that years of racing had exacted, the recurrent fear prompted by memory of the disastrous crash…all keyed in.

Campagnolo described the working of the derailleur and, Binda appearing dubious about it, demanded a bike, got some tools out of his bag and, one imagines, with concentrated intensity, fitted the gear. That done, he said to Binda: 'Now get on the bike'. Binda, like all the great champions a superb handler of the bike, rode round the garden working the gear. They struck a deal and Campagnolo equipment made its début in international racing.

Henri Desgrange had persuaded an Italian team to enter the 1937 Tour de France, with Gino Bartali, by now a big star – Giro d'Italia 1936 and '37, Giro di Lombardia 1936, as captain. Campagnolo made the trip to France. He loved being around racers, anyway - the buzz of competition, the company of bike men, the world that evoked his own unflagging youthful enthusiasm - but his purpose was tendentious. The French Simplex company had developed its own derailleur. The chain passed round a small jockey wheel slung under the chainwheel; a cable attached to a lever mounted on the down tube shifted a simple mechanism to pull the chain over the rear cogs and the jockey wheel took up the slack as the chain loosened. The mechanism was flimsy, the jockey wheel got easily clogged with dirt and mud, while the crude manner of hauling the chain sideways imposed considerable friction and therefore wear. Desgrange had banned its use in his race: too unreliable. However, the Simplex gear was much easier to work than Campagnolo's and the competition spurred him.

Riding the 1939 Giro d'Italia for Legnano, on bikes fitted with Campagnolo components, including the handsome rod derailleur, were the men whose rivalry would divide the Italian *tifosi* into two frenetic camps: *Bartalisti* versus *Coppisti*, the former in support of Bartali, winner of two Giri d'Italia (1936, 1937) and the 1938 Tour de France, and, the latter for his domestique, the 20-year old Fausto Coppi.[8] But, notional team loyalties gave second place to form, as ever 'the road decides', and there simply was no holding Coppi. Bartali had to give his brilliant *gregario* (folloewr) his head. Coppi finished in the pink. Sales of the Campagnolo gear rocketed and Aldo Zambrini, boss of Bianchi, hovered behind the new star, cheque book in hand, ready to swoop.

The war intervened.

Campagnolo realised now that he would have to engage full-time help in his workshop to cope with the demand for his hubs, gear and pedals which, to this point, he had not only been hand-tooling on his own but hawking round bike shops in a suitcase. He wrote to Enrico Piccolo, who had been working as a mechanic for an old racing rival of Campagnolo's, Severino Dartadi, enclosing enthusiastic write-ups about the derailleur in Milan's daily sports paper. Piccolo was doing military service in Capua but agreed to join Campagnolo as soon as he was discharged in 1940. He became the first full-time employee in the hitherto one-man band which, that same year produced the Campagnolo Cambio Corsa ('Racing Changer') derailleur gear, patented in May, every piece of the

---

8 Such divisions of loyalty are, of course, an Italian tradition – Capulets and Montagues, Guelphs for the Holy Roman Emperor, Ghibellini for the Pope, Binda v Girardengo, Binda v Guerra…

mechanism handmade, the cogs filed by Tullio, the master craftsman, himself.

Bartali avoided military service because he failed the medical. The army doctor told him that his heartbeats were so irregular, the pulse so slow (he'd long since been advised to smoke three cigarettes per day to boost the heart rate, a fourth if he won a race) that he couldn't possibly join up and sent him home. On 7 November 1942, three days after the decisive British victory over the Afrikakorps at El Alamein, Coppi mounted a bike fitted with wooden-rimmed wheels and raced round the Vigorelli cycle-track in Milan to break Archambaud's existing world hour record of 45.767km by 104 metres. (That record stood until Anquetil set a new mark of 46.159km in1956.) Soon afterwards, Coppi was drafted into the army but, captured in Tunisia by the British Eighth Army, he spent two years in a POW camp. Rumours even reached Italy that he had been killed.

Home from the war, he discovered that Bartali had signed a fat contract, all conditions met, for Legnano: once more he would be riding as domestique to the wily charmer, whom he'd ridden off the road in his first Giro. He approached Aldo Zambrini, director of Bianchi. In the ruins of post-war Italy, Bianchi, like many other manufacturers, had to relaunch itself and the presence of Coppi in the team was an undoubted publicity boon. Coppi promptly delivered Bianchi two consecutive victories in the Grand Prix des Nations, the classic international time trial, in 1946 and '47.

Campagnolo's commercial acumen now marched steadily alongside his technical genius.

His sponsorship of the sport was an essential part of his selling and he ensured the name Campagnolo became attached to every victory won by a rider using his components: equipment endorsements - 'The gear worked beautifully, I owe the win in no small part to Signor Tullio...'; the name Campagnolo emblazoned on every bit of literature abut the race – the list of riders beforehand, the post-race reports.

In 1947 Campagnolo began to export his components and in 1949 he made ten models only of a dual cable version of what he called his Gran Sport derailleur – one cable to move the chain from lower to higher cogs, a second to move it back. Clearly he was moving from refinement to refinement and the following year saw the advent of the true

Campagnolo derailleur gear, the prototype of all future models for some 30 years: the Nuovo Gran Sporto, the first rear mechanism to be used widely in the professional peloton. Fausto Coppi, now riding for Squadra Bianchi as he would for the rest of his career, won the Paris-Roubaix on the new gear (despite the fact that he considered it a disaster – there's no pleasing some people); Bianchi adopted the Nuovo Gran Sporto and the little workshop in Vicenza, its work force expanded to ten, beavered away.

Around that time, a young man of 20 had begun his own illustrious career in bicycle manufacture, filing lugs in the Gloria workshops in Milan: Ernesto Colnago. Another, Cino Cinelli, a fine racer – winner of Milan-Sanremo in 1943 and Giro di Lombardia in 1938 (2nd 1941, 3rd 1940) – hung up his wheels in 1948 after 15 years of competition and started his own business becoming the first to make aluminium handlebars and a saddle with a plastic frame. The company motto is *Crediamo in te, bici* In you, bike, we trust.

In his book about Campagnolo – *The Giant and the File* - Gianni Brera gives an insight into the intuitive way Campagnolo worked, the conjuring of ideas out of seeming banality, like James Watt staring at the steam kettle and *seeing* for the first time what countless millions had merely *looked* at. The problem of the bottom bracket, for instance: before the advent of the sealed unit, it was impossible to keep the bracket assembly watertight against rain, melted snow and mud spattering off the road into chain, gears, bracket, hubs. Even stripping down the entire machine after every dowsing could not stave off the gradual deterioration of the metal, especially in a moving piece of machinery, like the bracket, which underwent constant wear in the best of conditions. Seated at the dinner table one evening Campagnolo stares distractedly at the table cloth. It's wrinkled. The distraction is no more than the precious relaxed state needed for what has been a nagging thought process, not dissimilar to that of trying to retrieve a name from the memory. Brera records how, staring at the ruffled cloth, Campagnolo reached for a piece of paper and a pencil and drew the design for a bottom bracket into the walls of whose drum were cut grooves, indented ridges, to act as channels along which the infiltrating water would leak away. He takes the sketch to Piccolo and tells him to develop it.

Fausto Coppi spent most of his racing life in hock, continuously paying out alimony to his ex-wives, often having to spend contract money long in advance of the race itself. Some time in 1948, he told the Bianchi people that he was ready to join the team. Campagnolo caught the train to Milan and met Coppi at a restaurant. They haggled, Campagnolo held out, Coppi yielded and the two men shook hands on the contract – 5 million lire on account from a total of 23 million over three years. Days passed and Coppi did not acknowledge receipt of the cheque for five million lire that Campagnolo had sent in a registered envelope but without a return address, so as not to alert the competition for Coppi's services. Campagnolo phoned; Coppi knew nothing of any envelope but searched through an accumulating heap of fan mail and unearthed the envelope containing the cheque. Campagnolo was, at last, linked with the biggest name in Italian cycle sport sponsorship. Of its closest rivals, Bianchi and Legnano, the latter would soon disappear.

There is no question that riders liked Campagnolo's components, especially the Nuovo Gran Sport gear, but the charming, likeable Italian was a perpetual self-publicist, hanging out at races, getting to know riders, projecting his unquenchable enthusiasm for cycle sport and everything to do with its men and machines. Moreover, he played an energetic and central part in the increasing good fortune of Italian cycle teams in races beyond the frontier, especially the Tour de France and big classics like the Paris-Roubaix, typified by the careers of Bartali and Coppi, the latter in particular, providing a blaze of publicity for Campagnolo's components.

Bartali had won the 1948 Tour, ten years after his first victory, and came second to Coppi in 1949 (they also took first and second in the Mountains prize) with nearly 15 minutes over the very Italian-sounding Frenchman Jacques Marinelli. Every rider in the Italian team, including Fiorenzo Magni, (winner of the Tour des Flandres 1949-51), finished and they took the overall team prize. The following year, the Italians fell apart.

Bartali insisted on being captain and the directeur sportif, Binda, agreed on condition that Fiorenzo Magni, a Campagnolo protégé, be his second. However, Bartali was riding a Simplex, not a Campagnolo gear: the domestiques loyal to him would be able to supply him with a spare rear wheel if necessary and those few loyal to Magni theirs.

Different – incompatible – gears and hubs signalled contention. More to the point, Magni was the rising star, Bartali, now 38, surely waning.

Magni won the 8th stage and, in the Pyrenees, was heading for yellow. Bartali, suffering from cystitis, was not going very well and was also jittery. French fans were barracking the Italian riders and Bartali claimed he had been threatened by a ghastly old woman in black brandishing a large kitchen knife. Then he reported that, while descending a col at speed, a phantom black car had appeared out of nowhere and tried to shunt him off the road. His own brother Giulio had been killed by a hit-and-run driver during the 1936 Giro d'Italia and Gino hadn't touched the bike for two months. The trauma had surged back. Nonetheless, he regained something of his composure and his climbing legs on stage 11, first day in the Pyrenees, Pau to Saint Gaudens. The peloton had ridden through a cloudburst, pelting rain and near darkness which made the descents hideously dangerous. On the climb of the col d'Aspin, the French crowds were in a belligerent state. Robic and Bartali, trying to weave through the encroaching lines of angry spectators, went over the edge. A number of people scrambled down to help Robic, the Frenchman up, a good few of them inebriated. Bartali, the Italian interloper, had a rough time of it: he was insulted, punched, manhandled. Spitting vengeance, he won the stage into Saint Gaudens but had not long crossed the line when Magni came in and took over the race lead. Bartali's morale collapsed. Magni in yellow would expect full support of the entire team. At the hotel that evening, Bartali told Binda he was going to quit. Most of the team was riding a different gear from Magni's. Bartali was intransigent. Had he stayed, he might have neutralised the competition in the mountains – Kubler, Louison Bobet, Raphaël Géminiani – and left the rest of the Italians to protect Magni's lead into Paris. However, he would not budge. 'We have been subjected to violent aggression' he said 'and as a result we will not be at the start tomorrow.' *We*, notice, meaning 'Me and the *cadetti*, (the juniors)'. Binda, under such bitter pressure from the formidable Tuscan, whose bullying tactics had mired Italian solidarity a number of times in the past, not least in the umbrage he took at Coppi's refusal to play second fiddle, had little option but to withdraw the whole team. Magni packed a pristine yellow jersey in his case, along with two souvenir bidons, and went home. (He rode the next three Tours and won four stages.) It was an ignoble episode and, unhappily, in part due to commercial rivalry. Had the entire team been riding the same equipment, Bartali would have had no bargaining leverage for his petulance.

Top riders outside Italy were happy to puff Campagnolo's equipment – the Swiss Hugo Koblet, Tour winner 1951, Giro d'Italia winner 1950, Luxemburger Charly Gaul, Tour winner 1958, twice Mountains champion, the two Spaniards Federico Bahamontes, Tour winner 1959, six times Mountains winner, and his lieutenant Miguel Poblet, winner of two Tour stages. The Italian Gastone Nencini also won the 1960 Tour on a Campagnolo gear. The year after he did so, the Campagnolo company in its new factory overlooked by the Berici hills which rise gently up from the plain at the southern edge of Vicenza, became the first company in the world to use low-pressure magnesium casting. From the revolutionary material, both strong and ultra lightweight, which emerged from this process, Campagnolo fashioned wheels for cars and motorcycles as well as lightweight parts for military planes and satellites. The Wright brothers turned from the manufacture of bikes to make the first plane…Campagnolo did something like the opposite.

The region of the Berici hills is famous for truffles and wine. Campagnolo bought a vineyard there and, musing on the extraction of the cork from the bottle of good vintage, the struggle to liberate the liquid when the thirst is biting, the effort required to heave a stubborn stopper out, the risk of spilling liquid, he plied his file and made a screw-pull cork extractor. He seems, like Edison, to have been in a constant ferment of ideas, many of them unworkable but each one perhaps essential to the formulation of the ideas that did work. As Edison said, better to discard a hundred thoughts for the saving of one than to have had but one thought and that thought of little use, if any.

The list of great riders who rode on Campagnolo gears, hubs, brakes, chainsets is long and embraces most of the best. Professional bike riders are famously pernickety about their machines and equipment and with good reason. The bike is a frail machine, engineered to an extreme of weight and efficiency. Mechanical failure can lose a race or cause dreadful injury and a season's racing lost, if not worse. Madcap descents of the high mountains at dizzying speeds, sometimes coping with buffets of wind, driving rain, fading light, expose every rider to extraordinary risk: a slick of oil from a car, a patch of wet, a litter of gravel on the road can flip a tyre and the rider is down, possibly out. In the past, before indexed gear changing and bar-mounted shift levers, there was a real skill in changing gears: hearing a rival muff a change, the rear mech clacking, the chain running loose on top of the freewheel, a rider could sprint clear, gain 10, 20 metres before the rogue chain had settled and the cogs were biting again. It seems almost comical, now, given the high sophistication of modern equipment. In chancier times, Campagnolo and the others knew how dependable gears had to be to satisfy the precise demands of the peloton, how important was smooth, neat, swift gear-changing and the capacity of the mechanism to continue to work efficiently in all weathers, resistant to wet, mud, grit.

The advent of the Japanese cycle manufacturers into the European market will be treated of in a separate chapter, but it is worth noting here that at present Campagnolo gears offer the only competition from Europe to the rampaging Shimano. Campagnolo himself was, predictably, dismissive about the Japanese: *Copioni, de l'ostia* 'Copycats, by Christ'. Passionate about his work and the sport it served with such distinction, he was a stalwart of the European industrial base against stern competition from the east. That the name Campagnolo still has the distinctive ring of class, excellence and style is perhaps the best epitaph for the man from Vicenza with the file.

Somebody once said to him: 'You're another Leonardo da Vinci.' Tullio scoffed. 'I'm no genius, I'm a poor man who works day and night.'

If one might dispute the 'poor' – he'd drive past a bunch of cyclists and say he could afford the deluxe motor only because of them – one could never dispute the panache, dynamism and industry of the man.

He died in a hospital in Monselice, 45km south-east of Vicenza (he did not want news of his final illness to leak out) on 1 February 1983. Two days later, Eddy Merckx delivered a funeral oration to a packed congregation in Vicenza:

'Dear maestro Campagnolo, in the name of cyclists both famous and unknown all over the world, I bid you, here in this church, a heartfelt farewell. You share in our memories because you, like us, were a cyclist, you knew our fatigue better than we did, you gave us a helping hand, and you did so with that generosity and intelligence which came from your goodness both as a man and an industrialist. You were the most loyal and valued of our domestiques. The seven times that I crossed the Milan-Sanremo line first, you were with me. You were with me in the snow that day I rode to victory over the Tre Cime di Lavaredo[9] with more assurance than I had ever known. I shared every success with you. In saying goodbye to you, in the name of everyone present and all those who had wished they could be here, I wish to make it an act of faith. You will be remembered by cyclists of all ages and attainment as a cherished, an irreplaceable companion of the road. Above all, a great friend.

If I say this in my poor Italian I say it from an Italian heart because, thanks to you, with your name, you have attached a piece of Italy to bicycles all over the world. Your memory will live with us always. Farewell.'

On 24 June 1995, a memorial to Tullio Campagnolo was unveiled on the Croce d'Aune pass, above Feltre in the south-east Dolomites.

---

9 1968. A crushing 30km break which sealed the first of his five wins in the Giro d'Italia.

CHAPTER THREE
THE RALEIGH CYCLE COMPANY

Any account of the cycle manufacturing industry in Britain must give preoponderant weight to the history of the Raleigh company which dominated the industrial scene, national and international, for the greater part of the twentieth century. The founder of the Raleigh Company, Frank Bowden, qualified as a lawyer and in 1870, aged 22, took a job in Hong Kong where he spent a highly lucrative 15 years dealing in property and stocks and shares. However, life in the steamy climate of the Far East broke his health. Suffering, as he put it 'from an inactive liver, sleeplessness, bad circulation, varicose veins, rheumatism and general debility' he returned to England for medical treatment which may well have saved his life. He went to the spa town of Harrogate to take the waters at the chalybeate, sulphur and saline springs but a local doctor told him it wasn't a water cure he needed it was restorative exercise. He pointed out of his consulting-room window at a man riding a tricycle steadily round the town square. Three weeks before he'd been suffering from a partial paralysis and couldn't even move his legs. Cycling had brought him back to health and strength.

In late 1886, therefore, Bowden shipped a low-geared tricycle to Arcachon, a resort town on a sandy promontory of the Landes, the flat coastal region of south-west France, near Bordeaux. The steady-state, low-gear pedalling still recommended for '*supplesse*' not only restored his health; by early spring, the daily exercise had so strengthened him, body and mind, that he headed inland for slightly hillier terrain and, over a ten-day tour, cycled between 40 and 45 miles a day.

Thoroughly revived and brimful of energy, he returned to England and bought a safety bicycle from the Woodhead, Angois and Ellis works in Raleight Street, Nottingham. It had a diamond frame with an integral bottom bracket, rather than clamped on, as was more common. It had a 26 inch front wheel with anti-vibration forks, a 28 inch rear wheel, with 7/8 inch solid tyres (more wieldy than the usual ½ or ¾ inch) Moreover, by swapping freewheels, a rider had a choice, albeit fairly tedious to effect, of three gears. Bowden set off with his Safety that summer of 1887 for a continental touring holiday in France, Switzerland and Italy, and began to ponder 'the future of cycling for health, pleasure and business'. Why not apply the entrepreneurial experience he had gained in Hong Kong to the manufacture of bicycles ?

Things moved fast. He entered negotiations with the owners of the small firm in Raleigh Street and in December 1888 announced the inauguration of 'The Raleigh Cycle Company' operating from a much larger premises (formerly a lace factory) in an adjacent street. The firm grew rapidly, sales rose steadily and the number of models designed and manufactured excited enormous interest among public and sporting types alike. On a new and improved tandem Safety (after the Latin *tandem* which means 'at length') weighing 64lbs, W.C. Goulding and F.T. Bidlake covered 65 miles along the Great North Road out of London in 4 hours 5 minutes. Some while before, Bidlake had won a tandem race, partnered by the redoubtable George Pilkington Mills, over the 800 miles from Land's End to John O'Groats on a bicycle designed by Mills.

This was only one of a proliferating number of road races monitored by a newly-formed Roads Record Association. However, the National Cyclist's Union, who had been so sniffy about Mills' professional activities on the continent, now buckled to mounting adverse pressure from police, local authorities, the press and public opinion. The activities of the North Road Club in particular were singled out: they were heavily censured for turning an open stretch of highway into a racing piste rendering it permanently unsafe to anyone not on a bicycle. In 1890 the NCU banned all races on roads and, not long afterwards, F.T. Bidlake introduced time trials which could be passed off as no more than solo riders going about their lawful and unobjectionable business of getting from A to B by bike.

After the end-to-end ride with Bidlake, Mills was wooed by Bowden to join Raleigh as chief draughtsman. He at once embarked on the design of a purpose-built factory on a five-acre site in Lenton, a southern suburb of Nottingham, to accommodate the booming Raleigh concern. It opened in 1896. Raleigh's designers, engineers, mechanics, tool operators, managerial and marketing staff had been carefully schooled from the first and Bowden had shown himself to be a remarkably astute businessman. In 1891, racers mounted on Raleigh machines held a number of records - world and English quarter mile, Irish 50 miles, Italian 100 km, American 3, 4 and 5 miles - and in 1892 the American, Arthur Augustus ('A.A.') and 'Zimmy' Zimmerman, of the New York Athletic Club came to England. Bowden, well aware what a publicity coup offered, invited Zimmy to Nottingham to try out a Raleigh racing machine. In the USA, Zimmy had been riding an old-style, treadle-operated 'Star' bicycle which weighed 72lbs. In Lenton, he was introduced to a sleek, angle-framed, aerodynamic Raleigh with cut-out bend lugs, brazed seat stays and wheels with a combination of tangential and radial spokes, weighing a mere 24 ¾lbs. On this machine, in 1892, he took 75 wins, 10 seconds and 5 thirds. He won three of four events - 1, 5 and 50 mile - to take the British National title and, but for being involved in a big pile-up, would probably have won the 25 miles, too. He also broke the world quarter- and half-mile sprint records. Raleigh produced a poster to clarion their successes that annus mirabilis: A.A. Zimmerman Champion of the World, shiny dark hair centre-parted, bodily posture relaxed and powerful, ready to show his amazing speed, his gaze intent and direct. Behind him, on the verge of the road, beside their bicycles, stand a man in Norfolk jacket, plus-twos and cap, and his woman companion in full skirt, bodiced blouse and broad-brimmed hat. Alongside Zimmy is a signboard with Raleigh's list of wins for 1892. '2,300 Prizes. Unparalleled List of Riders…champions of Italy, Austria, South Africa, Wales.' Zimmy's hallmark high pedalling cadence, 125 rpm, was imputed to his early training in the chainless days on a high bicycle, where whoever could turn the big wheel faster would be sure of winning.

The boost that riders of Zimmerman's class and international renown gave Raleigh sales was incalculable, the encouragement to technical innovation in the Lenton works of huge benefit. In 1892, the Raleigh engineers introduced the distinctive tubular fork crown, a short length of round tube to which both steering head and forks were brazed. When the pneumatic tyres, wider than solids, arrived, enlarging the tubular fork crowns was a simple matter of lengthening the transverse tube. Other manufacturers who used cast crowns had to scrap all their stocks of castings and jigs to accommodate the fatter tyre. Mills visited America to see how the Americans made bikes and met one Edward Glover who was pressing lugs (the collars into which tube ends of the frame were brazed) out of sheet steel. Mills adopted the idea, directed that all lugs for the Raleigh should be made thus – including those holding the fork crown and the bottom bracket – and the famous 'All-Steel Bicycle', the Raleigh signature machine, began to roll off the production line.

 Mills also replaced the roller clutch freewheel he had designed – which tended to slip and jam - with an improved ball-bearing, ratchet and pawl version which proved to be 'practically frictionless, hard-wearing and thoroughly reliable'. He then designed the first back-pedalling brake. Mills was not only an exceptional engineer; his experience as a long-distance racer also made him alert to the need to produce machines which afforded comfort, reliability, smoothness and efficiency of action to the rider, whether for leisure or races. Such extremely high design and construction values lay at the heart of Raleigh's preeminence and it is, once more, an essential factor in the making of bicycles today: the demand for machines at every level of the range, which reproduce something of the ultra-quality racing machines. Indeed, for Raleigh a major selling-point was the lightness of their machines. A poster of 1900 shows a lissom young woman in tapered skirt, loose-sleeved cotton blouse and wideawake hat adorned with flowers, holding aloft a Raleigh roadster, chainguard, tool kit and all, with one hand, the other hand cocked sexily akimbo on her hip.

 By 1907, Raleigh was producing around 30,000 bicycles a year distributed from eleven depots round the British Isles and Ireland and Bowden decided to make the company public. The following year, Harry Green abandoned a first attempt to beat the Land's End to John O'Groats record, forced to stop halfway by raging winds even though he was ahead of schedule. He set off again only a few days later, survived nocturnal collision with a large heap of stones in the middle of the road and rode on with an increasingly painful knee. Having covered 323 ½ miles in the first 24 hours, he stopped to get the knee massaged and snatch an hour's sleep. Into the Lake District, he switched to a light Raleigh racing bicycle with sprint tyres and a single low gear. It was a bitterly cold night and when, at 4am on the third day, he rode into Edinburgh, his hands and wrists were numb with cold and the strain of holding the bars. Helpers rubbed them to restore the circulation. His digestive system was in wretched disorder but he pressed on doggedly and made the finish at 3.50am in a time of 2 days, 19 hours and 50 minutes, 2 hours and 52 minutes better than the previous record. The 11am edition of the *London Evening News* splashed news of his ride over three columns and Raleigh was soon producing a model that proved immensely popular: 'The Harry Green'.

Production continued to rise annually. The development of automatic tooling and machines which could work more accurately and between 20 and 100 times faster than even the best worker together with streamlining methods for making the many and various parts of the bicycle, increased output at the same time as reducing overheads.

In late 1914, an officer in the 10th Royal Hussars wrote to the Raleigh Company:

> *'I am at the front and use a Raleigh every day for despatch-riding, sometimes over very long distances. The roads are very much cut up with heavy transport but the Raleigh "sticks it" like a true Briton...I have been over the worst country out here, very often over fields, but my bicycle has never yet dodged its duty.'*

The machine is likely to have been either the 'Scout' or the 'Military' finished in khaki enamel. Perhaps he cycled past the lines of French cycle regiments going up to the Front, rifles slung over their shoulders, water bottle, ammunition pouch, food haversack, slung from their belt. No wonder that Tour de France riders, similarly laden, would also be called '*poilu*', ('hairy, shaggy'), the slang for soldier, 1914-18.

In its October 1914 edition, *Cycle Trader* reported that 250 men from the Raleigh Cycle Works had been called up or volunteered. Although the work force was severely stretched – the government had ordered several thousands of bicycles for the army and many motorists had switched to bikes to help the war effort – Bowden offered to devote a large part of the works to the manufacture of munitions. Just as the tooling in the old small-arms factories had been readily converted to the manufacture of sewing machines and bicycles, so now the reverse happened and the automatic machines which produced the intricate Sturmey Archer gears began to produce fuses [1] and the huge sheet-steel presses were turned over to the production of magazine pans for Lewis machine guns.

By the end of the war, nearly 5,000 workers were employed round the clock at Raleigh and, after peace was declared, the factory added full production of motor-cycles and motor-cycle gears to a massive production of bicycles. By March 1920, *Cycling* announced that 'touring and ordinary pleasure cycling is more popular than ever…taking these facts into consideration there is only one deduction to be drawn. There is going to be a boom, there is going to be a big boom in cycling.' By then, the Nottingham factory was making 2,000 bikes per week and when Sir Frank Bowden (he had been awarded a baronetcy in 1915) died in 1921, he had made Raleigh the biggest manufacturer of bikes in the world. The Nottingham factory produced its own gas and electricity and had its own wells providing water. Other firms had helped establish Britain as the foremost producer of fine bicycles – Rudge-Whitworth, Triumph, Swift, BSA and Royal Enfield, (alsomakers of the Lee-Enfield .303 rifle issued to all British troops.)

Henry Sturmey, an engineer, and James Archer, a schoolmaster, had patented their three-speed hub gear in 1902 and took it to Frank Bowden, head of Raleigh. Bowden was impressed, the Sturmey-Archer gear went into immediate production and became one of the great iconic items of bicycle kit throughout most of the twentieth century.

Raleigh publicity material led the promotion of cycling as life-style, the cheerfully romanticising copywriter employing phrases which have stuck in the language:

> *Is your life spent among whirring machinery, in adding up columns of figures, in attending to the wants of often fractious customers ? Don't you sometimes long to get away from it all ? Away from the streets of serried houses…only a few miles*

---

1 A fuse must be precision-designed and manufactured to be stable enough to withstand rough handling both in transit and by gun crews, to obviate premature ignition, but sensitive enough to explode on impact.

away is a different land, where the white road runs between the bluebell-covered banks crowned by hedges from which the pink and white wild rose peeps a shy welcome.

Sheltering among the trees you see the spire of the village church – beyond it that quaint old thatched cottage where the good wife serves fresh eggs and ham fried 'to a turn' on a table of rural spotlessness, for everything is so clean in the country...Rosy health and a clear brain is what Raleigh gives you...

However, the competition was marshalling. A heavy post-war slump in trade hit all manufacturing badly. In 1922 an Austin Seven and the imported American Model T Ford cost about £175, a standard Raleigh £14 and imports of lower-grade bicycles, selling for half the price, largely from Germany, were swamping the market. The Raleigh works manager called a meeting of shop stewards and work force and outlined the commercial problem: they simply could not compete on equal terms with the Germans. The workers agreed to work longer hours for a lower basic rate of pay in return for guaranteed job security. The result was that the firm managed to produce a bicycle for £10.10 shillings and, a year later, £8. 10 shillings. Their racing bicycle with a lugless, acetylene-welded frame sold for £11.10 shillings. (The lugless frame didn't catch on: racing men liked the elegant shaping and finish of the ornate lug.) The Raleigh name and the high standard of machine, above all the reliability which the cheap imports could not match, reclaimed a large proportion of the lost market. In 1923, Sir Harold Bowden, who had taken over the company after his father's death, declared: 'The tide has turned. Business is flowing towards England in an ever-increasing flood and, to my mind, the most satisfactory sign of all is the steady expansion of foreign trade.'

Raleigh's reputation had been built on innovation and the continual quest for improvement. In 1926, all models had rear hubs with a three-point bearing, renewable cups and dustcaps and, quick to exploit club pride among the cycling fraternity, what they called 'The North Road racer' was fitted with a new quick-release rear fork end. Continental cycle manufacturers won invaluable publicity from the use of their machines by the leading professionals, preeminently Tour de France riders. However, such commercialism stuck in the craw of the Tour's founder and organiser, Henri Desgrange, and to inhibit any influence manufacturers might have on his bike race, for a while he insisted that all riders use the anonymous identical machines, painted yellow (the colour of the paper, *L'Equipe*, which sponsored the race), provided by the Tour organisation. It was a noble, Spartan idea, in keeping with the stern autocratic 'father of the Tour', but doomed. The pull of advertising would not be denied for long. Operating in the strictly amateur world of sport, Raleigh enjoyed what might be called a more fresh-faced and innocent public image, derived from the exploits of chipper young men full of the joy of the road and willing to have a go.

In 1929, riding the same make of bicycle used by Harry Green in his end-to-end record ride, Jack Rossiter set out from Land's End followed by a support crew of Raleigh mechanics. The first man ever to ride all the hills in the final stretch without dismounting, a task made the more gruelling by fatigue and lack of sleep, Rossiter beat Green's 21 year-old record by 6 hours 28 minutes. (Rossiter next broke the 1,000 miles record; his time of 3 days 11 hours 58 minutes beat the old record by nearly four hours.)

Meanwhile, another man on a Raleigh, F.J. Davar, was cycling round the world. By May 1929 he had crossed South America from the west to reach Iquitos on the Lower Amazon, having so far travelled 47,000 miles through 36 countries. An American paper reported that:

> He was the first cyclist to cross the Andes…on a bicycle. Vampire bats, pumas, dantas [a fleet-footed beast the size of a bullock] and other weird animals investigated his bicycle in the Upper Amazon regions but left it at that, while he had to beware of the famous "death tree" which is said to kill anyone impudent enough to sleep under it. He was also the first to cross the Sahara, 2,900 miles, on a bicycle. The adventurous rider is now making his way north through Central America to the United States and reports that the Raleigh is giving him good service and is in quite good order in spite of its long and laborious journey.

Nevertheless, the Roaring Twenties had shot in with a fulsome blast of motor exhaust and, although there was an upsurge in cycling and outdoor pursuits during the economic downturn – the Great Strike of 1926, the steady spiral of decline leading to the Depression – the advent of cheap motor cars and accessible public transport was turning the riding of bicycles for pleasure into a more and more marginal pastime. To the 'great clerk class and the great shop assistant class' who, as *The Cyclist* had said in 1892, formed the majority of bicycle owners, could be added the tradesmen and factory workers who cycled to work. The clubmen 'scorchers' still took to the roads as they had ever done but the bicycle had, somehow, lost its cachet. Hoopdriver, the draper's- assistant hero of H.G. Wells' *The Wheels of Chance* (1896), experiences the delight of the young townie forging out into the hitherto unexplored countryside:

> *Here was quiet and greenery and one mucked about as the desire took one, without a soul to see...Once he almost ran over something wonderful, a little, low, red beast with a yellowish tail, that went rushing across the road before him. It was the first weasel he had seen in his cockney life. There were miles of this, scores of miles of this, before him.' And riding the bike gave him such a thrill he considered himself 'a bloomin' dook'.*

By 1934, Wells' opinion had become more jaded. The excited flush of the early days had decayed into something humdrum and mechanistic. Once Wells had said: "When I see a man on a bicycle, I have hope for the future of the human race." Now he was saying: 'The cyclist had a lordliness, a sense of masterful adventure that has gone from him now.' Was this more than just the sour musing of an old man already yielding to the pessimism which erupted in his gloomy *The Fate of Homo Sapiens* (1939) ? That 'lordliness' is the clue. The wealthy no longer rode two wheels. As the price of a bicycle fell, so did its attraction to the upper crust and princes of the church, like the Bishop of Chelmsford who was once champion sprinter of Essex. Society aspired to the motor car, the automobile, the self-propelling machine. Basing his assessment on a 1938 survey, conducted 'when conditions were as favourable as at any other time in the decade', a social historian found that the average British family income was of the order of £450 a year, with middle-class families earning between £550 and £600. The average industrial wage was £156 per annum and as many as 22 million people, of a total working population of some 25 million, earned around £260. The average semi-detached house could be bought for between £400 and £500 and as for cars, the cheapest saloon on the market, a new Ford 8, cost £117. 10 shillings, a Triumph Gloria family saloon cost £285. In 1933 Raleigh undercut both. Its 'Safety Seven', a convertible four seater with a twin cylinder engine, three-speed gearbox, top speed of 55 mph sold for £94. 10 shillings. Moroever, the secondhand motor was a good option. One Anthony Wood from Selsey in West Sussex remembered that 'before the Second World War you could buy a car of sorts for a couple of pounds. And you could get a good car, one perhaps only three or four years old, for £10. And you could run them on a shoestring.'

At the same time, Reg Harris, the future track World champion, was earning something like £2 per week and spending £1 on a pair of alloy handlebars. But he was a racing man, prepared to go into hock for the very best bits and pieces the market could offer. He would not be interested in a standard Raleigh, for which, in 1936, he would have to fork out no more than £4.97p. The following year, another racing man, Charlie Holland, who had recently turned professional with the Sturmey-Archer organisation, entered the Tour de France. His entire background was amateur, he was largely ignorant of bunch racing and wholly unblooded in the merciless arena of continental bike racing. He abandoned the race in the Pyrenees after a series of punctures put him way behind the time limit. His plucky riding endeared him to the French public and it is certain that the Tour organisers would have waived the rules to allow him to stay in the race, but he had a very straitened view on sportsmanship and would not entertain the notion.

The NCU continued to disregard racing: massed start competition put too high a premium on cash, luck, opportunism. The proof was easily found. Compare, for instance, the time for a 50-mile closed-circuit race in Dublin, 2 hours 15 minutes and 20.36 seconds, with the existing unpaced record of 2 hours 3 minutes and 38 seconds. Time - and time alone - was the true test of superiority and, thereby, of character, genuine athleticism and fair play. Professionalism was a by-word for cheating. On the big rivers of

England, for example, rowing had been a professional sport for years, practised by the working class, of course, very infra dig. Thus, without irony, *Cycling,* in the year that Holland briefly joined the continental peloton, reported:

> *At last the Amateur Rowing Association has decided to fall in line with other athletic bodies and to alter their amateur definition in the spirit in which other bodies regard amateurism. They are expunging that blot on their constitution which prohibits rowers who were engaged in manual labour or menial occupations [whatever that may mean] from participating in first-class rowing.*

The bicycle had undoubtedly taken on a more plebeian image and cyclists themselves, those who rode the bike habitually for pleasure, generally in the company of fellow enthusiasts, as opposed to those who harboured no romantic notions about having to ride to work in the rain and saw the machine as a utilitarian convenience and no more, had begun to be regarded either as wilfully eccentric or cheapskate. Bicycles meant *trade*, that despised occupation of the inferior classes. The side gate of even the most modest middle-class home bore a small metal plaque indicating 'Tradesman's Entrance'. Errand boys delivered groceries, greengroceries, newspapers, bread and cakes, meat, fish, poultry, confectionery, on bicycles fitted with large, front- mounted wicker baskets. Chimney sweeps, window cleaners, knife-grinders, postmen, telegraph boys, bill posters, rode bicycles, not to mention the ubiquitous summertime 'Stop me and buy one' Walls Ice Cream men and the autumn invasion of Frenchmen in berets and striped jerseys riding round the streets with strings of onions looped over their handlebars. Carrier Cycles of Wimbledon pressed the advantage of their delivery bikes: 'Makes a horse and cart unnecessary, saves the cost of fodder and enables you to employ a messenger boy instead of paying a vanman's wages'. Truly, the bicycle *was* 'the horse that eats no hay'.

For the cyclists themselves, the brisk and hearty outdoor crowd, the joy and enthusiasm of riding was as bright as it ever had been or ever would be. Mrs I. Cattaneo, who worked in the Rowntrees chocolate factory in York, was a member of the famous Clarion Club in the 1930s. The Clarion Club, founded in the 1890s, espoused radical socialist principles and a passion for the beauties of nature over the dirty squalor of towns. A cartoon in the

Clarion newspaper, shows a cyclist heading down a road towards a sunburst of Socialism, Prosperity, Good Will and Happiness, directed there and away from more ruinous fates by a signpost with three fingerboards: Clarion CC A1 Working Class Struggle for Power…CTC Capitalist Decay…NCU Death from Natural Causes. A silk top-hatted industrialist walks away in the opposite direction accompanied by a priest and a royal in crown and ermine; he carries two bulging money bags marked 'Stolen Gold' and 'Cyclists' Subs'. Mrs Cattaneo recalls:

> *The cycling club was the highlight of my life. I had never known holidays or been anywhere until we got this bike and went all over and had such good fun and such nice company…I didn't want money then 'cos I had this bike. We would pack up on a Sunday and we would call anywhere at these cafés, and they would give you as much tea as you wanted to drink for fourpence…I loved that cycle and I loved every Sunday.*

In 1932, Raleigh bought the venerable Coventry-based bicycle company Humber (originally from Beeston near Nottingham). Humber's success had, like that of Raleigh, been founded on the production of high quality bicycles, but the company was ailing and the takeover saved the Humber name from extinction. Within a year, Raleigh was producing 6,000 Raleigh and Humber bicycles a week and the 700 dealers who took orders for them had no difficulty in selling them. A move to buy another rival, Hercules, failed and in 1935 the Raleigh board made a momentous decision. Having just produced a saloon version of the Safety Seven, the company now dropped all its motorised lines, cars, delivery vans, motor-cycles, to concentrate on the essential Raleigh magic: bicycle and bicycle gears. The chief of the motor division bought the machinery, parts and all the stock to set up a factory in Tamworth from which emerged the famous car-cum-motor-cycle, the three-wheel Reliant.

The cheapest Raleigh was now selling for just under £5 and in 1939 Tommy Godwin handed Raleigh another advertising bonanza. In four days short of ten months, he covered 62,700, more than 200 miles per day; by the end of the year he had ridden 75,365 round and round the British Isles. During one week alone in June, in balmy weather, he covered nearly 2,000 miles. If the exercise seems a mite pointless, the reliability and speed of the Raleigh bicycle had once again been tried to the limit and found durable, and there is no question that such epic feats by lone individuals had a stirring effect on the public. In a famous two-image poster, a black cyclist, bare to the waist, rides away from a pursuing lion on his Raleigh roadster; the second image shows him full of smiles, pointing back over his shoulder with his thumb at the exhausted King of the Jungle.

As early as 1936, Raleigh had set aside an area of the factory for the production of shell cases; plant was brought in, much of it from Germany, and set up in a munitions shop by German technicians and engineers. As in 1914, the Raleigh works also specialised in the manufacture of fuses, a vital part of munitions, and accounted for the large proportion of fuses made during the War. A dud fuse is wasteful and, of course, damaging to morale. Production of bicycles therefore fell - to a mere 5% of the pre-war annual average of around half a million, and much of that for the military, including a folding bike for paratroops. Nevertheless, Raleigh bought out Rudge-Whitworth in 1943 – Dan Rudge began building boneshakers in 1869 – and, most important, benefited hugely by the addition of the Rudge dealerships to their sales network.

Wartime austerity and rationing hit the motorist hard. Enterprising taxi drivers converted their cabs into horse-drawn vehicles by removing the engine and front section of the vehicle and mounting a padded seat and small bogey wheels. Some cars were converted to run on gas – even ot the extent of strapping a gas plant to the car and fuelling it with coal, wood, chicken dung, rich in methane, or whatever was required. Petrol could be eked out by the addition of paraffin, which made the exhaust fumes stink, a dead giveaway. And, as the engine wouldn't start on a paraffin mixture, so the carburettor had to have two supplies attached, one for the adulterated solution, the other for petrol. Military vehicles ran on a petrol dyed pink, to make it distinctive. Sharp operators could remove the dye by adding two aspirins to a gallon and leaving it to precipitate; the dye fell to the bottom and the clear petrol could then be siphoned off. Or, the dyed fuel could be filtered through a carbon-granule gas mask, also available on the black market. However, the readiest alternative to running a car, was the bicycle, even for the high-ranking civil servant getting to and from his office on a tandem, piloted by his chauffeur.

CHAPTER FOUR
EARLY LIFE

He either fears his fate too much
Or his deserts are small,
That dares not put it to the touch
To gain, or lose, it all.

James Graham, Marquis of Montrose 1612 - 50

At 3am on the morning of 1 August 1921, the anniversary of Nelson's great victory at the Battle of the Nile in 1798, Theodora Chicken, née Ottawa, felt the first pangs of labour pains. Her husband, for reasons unexplained, summoned the Salvation Army. A vehicle arrived, Mrs Chicken was taken to hospital and, a few hours later, Bob Chicken was born, two days earlier than predicted. He was already keen to get on with things. His father, John William Chicken, had grown up in German Silesia, at the time a province of Prussia, where *his* father worked as a mining engineer, employed by a British company. On a holiday to Vienna, John William met Theodora Ottawa, a young Austrian woman, scion of a very wealthy Viennese banking family; they married and their first child, Cedric, was born in 1906. Interned for the duration of the First World War, Chicken brought his family back to England after the armistice and in 1919 set up in business, trading as William Chicken. He dealt principally in steel and composite metal tubing, including aluminium, for pharmaceutical use, but his mainstay was in gas barrel tubing for bicycle frames and WC flush pipes, imported from Karl Coppel of the Rühr town of Solingen, then one of the chief centres of the German iron and steel industry. [1]

---

1 Sword blades had been made in Solingen since the early middle ages and tradition has it that the craft was introduced during the Crusades by smiths from Damascus brought back by knights returning from the Holy Land.

The Chickens lived in a house near White Hart Lane, and Bob became a Tottenham Hostpur supporter at the age of 7. He loved football and dreamed of giving the game a serious try. He got as far as turning out for Tottenham Schoolboys against other north London boys' teams and was given a trial for Spurs, but it didn't go well. If his talent didn't match his ambition on the football pitch, his enthusiasm for the game and Spurs has never dimmed. In 2003 he co-sponsored an end of season home fixture with Birmingham City in celebration of 75 years as a member of the Supporters' Club.

In 1933, the family moved to Village Road in Bush Hill Park, a suburb of Enfield. Bob spent one term at Enfield Grammar School, but switched to the George Spicer, the Central School, Enfield, which offered more opportunity for sport. Bob's character and attitude to life and business amply fulfil the admonition of the school motto *Tenez Ferme* 'Stand fast, hold your own'.

He rode to and fro on his first bike, made by the Aberdale Cycle Company, the only major bicycle manufacturing company based in London, under the ownership of the Levy brothers, Joe and Leslie, which William Chicken supplied with tubing for frames.

He left school in the summer of 1937 to take up an apprenticeship at Ponders End in the drawing office of Edison Swan, Electrical Engineers and one of the first manufacturers of light bulbs in this country. From there he moved to Rubery Owen, Construction Engineers, a major manufacturer of steel-framed buildings. In their London Office at 53 Imperial Buildings, High Holborn – their main office was in Darlaston, south Staffordshire – he worked on the drawings for a steel-framed building for Speke airport. The company also sent him on a training course in technical drawing and design at the North London Polytechnic in Holloway Road, where he studied for 1½ years.

In November 1939, some six weeks after war declared, Bob joined up, the only one of four junior draughtsmen in the firm to do so. The others were given exemption because of the nature of the work and Bob might have claimed the same but was keen to join the Fleet Air Arm. Told that his youth and inexperience were against him, he was advised to apply to join the Royal Navy instead. He went back to the office to tell Ernest Owen, joint Managing Director of Rubery Owen that he intended to volunteer. Owen wished him luck and assured him that the firm would pay him a stipend for the duration of the war and that there would be a job waiting for him when it was over.

He marched into the nearest naval recruiting office in London, gave all the necessary particulars about himself and was ordered to report to the Royal Navy HQ at Chatham Barracks less than a week thence. He felt excited, uncertain, apprehensive.

The officer in command of recruit training, Commander Harvey, was a fierce disciplinarian. He needed to be; to turn young men of 18, some of them barely out of school, into sailors fit to serve in wartime, toughened against the stress of combat, admitted of no leniency. The conditioning period of about six weeks was strenuous and very demanding; the intensive instruction in PT, seamanship, naval practice and theory and all the basics of naval duties left virtually no time for relaxation.

Other aspects of life on the base weren't particularly agreeable either. Many of the regulars on were disdainful of these interlopers, so-called 'HOs', Hostilities Only. No more than mere amateurs or Johnny fly-by-nights in the eyes of the hardened old salts.

In early spring, 1940, Bob was at a dance in St Stephen's Church, Bush Hill Park. A stylish, practised ballroom dancer, he'd learned the intricacies – waltz, quickstep, foxtrot - at the Tottenham Royal, a bigger hall even than the celebrated gala venue in Streatham. This fateful evening at the church hall in Bush Hill Park he was partnering his particular favourite, Doreen Hill - an ample woman, to put it politely, but she must have weighed a ton, yet so skilled was she, blessed with such nimble footwork, she moved with astonishing grace, light as a feather, a wonderful dancer. They moved as one. In the middle of one dance, the caller announced a general Excuse-me: anyone, man or woman, could move up, interrupt a couple and take over. Bob had spotted Christina earlier in the evening, sitting at the side of the hall. She was tall, very attractive, blonde hair, brilliant blue eyes and, suddenly, he saw those brilliant blue eyes trained, close-to, on him.

'May I have this dance, please ?' she said.

The rules of the Excuse-me were clear; Doreen Hill gave place and Bob continued the dance with Christina. Except that she could hardly dance at all. He tried to teach her the rudiments, there on the dance floor, without much immediate success but, if she could not dance much, she had, for good and all, walked into his life and he into hers. The first courtship was brief. Three months later he was posted overseas.

Christina, born in June 1922, enrolled in the Auxiliary Fire Service, AFS, later the National Fire Service. She had wanted to join the Women's Auxiliary Air Force (WAAFs) but her parents refused permission. So, she volunteered to help with the vital ancillary services for the fire fighters. She underwent an intensive training period which included driving lessons at a depot in Highgate, north London – clambering up into the high three-ton Commer trucks with the crash gearbox, double-declutching for every change - as well as lessons in the basic engine maintenance and mechanics. To pass her Heavy Goods Vehicle licence, she was required to drive into London and through the narrow streets of Soho, the lorry so wide it nearly touched the buidlings on either side. There was, at least, no traffic to cope with. At the driving school, in an officers' instruction depot in Crouch End, women auxiliaries were taught alongside men and the general judgement was that Christina, a rather refined, self-effacing young woman, had no chance whatsoever of passing the rigorous exams, practical and written. However, the apparent gentleness of character disguised a formidable spirit and will and she excelled.

She spent some time operating the switchboard monitoring the despatch and tracking of fire appliances as they were called out, ferrying wages to and from army bases, then, as demands on the service grew heavier, particularly during the Blitz, driving the small grey trucks containing mobile kitchens to the firemen's recuperation centre at Upshire, near Waltham Abbey on the northern edge of Epping Forest. As men who had been fighting the fires in Coventry and other hard-hit targets of the Luftwaffe, were brought out of the zones of action to the rest areas, Christina and others like her would drive out, usually at 3 or 4 in the morning, to Upshire, Silverstone or closer at hand, the fire station at St Pancras serving a sector in north London which suffered badly during the Blitz. Based first in Enfield and subsequently at Hadley Woods, near Barnet, she also had to ferry other young women of the AFS to and from lectures at Cholmondley House in Highgate, as well as driving vehicles for repair to various garages and depots. Taking out the mobile kitchen units or Army Transport Vehicles from the motor pool, she would sometimes bring help and succour to areas hit by a bombing raid. On one occasion in Enfield she saw a woman, still alive, lying on the floor of a house caught in the blast from a bomb which had dropped on a church opposite. The walls to either side of her had been hoisted up by the concussion of the explosion and then sunk back almost exactly into position, albeit severely buckled. The woman had survived what must have seemed a certain death by the merest chance. Such was the appalling shock of war and the slim dispensations of luck.

Eventually, Christina decided that she would try to become a nurse but was rebuffed: there were restrictions on personnel who had volunteered and moving from one service to another was not possible. So, to her chagrin, her wish was denied.

Towards the end of the induction period at the naval base in Chatham, all recruits had to pass an IQ test, embracing general knowledge and a searching enquiry as to why they wanted to join the Navy. Having been accepted for service, (and some of the older, better qualified men were selected for officer training), they were asked which branch of the navy they wished to join: as a Seaman [general shipboard duties], Stoker [maintenance of engines, boilers etc], and, the elite of the three, Signalman [mastering communication by means of flags – an old system formalised by Sir Home Popham in 1803 - as well as telegraphy with morse code and Aldiss lamp]. Bob chose and was admitted to the Signals branch and, given the choice of a posting to Lowestoft, Devonport or Portsmouth, opted for the small ships base for trawlers, mine-layers and mine-sweepers in Suffolk, known as the 'Sparrow's Nest'.

Life in Lowestoft was dull, dismal, monotonous. The ratings had little with which to fill the idle hours; they did no training and virtually the only thing they were required to do was guard duty – four hours on, four hours off round the clock, carrying a loaded rifle which no one had even taught them how to fire. After three weeks of this tedium, Bob asked for a draft to a ship and was assigned to the Mediterranean Fleet, based in Alexandria.

On 1 June 1941, after a brief stopover back at the Chatham barracks, he took a train to Greenock in Scotland to join the S.S. *Orbita*, a merchant shop of some 9,000 tons commandeered to transport around 5,000 squaddies and matelots, packed into the entire space of the hold like sardines. They slept in hammocks slung so close together that any slight elbow movement and they'd nudge their neighbour. Turning over was a trial. Two days after boarding, they headed south, with no escort or air cover, across the Channel, down the west coast of France, past Spain and North Africa, to an overnight stop, after 11 days at sea, in Freetown, Sierra Leone, then a British possession. They refuelled with oil. The sun blazed in 100° of heat. There was no shore leave. The food served up from the galley was pretty awful.

The ship rounded the Cape and docked at Durban, 14 days later. Sailors and troops transferred to the *Niewa Amsterdam*, an ocean liner built just before the War and commandeered from the Dutch, together with additional military personnel, for a week-long convalescence period: plenty of shore leave, with overnight passes. They slept on board but the luxurious sleeping quarters and a distinct improvement in the quality of the cooking were mightily welcome. Hitchhiking into Durban town one day – and hitching was the principal means of off-duty transport from bases wherever they were – Bob was picked up by a family, the McLarens, who befriended him, took him to see the sights of Durban and then home to their house for dinner. He saw them several times thereafter.

From Durban, they sailed up the east coast of Africa to the Gulf of Aden, across the Red Sea and into the Suez Canal where they disembarked at Port Tewfik on 23 July. Here they transferred to a train of cattle wagons and then open motor trucks for the last leg of their journey to Alexandria. Their destination was a large camping site in the desert at Sidi Bish, a naval drafting station called HMS *Sphinx,* about 10 miles west of the port. They were quartered in large, ridge tents and slept in hammocks slung from 3' staves so that they lay about a foot off the ground. Life in Sidi Bish was peachy. They idled away a fortnight of total relaxation, playing football on the sands and doing not much else.

On the morning of Tuesday 2 September, Bob was drafted to HMS *Queen Elizabeth*, flagship of Admiral Andrew Brown 'Cuts' Cunninghman, Commander-in-Chief of the Mediterranean Fleet, as signalman in the signals communications division. As he walked up the gangplank onto the mighty battleship, huge in size, every inch of it quite spotless, the impression of majesty combined with the weight of expectation was overwhelming. He suddenly felt part of the Royal Navy, heir to the great tradition of Nelson, the splendid history of Britain's maritime exploits, for the first time. Anchored alongside them in the naval base were the battleships HMS *Barham* and *Valiant*, the light cruiser *Naiad*, heavy cruisers *Ajax* and *Coventry*,[2] the destroyers *Jervis, Jackal, Hero* and *Kingston*. This most powerful naval force was subjected to intermittent heavy night-time aerial bombardment from that September on till the severe depletion of the fleet in December. On board the *Queen Elizabeth* he embarked on his first training since Chatham.

The routine was strict but good-humoured and pleasant. Respected commanders observe the old axiom that a happy ship is a good ship. A ship's company will always work harder and more responsively for a captain they respect and have time for. Plunging into duties was a relief from the boredom of the relatively disorganised traipse out from England to the real theatre of action. The seniors on board were patient with the new bugs; practical training – identification and hoisting of flags, Morse code – supplemented the theory taught in lectures on the reading of charts, the interpretation of fixed and flashing lights, the measurement of tides and currents, the laying off a course, the setting of buoys, anchors and cables…all the vital minutiae of basic seamanship. The training was interspersed with Mess Deck duties, cleaning and cooking. [3]

Meanwhile in the western desert, the Long Range Desert Group, the Desert Rats, a behind-the-lines strike force of commandos travelling in jeeps and small trucks, were beginning operations.

---

2 A cruiser may be defined as the smallest ocean-going warship but the largest that can be built in numbers. The original 18th century 'cruizer' described a rated warship on detached duty.

3 Mess Deck was also used as a generic term for the ordinary seamen as a body.

They were allowed a lot of shore leave in Alexandria but no overnights. On Sister Street, home to a row of legalised brothels, there'd always be queues of at least thirty or forty men, mainly army. Before the standard issue of government purchase condoms by the Purser, the ship's commander advised his ratings: 'I don't care a fish's tit how you get on with the ladies ashore but make sure you wear a top hat.' Coming back late one evening to catch the Liberty Boat, Bob saw it cast off just before it was due to leave, ran along the jetty as fast as he could, hollering for them to wait, leapt clear into the water, just managed to grab hold of the side of the boat and was hauled in. The Petty Officer in charge of the lighter detail would often set off before the appointed time, either because he got fed up with waiting or, more likely, seeing the laggards strolling back, no cares in the world, pissed and replete, he decided to teach them a lesson and have a good laugh at the same time. On another occasion, Bob safe on board, he watched as two matelots came in late, ran to the dockside hollering 'Wait ! Wait !' jumped for it, and were left, floundering, plainly visible in the moonlight, knowing that when they did make it back on the next boat twenty-four hours late, their shore leave would be cancelled for a week as punishment for going AWOL. Man overboard ? Rating in the drink.

On Sunday 12 October, the fleet left harbour for exercises along the coast west towards Tobruk. At dawn next day, they were put on red alert: a squadron of Italian torpedo bomber aircraft had spotted them and moved in to attack. They sheered away after several near misses, returned next morning and were beaten off by a sustained heavy barrage of naval guns. The fleet regained port just before midnight.

An all-night leave scheduled for Monday 17 November was cancelled at the last minute and the ship's captain gave the order 'prepare for sea'. The entire Battle Fleet left harbour early next day with fighter aircraft cover. At midday, a lone Ju88 bomber flew over and was sent packing with a salvo from the guns.

After a brief respite, the fleet was again ordered to sea on Monday 24 November: the First Battleship squadron under the command of Admiral of the Fleet 'Cuts' Cunningham, with escorting destroyers left harbour at 6.30am, loaded with supplies of food and munitions for the beleaguered 7th Army in Tobruk.

At 4.23pm on 25 November 1941, as the fleet carried out a normal zigzag evasive manoeuvre, the 35,000 ton battleship HMS *Barham*, second in line of the three Fleet battleships, was hit amidships by four torpedoes launched by a German U-boat. Geysers of water and columns of smoke shot skywards and gradually enveloped the Barham. Bob, off duty on the flag mess deck with some others, drinking tea, didn't hear the explosion, and when a rating rushed in and said the Barham had been hit there was a chorus of 'Don't be wet'. However, when they raced up onto the upper deck, they could see the ship, no more than 80 metres away, listing at 45°, and men leaping from the upper rail into the water. Risking a charge by leaving his station without permission, Bob dashed below to fetch a camera and came back in time to take a picture of huge clouds of dense black smoke billowing from the stricken vessel. The *Barham* went down 4 minutes 45 seconds later. Some 700 men survived, many of them actually saved by the massive force of the explosion which blew them high into the air from the interior of the ship. About 600 men perished, including the ship's captain G.C. Cooke. Vice-admiral H.D. Pridham-Wippel was picked up out of the water an hour after the ship sank.

The terse prose of naval logbooks somehow best captures the dreadful tragedy of a sinking and the loss of life. A position at sea, latitude and longitude. A date. A time. The name of the ship. Nearly 600 people lost.

Captain Morgan of the *Valiant* reported that the submarine had been visible for about 45 seconds and, simultaneously with their efforts to ram her, they opened up with pompoms. However, she was so close that they could not depress the guns sufficiently and the shells passed over her conning tower even as she dived. Morgan concluded that the torpedoes had struck Barham between her main mast and funnel and the final explosion was almost certainly her magazine of six-inch shells going up – it wasn't loud enough for the fifteen-inch magazine.

Shortly after the loss of the *Barham*, there were alerts, relayed by tannoy, to all ships at anchor in Alexandria, to be on the watch for Italian commandos on submersible assault craft trying to get past the harbour boom. But, one night, as the boom was raised to allow an Egyptian trawler to enter the harbour, two Italian assault crews sneaked in on their 'chariots' (also known as 'pigs') and laid limpet mines on both the *Queen Elizabeth* and the *Valiant*. Both ships settled on the harbour floor on an even keel in shallow water. Bob, in his hammock on the Mess deck below the waterline, heard a dull thud somewhere below and, some time later, saw oil seeping through a seam onto the narrow passage of the Mess deck.

The Italian commandos dumped their craft, swam to a buoy and were picked up as POWs. News of their capture was suppressed. They were segregated, allowed no communication with the outside world by letter or message and, as Cunningham put it, 'They will just die for six months and I hope give the Italians the impression that they perished in the attempt.' Bob was one of several personnel to leave the now incapacitated *Queen Elizabeth* to transfer to HMS *Cleopatra*, flagship of Admiral Philip Vian.

The sinking of the *Queen Elizabeth* and *Valiant* was hushed up, the ships' companies carrying on the daily on-board routine and deck ceremonies as if the ships were ready for sea. They even painted the sides. A fine photograph shows the *Queen Elizabeth* bows on, the white ensign of the Royal Navy streaming at full spread in a stiff breeze and Admiral Cunningham saluting on the foredeck below the forward big-gun turrets. Three weeks after the attack, a signal came through that the recently commissioned HMS *King George V* was on its way to join the fleet. No one could believe it, but, sure enough, the familiar silhouette of the new battleship appeared, hull down, on the horizon. It was, in fact, the venerable battleship HMS *Centurion*, which had fought at Jutland, rigged with wooden gun turrets and superstructure as a decoy.

The Battle of Sirte, March 1942

By 1941, Axis forces dominated the crucial sea-lanes at the heart of Europe. Turkey and Spain remained neutral, but most of North Africa was held by Italy with German reinforcement. Vichy France had assumed command of the French mandate of Syria. The British had troops stationed in Egypt, as part of a 20-year defence pact, and although they held the all-important naval base of Alexandria together with Malta and Gibraltar at the western gate into the Atlantic, access to the Arabian oilfields and the Suez Canal now lay under aggressive threat. Malta had been essential to the Royal Navy's presence in the Mediterranean since 1814 but its position, athwart the straits between Sicily and Libya, both Italian controlled, could no longer be considered viable. The Royal Navy's ascendancy in the Mediterranean, unchallenged for 150 years, was suddenly in peril.

Mussolini had renamed the Mediterranean 'Mare Nostro' - Our Sea - and, for the moment at least, the braggadoccio held. The Italian navy, the Regia Marina, sailing out of Naples and Taranto, patrolled the waters at the extreme range of the aerial radius of British flights out of Malta, blocking the route of Allied shipping between Alexandria and the Atlantic. Troops and supplies had to come either the long way round, via the Cape of Good Hope and the Red Sea, or risk the exposure of convoy across the Mediterranean. The 160-mile-wide corridor immediately west of Alexandria, between Crete and Cyrenaica, the eastern coastal sector of Libya, thoroughly deserved its grim nickname: Bomb Alley.

The overriding problem facing the convoys making the dangerous journey from Alexandria to Malta (approximately 1,130 miles) was that escort ships could carry only sufficient fuel to take them about halfway before turning back. Fuel supplies in the western stations was exceedingly limited. So long as Malta could send out air cover and escorts to take over the protection rôle, a convoy had a fair chance of surviving the combined assault of Italian navy and air force as well as the Luftwaffe and a growing threat from the German E-boats, small, elusive, torpedo-carrying, very speedy, high-powered attack vessels. Another besetting problem was the lack of fast supply ships. All convoys must sail at the pace of the slowest vessel. A battleship could achieve about 23.5 knots, a light cruiser up to 32.2 knots. The Italian cruisers were reckoned to be capable of 37 knots though, in reality, it was closer to 30. The speediest merchantman could steam at a maximum of 14, but more usually 12, knots; the slowest at a mere 7-8 knots.

On 20 March 1942, at the dark of the moon, a convoy of four merchant ships, MW 10, sailed out of Alexandria: *Clan Campbell, Pampas,* the Norwegian *Talabot* and *Breconshire.* Loaded with food and fuel for Malta, they were protected by 3 new Dido-class light cruisers armed with dual-purpose (anti-aircraft and naval attack) guns: *Cleopatra* (flagship of Rear-Admiral Vian, in command, signalman Bob Chicken on board), *Dido* and *Euryalus*; an anti-aircraft cruiser, *Carlisle*, for close escort; and 18 destroyers in three Flotillas.

Vian, formerly a destroyer commander, had fought at Jutland. He was acerbic, complex, widely disliked, hard on himself and hard on those under his command, but his courage and tenacity were never in doubt and Cunningham described him as 'a superb fighting sailor'. Yet on the eve of embarkation, Vian spoke of convoy MW 10 as being 'a desperate measure', which must mean that he had made a dusty assessment of the chances of getting through. It was a view shared by others. Middle-East Command observed that:

> *It appears useless to try to pass in a convoy until the air situation in Malta*
> *Has been restored and the military situation in Cyrenaica improved.*

The Chiefs of Staff replied:

> *Malta is of such importance as an air staging point and as an impediment to the*
> *enemy reinforcement route that the most drastic steps are justified to sustain*
> *it....No consideration of risk to ships need deter you.*

Italian reconnaissance reports – from air and submarine surveillance – alerted their shore command to the presence of the convoy on the afternoon of Saturday 21 March, probably confirmed by four German troop carriers sighted by the convoy sailing for Crete from Africa. Early next morning, 22 March, the battle group at Messina rendezvoused with Admiral Iachino aboard the *Littorio* and his escort of four destroyers of the 11th flotilla out of Taranto. Iachino's fleet was making 23 knots; Vian's convoy, still provided with fighter cover, could manage only 11 ½. He would certainly not be able to avoid interception before meeting the ships of K Force unless he turned south, thereby consuming extra fuel he could not afford. The detour might not deliver any great advantage, anyway. The Italians would have to be faced.

A storm was brewing. The British ships were steaming to windward ahead of a stiff, 25 knots blow from the south-east. This threw a heavy sea onto the bows of the oncoming

Italian ships and slowed them down marginally. Bob Chicken recorded in his diary: 'Sea rather rough, sea-sick.'

At around 9.30am, four Ju 88's overflew the convoy in thick cloud and driving rain. At 9.35am, five Italian S.79 torpedo bombers flying out of Libya spotted the ships and let their 'fish' (i.e. torpedoes) go, but too erratically to make a hit. The British ack-ack fire brought one down and, just after 11am, gave another four S.79's a sufficient pasting to make them send their torpedoes wide of any mark.

2.10pm. Captain Bush of the *Euryalus* spotted the Italian ships' masts looming over the horizon and signalled three battleships to the north. Vian at once ordered the *Carlisle* and her accompanying destroyer to lay smoke across the wake of the convoy, while his squadron and the fleet destroyers moved ahead as a strike force, leaving the remaining flotillas to continue as close escort to the convoy.

Soon, the entire British force was enveloped in smoke, whipped forward by the stiff following blow. Vian's strike ships made rapid forays out of the screen and inflicted some damage on the Italians with torpedo and gunfire. Captain McCall of the *Dido*:

> *Outside the smoke screen, visibility was good. Time and time again we dashed out to sight the enemy and fire a few salvoes. When the enemy shells got too close, we retreated under the blanket, altering course as soon as we were unobserved, to mislead the enemy.*

Shortly after 1pm, Signalmen Bob Chicken and Yeoman Thorpe, on board Vian's flagship, the *Cleopatra*, were ordered to hoist the Battle Ensign. Bob records that 'it was a thrilling moment . . . a grand sight to see the brilliant ensign of the Fighting 15th fluttering in the grey sky over a stormy sea in a high wind.'

The Italian cruisers came on in line abreast, firing at extreme range, then swung round in retreat, attempting to lure Vian onto the heavy guns of the *Littorio*. Vian pursued. 'As our 5.25's opened up' Bob Chicken wrote, 'for about ten minutes all hell broke loose, nothing but smoke, the flash of guns, the hissing of shells and an acrid smell of burning.'

The British fleet harried and snapped with such energy and determination that after an hour the Italians had had enough and disengaged.

Vian signalled to Harwood 'Enemy driven off' and rejoined the convoy. No sooner had escorts regrouped with the ships of the convoy than the *Zulu* sighted the enemy again. Almost at once, a salvo from the light cruiser *Bande Nero* hit Vian's flagship the *Cleopatra* at a range of some 1 to 1½ miles, wrecking the radio and radar installations and killing fifteen men. Her front three turrets blasted away at the advancing Italian ships and her rear two turrets hammered at the air attack, as the *Cleopatra's* crew set to to rig a jury radio aerial.

As enemy planes screamed past overhead, the air heavy with the detonation and echoing rumble of heavy guns, the smoke-laden skies torn with the burst of shells, signalmen Bob Chicken and two friends, Bill Hastings and Mick McGonnegal were hauling a flag hoist up to the masthead. Part of the bunting caught on the W/T (wireless transmitter) insulator and, in Chicken's account, 'at once Yeoman Thorpe shouted "I'll clear it" and up the ladder he went. The bunting was snagged about 8 feet above our heads and he started setting it free. A few seconds later, he called down to McGonnegal and me – we were holding the halliard, "Give me a hand with this." He had been up there no more than five seconds when we were hit. All I remember is opening my eyes as I knelt on the Flag Deck – the first thing that caught my eyes was blood, bits of flesh and a sickly smell. I looked round and saw McGonnegal lying full length on the deck, badly mutilated, both his arms had been blown off. It was a ghastly sight. Of Yeoman Thorpe I could see nothing. He had been blown to pieces. McGonnegal was still alive, though unconscious. Together with a Scots fellow, we lay him in a stretcher and took him below to the Canteen where, later, he died.'

At 6.56pm, the entire Italian force withdrew, ordered not to risk combat after nightfall. The guns fell silent.

However, the escort fleet had now reached the limit of its fuel and turned back to Alexandria. At first light on 23 March, still some way short of safe haven, and battered by a gale force wind, MW 10 ran the gauntlet once more. The Ju 88 attacks began at

7.15. The *Pampas* was hit by two bombs which, mercifully, failed to explode and, together with the *Talabot*, she limped into harbour. Me 109's strafed the *Breconshire* as she neared the island in heavy seas. She began to drift. The *Penelope* could not get close enough to take her in tow, so she anchored off Marsaxlokk bay, at the southern tip of the island. The *Clan Campbell*, ploughing on at a bare 7 knots, was hit and sank before making harbour. On 26 March, the *Pampas* was hit and sank in the Grand Harbour, the *Talabot* was set on fire and, a lading of ammunition still in her hold, Lieutenant Copperwheat of the *Penelope* laid demolition charges to send her to the bottom before she exploded. He detonated the mines from a distance of only 40 yards, was injured but survived. On 27 March, after four days unremitting attack, the Breconshire, laden with oil, overturned in Marsaxlokk bay.

Of the 26,000 tons of supplies loaded at Alexandria, a mere 5,000 had been disembarked, a further 1,522 tons salvaged from the wrecks.

Vian, re-entering Bomb Alley on the return trip, enjoyed some protection from the continuing heavy weather; sporadic attacks by German and Italian bombers continued till after dark but to no effect. His battle-scarred ships sailed wearily into Alexandria at noon on 24 March to a 'tremendous reception by the ships in the harbour' – Royal and Merchant Navy and Allied, sirens sounding, thousands of crewmen lining the decks cheering continuously.

As a tactical victory, this Battle of Sirte ranks as one of the finest naval engagements ever fought by the Royal Navy, a triumph of an outnumbered and outgunned force fighting under the direction of a brilliant and determined commander in most severe weather conditions. Vian was knighted immediately. As Winston Churchill's telegram of congratulation put it:

> *That one of the most powerful modern battleships afloat attended by two*
> *heavy and four light cruisers and a flotilla should have been routed and*
> *put to flight with severe torpedo and gunfire injury in broad daylight by*
> *a force of five British light cruisers and destroyers, constituted a naval*

episode of the highest distinction and entitled all ranks and ratings concerned and above all their Commander to the compliment of the British nation.

Yet, Malta remained in jeopardy. The convoys would continue to sail the final leg of their already precarious journey unprotected. Churchill's telegram begins by expressing 'the admiration which I feel at this resolute and brilliant action by which the Malta convoy was saved'. It was a hollow claim devoid of any propaganda value: the Germans could see the upturned hulls and the broken remains of MW 10. Tragically, Vian's brilliant victory had made very little difference in practical terms to the beleaguered island.

For Bob Chicken, having survived his fifth action in the Mediterranean two months short of his 21st birthday, grief at the death of those two fellow crewmen, in particular his friend McGonnegal, mingled with the indelible pride in having taken part in the battle. Such is the cost of war and the punishment of friendships formed in wartime, the anguish of loss still sharp even 60 years later at the vivid recall of the entry in his diary for Sunday 22 March: 'Terrible day.'

Shortly after the fighting ships of MW10 returned to safe haven after the engagement off Sirte, Bob writes: '2 April. Received airgraph from Christina. Wrote her in evening regarding engagement.' She accepted his proposal of marriage gleefully.

A month later, after an afternoon's sunbathing followed by 'over the side for a swim', Bob reported to the Sick Bay feeling rotten. He'd caught a mild dose of malaria with dysentery thrown in and spent the next fortnight in hospital on shore, being nursed back to health on three successive diets: fluids, fish and chicken – poultry, that is, not his own self-care remedy. Discharged on 19 May at 6pm, he reported to the sick bay of the HMS *Canopus,* a shore station, for a week's convalescence and light duties.

At 5pm on 13 June, the day that Rommel began his definitive push on Alexandria with tanks and armoured vehicles, closely followed by waves of infantry, the Mediterranean fleet raised steam and left harbour. At 9am next morning, it joined another convoy and headed into Bomb Alley, where it was heavily strafed by a strong force of Ju 87s and 88s, attack after blistering attack. Almost every ship suffered a near miss. Bob and the other signalmen spent the whole of this desperate day on the Flag Deck, the battle raging – the incessant shriek of aircraft engines, the deafening roar of the guns, a nauseating apprehension that the ships they stood on and the men alongside them were on the point of being blown sky high. Throughout the following night, the ships, caught in the light of flares dropped by planes, endured further attack from E- boats darting in and out of the smoke-veiled shadows firing salvoes of torpedoes.

The surviving ships regained Alexandria at last and Bob cannot have been the only one to be 'tired out' after 18 hours a day on watch. Some wag in the 4th Cruiser Squadron sent round a signal: 'We thank you for your week end in the Med. There was never a dull moment. We wish you good luck in your very tough job.'

Gallows humour seemed, on occasion, the only manageable response to the horrors of conflict.

On 2 July, Bob and his pals Povah and Honeyball walked up through to the top of Mount Carmel (where Elijah conducted his duel with the priests of Baal) above Haifa, sat in a café in the surrounding woods for a drink and gazed out at the glorious view that opened up below them. Northwards, they could see what had once been perhaps the most famous seaport on the Levantine coast, Acre (Akko) taken by the Crusader army of Richard the Lionheart and Philip Augustus of France in 1191, fortified in massive style and held for a hundred years as a main bastion of the Christian Kingdom of Jerusalem. Behind them, to the east, the pale outline of the Galilee Hills was caught in the twinkling haze cast by that magical, crystalline light which so captivates anyone visiting the Holy Land for the first time. They returned to the ship full of what they had seen at the end of what Bob called a 'grand day'. As usual, in the close, sticky heat of the Mediterranean, Bob slept on the upper deck.

Back on board they returned to a humdrum round of duty, interspersed with signals exams, cricket, swimming, shore leave, news from the Russian front and the war in the desert, visits to German town in Haifa, dances in the Army Recreation Hut, the results of the exam – Bob was rated Signalman 1st Class on 23 July (the rank for HOs; regulars would be made Leading Signalman) – and the celebration of his twenty-first birthday on 1 August:

> *Went to sea for gunnery exercise. On return to harbour at 3.30pm I drew the rum and was given sippers by all 12 drawers. A total of more than 8 tots. Shortly afterwards I knew nothing, was sick "out on my feet" was taken for shower bath and then put to [bed] "head down".*

The navy issued a daily tot of dark rum which, for ordinary ratings, was diluted with water as 'grog' to make sure they drank it at once.[1] The treacly rum, which, I'm assured, had a taste like no other rum, rapidly went sour when mixed with water and, therefore, could not be hoarded for a binge. The bosun's whistle piped the call at midday, before the main meal, to the accompanying cry 'Leading hands at messes muster for rum'. The duty man from the mess, the 'disher-outer', collected the rum from the oak barrel, which sported a brass plate with 'The King, God bless him' engraved on it, in a metal measure called a fanny.[2] The disher-outer then returned to the mess and, as the marker-offer recorded the ration for each man on a round pad, poured the tot, man by man, as they came up with their glass tumblers. As a special treat, mates could give away 'sippers' to a pal or, as here, to a birthday boy: namely a sip of their grog, the quantity regulated by custom; in special cases he could grant 'gulpers'. For 'sippers' the recipient would hold

---

[1] Rum mixed with water was called grog after 'Old Grog', Admiral Vernon, who first issued the order for dilute rather than neat spirits in 1740. He habitually wore a cloak made of grogram, a coarse fabric of silk, mohair and wool, often stiffened with gum.

[2] Fanny Adams, a young girl, was murdered in 1812, her body cut into pieces and thrown into the river Rother at Alton in Hampshire. Hence 'Sweet Fanny Adams' meaning 'nothing at all'. Towards the end of the century her name was adopted as naval slang for tinned mutton and subsequently, from the shape of the tin, also the can for liquor.

his tumbler with his forefinger overhanging the rim to the depth of the first joint, to limit the amount poured in; for 'gulpers' the measure was extended to the second joint of the finger. The accumulated surplus in the can went to the beneficiary of the dividend. The issue of grog in the navy ceased some time ago.

 The pleasure of a visit to 'clean, modern Tel Aviv. Most wonderful beach' gave way to another hair-raising spell of action. At 4.30am on the morning of 12 August, the crewmen of the *Cleopatra* had to rise and shine for sailing at 5.30. All available HM warships and several merchant ships had been ordered to set out from Alexandria, Port Said and Haifa. They steamed steadily north-east all day but, shortly after night fell, the convoy ships and most of the warships as escort, turned west and made for Gibraltar under cover of darkness, leaving the two cruisers with four destroyers to steam full ahead towards Cyprus, which hove into view on Wednesday morning. The flotilla spent the day cruising the waters round Cyprus, undetected by enemy aircraft. Bob recalls seeing a black mass in silhouette off to starboard: it turned out to be the coast of Crete, some 3½ miles away. At about 10.15pm, he turned in to snatch some sleep but was wakened by the first burst of firing. RAF marker planes were already flying over the island, dropping flares to illuminate the targets. It was, said Bob, a spectacular sight: the bursting aerial flares, the red, white, blue and green ack-ack tracer fire, 'flaming onions', coursing up into the sky from the ground. Then, in his diary, using an age-old expression of the senior service, 'our guns spoke', adding the fiery explosion of their shells to the dazzling pyrotechnic display. Only after a good five minutes of this naval bombardment did the shore batteries reply. Shells hissed overhead, one hit the water only twenty yards from the *Cleopatra's* side, sending up a huge fountain of spray. The *Arethusa* was in the thick of things too and, suddenly menaced by two E-boats astern, let loose with her rear turret four-inch guns, blasting away into the murk, to drive them off. The engagement lasted 14 minutes, all the big guns of the flotilla blasting away non-stop, meting out a fearful pounding on the shore batteries, until the barrels rested, their grey paint blistered off with the heat of the intense firing, and the ships slipped away, back into the cover of the deep black night. In his diary Bob writes, with that no-fuss unemotional concision which is the characteristic of entries in navy ships' logs: 'Got away OK.'

On 15 August, they left harbour for Port Said. 'Busy all day in the SH [Signals Hut],' Bob noted, 'with little cooperation from the Bosun, who was breathing down their necks incessantly. Nerves got badly frayed.'

Although the watch had been granted shore leave, Bob carried on writing up the logs until 8.15pm. The Bosun gave him another surly order too many. The tension burst and the two of them, rating and non-commissioned officer, had a blazing row. The Bosun slapped down a mean-minded punishment. Still smarting, Bob records: 'The Navy has no fairness.'

Shortly afterwards, Bob was drafted, with three others, to the naval submarine base at Beirut, in Lebanon. They travelled by train on Tuesday 25 August, first to an overnight stop in Haifa and on to Base Beirut by 8 o'clock on Thursday morning.

His diary records: *'27 August. In evening, Jock and I went ashore . . .went to pictures then few beers and eats. Returned about 10pm though leave is still midnight. Don't think much of this place'.*

16 September brought news of the loss of three destroyers detailed to land commandoes near Tobruk whose mission was to destroy the shore installations and the fuel and ammunition dumps before Rommel's Afrikakorps arrived. These were ships crewed by men familiar to Bob and his friends. Friendship was very precious in the circumstances of war and, by the same token, often short-lived. After arriving in Beirut, Bob made particular friends with one Bill Llewellyn and, when Llewellyn got his papers for home, there was the inevitable sharp pang of another strong bond no sooner forged than snapped. On Bonfire Night, 1942, Bob writes: 'Bill left the Base for the *Orion*. Funny how each time I make a really fine friend, within a few weeks we are parted. First Duke, then Bill Murray and now Bill Llewellyn.'

It is unarguable that no one who has not endured the horror of war can plumb the degree and scope of the fear battle evokes. The first experience of conflict, the shock of battle, has temporarily unmanned many who later showed enormous courage. Battle-hardening does not necessarily inure to the ghastly effects it has. The melancholy of war afflicts those who have fought juist as it repels those who have not. Caught up in the routine inhumanities of war – unquestioning obedience to apparent insanity, the only fear tolerated a visceral dread of being caught in cowardice, implacable violence, a strict and blameless condition of employment, obliteration of conscience, suppression of imagination, of moral and emotional repugnance – friendship may be the one constant of humanity that remains and the loss of friends to enemy action, the exact replica of your own action, a poignant gauge of what a man in uniform is duty-bound to give up in serving the greater inhumanity.

Letters and airgraphs helped relieve the ache of being so far distant from home, the future so uncertain, and on 25 November: 'Red letter day. A long airmail from Christina and also a short one enclosing the photograph I have been longing to receive. Am terribly pleased with it.'

 But, monotonous stints of duty apart, life in Beirut was looking up. After over a year's more or less continuous active service, the rest and relaxation in a safe posting came as a huge relief. More and more frequently released from duty early, in the afternoon Bob made for the ABC café in the centre of Beirut. This was the 'in' place: the most popular rendezvous for the Lebanese, drawn by its lively atmosphere, friendly company, jazz, dancing, conversation, joie de vivre, and it suited Bob to a tee. He quite soon made friends with the owner, Fuad Khattar, and, after only a few visits, was invited by Fuad to his house in the smart residential quarter of Ras Beirut, to meet his mother and three brothers. Each of the four young men ran their own business but, far from being dull commercial drones, they enjoyed an ebullient bachelor lifestyle with a wide circle of elegant and charming young men and women. Bob joined the circle and thereby met two close friends, both students studying at the American University in Beirut: James Saghi, a devout Christian from Iran, and Akbar Oskoui, a Muslim, both destined to become life-long friends of Bob. Through them he met a good many other well-respected and educated Lebanese, all English speakers and keen to use the language. Although socialising in Lebanese homes was strictly off-limits to all naval and military personnel, Saghi, much the same build as Bob, loaned him a civilian suit, into which he'd change at Saghi's house, and off they'd go to parties, cocktails, soirées. The eight months he spent in the city were a formative time in his young manhood. In a daily life hedged round with cheerless officialdom, timetables, service regulations, duty and divisions (crew inspection), even the familiar brief intermission of shore leave – a few hours of entertainment and the tender back to the ship – the excitement, the gaiety of becoming part of a social group where he mixed with cultivated, sophisticated, bright and vivacious young men and women of his own age but from a very different culture, was a godsend and life became even sweeter when he was transferred to an onshore installation in the city.

The Port War Signals Station (PWSS) in Beirut processed inter-Fleet signals and communiqués from the Fleet Commander in Alexandria, with additional duties of transmitting meteorological reports as well as relays of information about shipping to Lloyds of London.

On long weekend leaves, two or three days, hitching his way, Bob grabbed at the chance to explore the region: Jordan, Syria, Palestine. He went to Jerusalem, to Haifa, Jericho and the Dead Sea, to Baalbek – the vast ruins, including those of its mighty temple, ravaged by earthquake, but one of the grandest architectural achievements of all time – to Petra, 'the rose-red city half as old as time' lying in a rock basin on the eastern side of the Wadi el-Araba in Trans-Jordan, to Aleppo, the great city in Syria, which dated back to 2000 BC when 'the kings of Aleppo held a great kingdom'.

Despite a long period of depression that summer, brought on by homesickness, rows with a martinet of a Yeoman of Signals and the inevitable toll of accumulated stress in action, Bob's time in Beirut planted a love of the city, of its people, of the life it brought him, richly varied and full. What the war had taken away – the fancy-free years of early manhood, it repaid with life in Beirut. Others he had known and served with had not been so fortunate; many had lost their lives. Amid the perfumed airs of Beirut, morning and evening, the sense of having been spared for some purpose, even if, for the moment, the purpose was to eat drink and be merry for tomorrow . . .well, who knew what, tomorrow? . . . the vibrant awareness that he was being given a precious, unforeseen chance to build on and learn from this experience, an experience he could certainly never have dreamed of in Bush Hill Park, was profound. It is no exaggeration to say that it informed and helped shape the rest of his life: his atittude, his energy, his great thirst for all that life could offer in work and play.

In 1941, General de Gaulle, leader of the Free French Forces at his HQ in London, promised the Levant states, Syria and Lebanon, their independence, as guarantor of their siding with the Allies, the position of whose forces in the Middle East was, by now, precarious. But de Gaulle had neither authority or power to make such an undertaking. The promise, welcome as it was to peoples who hated the French mandate in Lebanon, bore little weight: words without visible substance. Earlier that summer, the Vichy French administration in Lebanon had invited the Luftwaffe to fly in to their aid thus compromising dangerously an essential base of Allied military operations in the vital Mediterranean theatre of war.

The Arab States – Egypt, Iraq, Transjordan, Saudi Arabia, the Yemen, Syria, Lebanon were now banded together in the Arab League. Unity, it seemed, at last. Writing in the *Sunday Express,* Major-General Sir Edward Spears, head of the military mission in Paris **in** 1917 and now Conservative MP for Carlisle, said of British obligations to the League:

> *If we ran away from our pledges, then inevitably they would turn*
> *against us. They consider we let them down badly after the last war.*
> *Should we do so again, these chivalrous people would deem our word of*
> *no account; they would hate and despise us.*

After the arrival of the Allies, both Syrians and Lebanese looked to Britain (not France) to help them attain the promised independence. The French procrastinated for two years but finally allowed elections in August 1943. Nationalist majorities were returned in both Syria and Lebanon and, to the dismay of the French, nationalist governments took office. Three months later, the arrest of the Lebanese president and ministers, carried out, according to the French delegate-general, on the orders of de Gaulle, resulted in crisis.

Bob writes about the growing tensions in the city, and the groundswell of opinion against the French occupation. On afternoon watch at the Port War Signals Station on 7 November 1943, he saw a large crowd gathering in the street below. It was quite obvious that they were angry beyond any appeasement by appeal or speeches. Fury at the suppression of independence even as it had been granted, was about to erupt into street violence.

Next morning, all British military leave was cancelled, French military forces moved in to restore order and martial law was imposed. A relative calm was restored but the situation remained extremely tense, despite bland announcements – 'crisis averted' – issuing from London.

In late November, Christina went into hospital for an operation and, as she recuperated, sent Bob a lock of her hair, a small comfort to help ease what was a difficult time of service in Beirut. Bob was being constantly harried by the harsh-tempered Yeoman of Signals, who for instance – and quite against doctor's advice – put him on 24 hour watch as soon as he left the sick bay after a severe bout of tonsillitis. The lingering knee injury sustained in a football match – a wild kick – swelled intermittently and gave him considerable pain and discomfort. He was also permanently tired out from lack of sleep ('…shall have had 2 hours sleep in last 40'), frequent 48-hour watches and a bad cold that brought back the sore throat. The diversions of watching football matches, evenings at the ABC café and dinner with his Lebanese friends – James' birthday party on New Year's Eve he pronounced 'a success' – became more and more vital to his well-being.

At 0045 hours one Saturday morning, 'Back PWSS in matelot's rig', the party was over, so too the eight months stay in Beirut. Bob's brief entry in the diary makes his feelings plain: 'Found it hard saying goodbye to them all, especially James.'

Bob and the others left Beirut on Sunday 6 March by train back to Alexandria via Haifa. The lull in Alexandria was tedious: 'two night watches on the outer boom. What a job ! . . . Did my shopping buying cosmetics, shoes and stockings . . .Then harbour party again. Detailed for night on a caique [a small, Levantine sailing craft] – anchored to target in harbour. Hurry along U.K. draft!'

Three big 'troopers' (troop ships) entered Alex about 5.30 on the evening of 20 March and their arrival set off a big buzz of rumour that a sizeable home draft was impending. A week later, Bob and his friends Dinger and Collins, were ferried out to the HMS *Centurion* across the harbour in a high gale, the turbulent sea pitching the small boat about wildly. They very nearly capsized and had to turn back and try again from another jetty. Soaked on arrival at the steps up the old battleship's side, they slept that night in hammocks, the first time in one and a half years, and without pause or ceremony the ingrained shipboard duties and routine resumed: cleaning signals lamps, clearing decks for 'Skip's rounds' – the Captain's inspection – standing to for divisions, and so on. Night passes for shore relieved the monotony, but the eagerness to be on their way home plucked at them all constantly.

Final stocking of the ships was set for 6 April, Maundy Thursday. Bob 'wrote final letter to Christina.' His diary entry for Friday 14 April reads *Journey appears to be very slow . . . Same dreary speed 6 – 6 ½ knots.'* It was, however, *very quiet*. The sun shone, the sea was smooth. As they rounded the southern coast of Spain off the Golfo di Almereia, they could see the snow-capped peaks of the Sierra Nevada mountains, their flanks burnished in the chrome light of the Andalusian sun and at 1930 that same day, Friday 21 April, they tied up to a detached mole under the great looming bluff of the rock of Gibraltar.

Monday 1 May 1944

> *Captain told us of putting in at Pompey in about 10 days. This we already knew.*
>
> *Steering 000° [due North] about 700 miles west of the Spanish coast in the open Atlantic, the Centurion was constantly updated on U-boat dispositions. Lieutenant McClough gave a talk on "Inside France Today" and the Bay of Biscay lived up to its foul reputation by blowing up a squall and swamping the ship with a heavy downpour of rain.*

At about 11.45am on 11 May they passed the Scilly Isles, spotted the Lizard Point three hours later and, at 2200 hours, the ship sailed into The Sound outside Plymouth harbour. It had been almost three years since Bob had left Britain.

Going on shore, he was astonished at the huge numbers of American GIs in town and, next day, steaming on to Porstmouth, they passed 'a terrific number of invasion craft in Solent'.

Sunday 14 May 1944

> *Up at 0615. Left ship at 0745. Arrived home at 1pm. Greeted by dear Mother. Changed into civvies. At 4pm to 'Avoca' [Christina's parents' house] and to my joy Chris herself opened the door – to me heaven itself she looks everything I knew she would – to me she has become my life.*

At 0845 hours the following morning, Bob caught the train back to Portsmouth and rejoined the ship. A new crew came aboard soon after and Bob and the others left for Chatham – 'terrible, a prison' – where, because there was no bedding, they had to sleep fully clothed on benches in a bomb-proof tunnel.

Leave came and Christina tried, but failed, to obtain a grant of leave due her, from service duty driving ambulances and lorries.

Tuesday 30 May1944

> *From phone conversation with Chris, gather that the leave (she is entitled to) has been refused her. For King & Country. Bullshit !!!*

Her leave of seven days finally came through on Saturday 1 July. Bob's ended that Monday.

He caught the train north to the Signals Station at St Abb's Head, beyond Berwick. It was a soft number, mainly weather reports, no strategic signalling. He had plenty of extra money and paid for Christina to come up to visit for the last days of her leave. He wangled another visit south before the momentous twelve days leave which, partly because of working additional night watches, he'd managed to move forward to 19 September.

Friday 15 September

> *Since being back in this country, the great love Chris and I held onto for 3 years has more than confirmed itself, and it seems to grow daily. We have made the decision and marry this year on Sat 23rd Sept. God grant us every happiness and success.*

Two days before the wedding, Bob was at home and records: 'Words with father. Lisa [his sister] intervened and unintentionally supported him, causing me great mental harm. Thank God all is to end soon. Mother gave me great support.' Lisa, a rather severe, Germanic young woman, had always had an unhappy knack of rubbing Bob up the wrong way.

It was 'a great and beautiful wedding we are told' and they spent their first night together in London before travelling up by train for a four-day honeymoon at the Norbreck Hydro hotel on the coast road just north of the 'famous seaside place called Blackpool / That's noted for fresh air and fun'. The Norbreck, a large crescent-shaped edifice overlooking the Irish Channel, offered seawater hydrotherapy to supplement the fresh ozone breezes of the legendary resort.

Bob and Christina went dancing at the Tower Ballroom and the Spanish Hall. They spent two evenings at the movies and one at the theatre where they saw Firth Shepherds 'Junior Miss' which they pronounced 'a great show'. Their only honeymoon photograph was taken of them on the North Pier, a gale wind blowing. They returned to London and, on Tuesday morning, said a disconsolate goodbye as Bob headed once more north to the lonely outcrop of rock looking out over the North Sea and Coldingham Bay.

CHAPTER FIVE
CIVVY STREET

In the early months of 1945, the Allied armies were closing in on Berlin. It was patently clear that Germany was on the point of collapse. (Attacked from the west by American and British forces, from the east by the Soviets, Berlin capitulated on 2 May.) Bob was demobilized ahead of time in February because of his expertise in engineering draughtsmanship. Over six harrowing years of war, Britain's resources and exchequer had been exhausted and he and countless others with specialist skills were urgently needed to begin the vital task of national reconstruction.

He reported to the Admiralty in London where he was issued with a heavy but quite well-cut demob suit, dark blue cloth with a white pinstripe, shirt and socks. He kept all his old naval equipment, including black shoes and underwear. There was no ceremony: he just walked in, collected the mufti togs, and walked out, onto civvy street once more. A few weeks later, a small brown cardboard box arrived from the Director of Navy Accounts at Foxhill Hutments in Bath, addressed to 'R.J. Chicken of 109 Park Avenue Potters Bar, Middx', (where he and Christina now lived). The medals it contained were four of a number of different service decorations 'instituted in recognition of service in the war of 1939- 45, namely: the 1939-45 Star, the Africa Star, the Defence Medal and the War Medal 1939-45.

He returned to work at Rubery Owen to honour his pre-war commitment but was already beginning to involve himself with his father's business, seeking to open up new foreign markets, for instance through one of his Lebanese contacts, George Naassan who worked for A.B.C. Stores in Beirut.

In a letter of 28 November 1944, congratulating Bob on his marriage, Naassan expressed the intention of A.B.C. to trade 'not only in cycling accessories . . . but other business fields such as securing manufacturers' representatives . . . ' These other fields cover a bewildering variety of goods, from ping pong balls to porcelain and shirt poplin, underwear of all sorts, hair combs, glassware and nails of every variety, and all manner of articles in bakelite, such as soap boaxes, plates, cups and saucers.[3] There was scarcely a home in post-war Britain that did not contain some bakelite article or other – radio, crockery, container, butter dish – in a cold custard cream colour, or gravy brown, pease pudding green, soap white . .

By March 1945 Naassan was telling Bob that he had been able to inform Chicken senior that 'restrictions on cycles and cycling accessories have been removed and the importation of these does no longer require the blessing of the Middle East Supply Center . . . I was very thrilled to note that it is your intention of going in with your father, mainly to open up a further line – trade and exchange with the Lebanon, and can foresee that business will result to our mutual advantage.'

News that Bob and his father were going to join in partnership was premature. William Chicken was far from enthusiastic about letting slip any control in his business yet awhile. Bob's elder brother Harry had joined the business already to concentrate on reviving the import of pharmaceutical and sanitary tubing with Kronprinz, but he left after about a year to join a newly established firm specialising in a range of pharmaceutical products.

Relations between father Chicken and his younger son Bob had always been volatile, and the young man, home from a theatre of war, after three years tempering of his spirits and character, was not over-inclined to kowtow, either. The inevitable cessation of imports from Germany during the War had hit the Chicken firm hard.

To bolster his business, John William Chicken turned to firms which he had been supplying with tubing and bought up from them surplus cycle component parts, in the main saddles and tyres and cotton rim tape which came in large bales.

---

[3] Bakelite, invented around 1909 by L.H. Baekeland, was a condensation of phenol or other phenolic bodies and formaldehyde, used as a plastic and an insulating material. The substance was brittle but much used until more versatile plastics came in.

Apart from the most famous saddle-manufacturer, Brookes, there were several other companies making them, notably Lycett, Manfield and Wrights. Chicken had a good relationship with Wrights so he was able to buy from them direct and it was this subsidiary business which kept the firm afloat during the stringent period of wartime.

In early May, Bob received heavy news: his elder brother Cedric, a Lieutenant Colonel in the Indian Army, a dashing man in heroic mould who had always given him great encouragement despite the wide gap in their ages, had been killed in action during the offensive to drive the Japanese out of Burma. It was a sickening blow. Another brother, also older, Dick, an army Corporal, had visited him in Beirut – a brief but welcome reunion – but plans for Cedric to come had been put off. Now the dying phase of the war in the Far East had robbed them of him.

When Bob and Christina's first son was born, in July 1945, they named him Cedric in memory of Bob's beloved brother.

Naassan wrote in commiseration.

> *My dear Bob,*
>
> *I was most pleased to receive your letter of May 26th but at the same time was shocked by the sad news of the death on active service of your eldest brother Cedric . . .I can feel how good and clever he used to be from what you used to tell us about him . . .*
>
> *There is a big flow of British goods coming to this country, amongst which are cycles, cycling accessories, electric appliances and quite a number of other commodities and there is no reason why not to start [exporting] immediately . . . I suggest that you simply locate an article, offer it stating quantity and price, and I immediately apply for an import licence . . . For instance, if your father has, say, some cycling accessories that he can export, you simply write to me an airgraph detailing what he can send, giving quantities as well as prices and I can start doing the job here.*

Towards the end of 1945, Bob went in to see H.E. Dawson the Managing Director of Rubery Owen in the London office to ask for a rise in salary. Now that he was married with a child, he needed to earn more money. Dawson appreciated Bob's position but could not afford to pay him a full draughtsman's wage; Bob was still learning. Bob countered: he was keen to get in on the sales side, certain that he could do well in that direction. Dawson told him, with regret, that the company had no place for him there. They shook hands and Bob left to join Clarke, Hunt & Co., a Light Steel Manufacturers and Sanitary Engineers at their Middlesex Iron Works, what Bob calls a firm of general metal bashers. The works were located in Enfield, closer to where he lived, and the wages – £ 2 / 10s per week – significantly higher than what he was getting at Rubery Owen, though far less than a miner and at a time when manual workers were earning £ 5 per week. He worked in the drawing office as an estimator, principally for fire escapes, but also steel coal chutes, staircases, and framework structuring for major building projects. He made detailed drawings from which he could then cost the materials required, construction and installation. Huge quantities of ironwork had been commandeered to boost the war effort – park and domestic railings, tramlines, even fire escapes on old buildings – and general metal bashers swung into action to replace them.

The Chicken-Lebanon connection wasn't making progress. Despite the contretemps between France and the Lebanon, French goods inundated the Lebanese market in which they had for so long been the principal supplier. However bicycles were still in great demand and in February 1947, Naassan pressed Bob to sound out the various cycling manufacturers in Birmingham to try to secure say fifty cycles with double-bar frames 'and I am positive that your efforts will be successful.'[4] He also expressed interest in acquiring outlets for 'poker chips, glass marbles for boys, good quality playing cards, etc.'

---

[4] The 'double bar frame' is one with two top tubes, i.e. reinforced to withstand rough roads, which Raleigh used to send to developing countries.

In reply, 'from our own post-war built Bungalow' Bob reports, ruefully:

> *I have again made tentative enquiries regarding the exportation of cycles, and must express my regret in informing you that at the moment every cycle manufacturer I have approached has duly informed me that their orders for cycles and component parts are ear-marked for export a total of many months ahead for delivery – thus affording little opportunity. To this may be added the recent cut in steel to the Cycle Industry, which you may be sure will be severely felt in this country and abroad.*

No, George, Britain is at present in a most difficult economic position and one which the Labour Government seems incapable of handling along the lines of real recovery. However, the people remain confident of better times – in all probability under a different Government, and I can assure you that at the earliest moment, when conditions do improve, we will enter into a business relationship. As matters stand, our prices compare most unfavourably for all commodities with those offered by the States [whose goods, as Naassan had pointed out, could "still be got cheaper in Lebanon than in England"] – only in workmanship are our goods warranted.

At the end of the War – German forces surrendered unconditionally on 7 May 1945, Japan capitulated on 2 September - Britain's indebtedness was calculated at $ 14,000 million (U.S.), the largest of any country involved in the fighting.

She alone had fought from day one to the bitter end and, in the five years since being declared 'broke' in 1945, she had strained her resources to the absolute limit. An estimated 28% of the country's wealth had been obliterated during the War.

When hostilities ceased, at last, there was a general clamour for things to be done and to be done fast, houses built, infrastructure replaced and mended, systems renovated: the men and women who had made such punishing and chronic sacrifices for their country now looked to it for decent compensation for all they had lost. The populace, united against the common danger, now rounded on the Conservative Prime Minister, Winston Churchill, as the archetype of the officer class to whom they had had to answer for too long, and voted in a Labour government in 1945 with a huge majority of 183 seat over the Conservatives, who had dominated the wartime Coalition government. As a Welsh sergeant said at the time: 'When I joined up I was red. Now I'm bloody purple'.

The emotional shift from a war footing to that of peace was, in some ways, hard to accommodate. Life under arms, frequently brutal and unpleasant, had, nonetheless, a certain frivolity, too, a glamour. In the crucible of risk there is a firing of the spirit. As William Hazlitt said: 'Danger is a good teacher and makes apt scholars.' Away from where the danger was at its height, in battle, the prevailing disposition was coloured by the emergency: eat, drink and be merry for tomorrow we die . . . us or our friends. For servicemen, at least, living in the shadow of death, everything – food, drink, clothing, entertainment – was more or less *found*. The BBC – home of the Forces Network, precursor of the Light Programme through ITMA, 'big-hearted' Arthur Askey, Tommy Handley and the forces' sweetheart, Vera Lynn amongst others – had kept them chirpy and amused during the War, laughter and sentiment to cushion the hardships. Many army men, in the experience of the novelist Anthony Burgess, serving with the Army Education Corps, had their own version of 'BBC' for morale-boosting and basic velleities: 'Beer, Baccy and Cunt'. When life is precarious, keep it simple. After the wild junketings and delirium of victory, when the lousy war was over, the troublesome peace began.

In its manifesto, the Labour Party undertook to make no baseless promises. Mindful of the débâcle that had followed the First World War, when the men coming back to 'a home fit for heroes' were sorely disappointed, the Labour party declared that: 'The future will not be easy. But this time the peace must be won'. It would entail, Atlee said, 'a revolution without tears'. For, no matter that everyone had yearned for peacetime for so long, when it did come at last it came as something of a shock. Connubial bliss, babies and ration cards had not the same vital appeal as the reduced needs of the embattled serving man or woman or the frisk of risk. For a start, life was grey, lacking in excitement and mischief. The larks and camaraderie of close service friendships – at home and abroad – had yielded place to the everyday process of settling down to job, marriage and the vagaries of the future. One is reminded of Florence Nightingale who, overhearing a group of men vapouring about the joys and pleasures of paradise to come, retorted: 'Actually, I think heaven will be quite *rigorous*' in a severe tone which implied that it most assuredly *would* be rigorous if she was there and had anything to do with it.

The ecstatic welcome for the returning serviceman to the wife and children he hadn't seen for years, the children only as infants, in some cases preceded a difficult, even painful, period of adjustment. The standard joke – 'the second thing I do when I get back home to the wife is take my pack off' – soon staled in the reality. Stories abound of the young boy opening the door to the tall man in khaki with a kitbag over his shoulder and shouting to his mother inside the house: 'Mummy, there's a strange man at the door.' A Mrs Crane recalls how, after her husband came home, their children . . . just stared at him, round-eyed you know, and when he kept saying "Don't do this" and "Don't do that" [as a man who'd been under orders for so long himself was prone to do] they said: "Mum, who's that man that keeps coming in our house and staying all night?" I said: "It's your father." And they'd say: "Well, we don't know him – who is he? Tell him to go away."

Hard it was for both adults and bewildered kids, the father being so disliked by his own children and the mother, who probably sympathised more readily with them than him, caught in the middle.

During the War, people had pulled together. The Blitz had pitched civilians into the front line and it bred a new and more confident spirit of egalitarianism. The men had been fighting for King and Country on the war front, those who stayed behind had equally been fighting for King and Country on 'the home front'.

Sir Tom Hopkinson, editor of *Picture Post* a very popular illustrated weekly magazine, a national institution, recalled how:

In any office such as ours, besides the day's work we would go on fire-watching at night and a managing director would fire-watch with the office boy and the junior typist, five or six people, and then they'd all doss down in great discomfort in one of the offices with the rugs that were provided for the purpose. And then the visible signs of any difference in class disappeared.

Democratic conventions even invaded the army. The officer class had once held itself quite aloof from the lower ranks – Earl Cardigan, having delivered the Light Brigade to the batteries, at once rode back down the valley 'thinking it no part of a general officer's duty to fight with private soldiers'. The word 'private' in the military context means 'without privileges'. Such an imperious attitude no longer washed; many officers were new to the forces, HOs, and were promoted by selection after they had joined up or else through the ranks, on merit, during service. Many of them would have no truck with the tommy-rot of a ruling class by virtue of birth. Leadership was recognised as an innate quality regardless of family roots. (As a pacifist slogan of 1940 put it: 'A bayonet is a weapon with a worker at each end.') There was no room for toffee-nosed boobies in a citizen army. Junior ranks who found themselves being bullied and bossed about by second- and third-rate nonentities whom they actively despised, no longer subscribed to the idea that rank had aught intrinsically to do with superiority, either moral or intellectual. Insubordination, once the object of Draconian punishment and always unthinkable, could not be so easily quashed, now. The socialist spirit was abroad, in part fed by a new enlightenment in a hitherto ill-educated working class fostered by the Army Bureau of Current Affairs which directed that all personnel should receive at least one hour's education per week, in the form of group discussion. Platoon commanders led the conversation with the help of ABCA bulletins on such subjects as the military course of the war and surveys of current social, economic and political affairs. This intellectual enfranchising of the masses caused dismay in some quarters. The MP for Penryn and Falmouth, Maurice Petherick, wrote to Churchill's Parliamentary Private Secretary in 1942: 'I am more and more suspicious of the way this lecturing to and education of the forces racket is run . . . for the love of Mike, do something about it, unless you want to have the creatures coming back all pansy-pink.'

David Niven, a regular soldier before the War and a Commando during it, said that

> *'One thing stuck out a mile in these [ABCA] debates – the vast majority of men who had been called up to fight for their country held the Conservative Party entirely responsible for the disruption of their lives and in no circumstances would they vote for it next time there was an election – Churchill or no Churchill.'*

Their chance came in July 1945 and they grabbed it.

Sir Stafford Cripps, first President of the Board of Trade and then Chancellor of the Exchequer in the Labour administration elected in 1945, introduced economy measures to aid recovery of the country which was still, effectively, conducting life as if under siege. Clothes, petrol, and foodstuffs were rationed; import of goods was curtailed. The economist John Maynard Keynes, appointed as first British governor of the International Monetary Fund and the International Bank established in 1944, at once negotiated a Lend-Lease agreement with America through the incumbent President, Franklin D. Roosevelt – supplies delivered free of charge to shore up the massive deficit. However, after the defeat of Japan in August 1945, the new President, Harry Truman, cancelled the Lend-Lease programme and Keynes had hurriedly to negotiate a loan in order to fund an increase in exports and to amortize the war debt. There was a stringent condition, however: within a year of the grant, sterling was to become freely convertible into dollars. Britain had little choice: wheat, petrol, cotton, tobacco and so on flowed from America to the UK, but there wasn't much that could be exported in return. By the spring of 1947, Britain was buying 47% of its imports from the USA and the dollars of the grant were being spent fast. Investors exchanged pounds for dollars and the loan was quickly all but exhausted. Britain was, once more, on her uppers. A popular song of the time has a taxpayer saying: 'Only yesterday at tea, The Chancellor he said to me, I wonder what it feels like to be poor.' There were shortages of beer, coal, food, cigarettes, cakes and ices, housing, clothes, electrical power, coupons for blackout material that, in the absence of the Luftwaffe's night raids, could at least be put to use as curtains. Indeed there were shortages of everything whose supply *could* be shortened. As late as 1949, a butcher's shop in Birmingham was whimsically advertising for help on a blackboard in its window: <u>WANTED </u>FOR NEXT WEEKS TRADE   MAGICIAN OR ILLUSIONIST.

 As their manifesto promised, Labour nationalised the Bank of England, the aviation, coal mining, iron and steel industries, energy production – gas and electricity – and railways. Cripps was a gaunt intellectual, a rather humourless devotee of progress without pleasure. He slept but three hours a night, rose at 5am and took a cold bath, never touched alcohol and applied his own pious rectitude unswervingly to economic asperity and cuts in the standard of living. He invested the rationing of food, clothes and petrol with a sort of moral asceticism. His driving principle was 'austerity' a word first planted in common circulation by Oliver Lyttleton, Conservative President of the Board of Trade, in 1941. Winston Churchill once said of Cripps: 'There but for the grace of God goes God' and he was commonly regarded as something of a joke. Men in pubs asked for a packet of 'Sir Staffs', that is *crisps*. His puritanism may have served the immediate pressing need, but the asceticism clinging to him, and thereby the nation, was unrelentingly dour. It was a time of weariness and privation, vividly evoked as a backdrop in George Orwell's *Nineteen Eighty-Four* – actually 1948 post-war Britain, crippled spiritually and materially, and blighted by what Orwell saw as the general and catastrophic erasure of moral choice. People living on boiled cabbage which meant that, like the squalid tenements in Dostoevsky's *Crime and Punishment,* the cloying stink of the overcooked vegetable permeated everywhere. Meat rationed to a couple of slices of fatty corned beef, and one egg a month and that usually bad. Privations are manageable when they have to be endured with what some called the luxury of danger, the buzz of a gamble, even extreme hazard. There seemed, in such circumstances, at least to be a point to the hardship. The adrenaline fix gone, surviving on short rations is naught but a misery. These were days when hungry people looked rancorously at what some profligates tossed into the pig swill buckets. What a waste. Indeed, Orwell had wanted to give his book the title *Nineteen Forty-Eight* but the publishers wouldn't have it.

Bob and Christina were luckier than most – they, ate least, had a house to live in – but the stringency of postwar living conditions impinged on everybody. The shortages, the psychological and emotional tumble from the euphoria of victory and the joy of homecoming to a horizonless future, made living in this uncertain limbo of peace very difficult. The overarching sense of purpose during the war, the sense of serving a greater cause and doing one's duty, was suddenly gone and the daily necessities and obligations were, by comparison, mundane, indeed: work, domestic drudgery, nappies, bills and rationing.

When Clement Atlee took office, the basic food ration per person per week was:

1s. 2d. worth of meat

3 oz bacon and ham

8 oz sugar

2 ½ oz tea

2 oz butter

2 oz cheese

4 oz margarine (invented by the French chemist Hippolyte Mege-Mouriez in 1869)

1 oz cooking fat

1 egg per fortnight (dried eggs were a versatile addition to the larder – 4oz of dried egg was equivalent to nine large eggs and could be used in cakes or as scrambled egg.)

2½ pints liquid milk (dried milk was also available)

12 oz sweets (including chocolate) per fortnight

A customer had to register with one grocer for twelve months in order to obtain this staple supply. Hotels, restaurants, boarding houses, factory and works canteens were also subject to rationing. Restaurants were restricted to three-course meals at a maximum price of 5 shillings. Coffee was extra. In the orchards of the Garden of England, lively scrumping of apples supplemented the diet. An army Catering Corps colonel of my acquaintance told me that, just after the War, a Paris restaurant of some repute grandly offered, for pudding *Une pomme anglaise*.[5]

Queuing swallowed hours of every housewife's time. Harrassed women joined queues more in hope than expectation, often because they knew something must be on offer, even if, stuck for hours at the tail end of the long, long queue, they had not a clue what it would be. A cut of meat or a scoop of offal for dog or cat food? Kids were sent out on queue duty. Cigarettes and tobacco were hard to get. The resentment felt by many people during the War, seeing Churchill with his famous cigar and they restricted to five fags a day, fuelled the Labour victory. On one occasion, during a visit to the East End of London, Churchill spoke to a large crowd, assuring them 'We can do the job'. A voice in the crowd hollered back acidly: 'Who's this *we*?' Razor blades were in very short supply. A contemporary short story began: 'It was the fifty-fourth day of the new razor blade..' When the first shipment of bananas since 1940 arrived at Avonmouth on New Year's Eve, 1945, the Lord Mayor of Bristol hosted a civic reception on the dockside. 'Yes, we have no bananas,' they'd sung mock cheerfully round the old Joanna in the pubs 'we have no bananas today.' Victor Ceserani, the chef at the exclusive Boodles Club in St James, was greeted by his wife when he came home one night as usual at 10pm: 'I've got a wonderful surprise for you, darling.' She went to the cupboard and produced a banana. 'We looked at it with reverence' he said. 'It was the first time we'd seen one for years.' They peeled it very carefully and ceremoniously, cut it in half and put the halves on two small plates, then ate their portion, slicing it as thinly as they could to prolong the enjoyment. 'Looking back now' he said 'it sounds stupid, but that's absolutely true.'

By August 1946, the basic petrol ration allowed private motorists to drive 270 miles per month. Importing oil from America so drained dollar reserves that by June 1948 the

---

[5] Food rationing didn't end until 1954, and when James Saghi visited the Chicken household in the late 40s, he wanted to buy sweets for the two young Chicken boys – Robert had been born in 1949 – and, not understanding how precious the oblong tickets of low-quality buff paper were, used up an entire month's supply on his presents of toffees and pear drops.

monthly ration was a mere 90 miles. The petrol used in commercial vehicles contained a red dye and its discovery in the tank of a private motor led to criminal prosecution.

Naturally, rationing encouraged under-the-counter transactions by shopkeepers who surreptitiously kept back goods or special cuts of meat for favoured customers who could pay a bit extra. During the war, knackers' yards supplied restaurants on the hush-hush with horsemeat – very tender, in fact – as a substitute for beef. The black market thrived – 'on the black' meaning engaged in shady commerce dates from about 1943. Spivs, small town touts and racketeers in sharp suits traded in clothes coupons, buying for 6d selling on for 3s 6d, wheeling and dealing 'at the back door' – frequently on a barter basis – in clothes, hats, camiknickers, rayon or lisle stockings, in fact anything saleable, commestible or material that came their way.

On 14 May 1946, a story appeared in the *Daily Express* about the discovery by detectives of a ton of gelatine in a back room of a hotel in Barnsley. It was the headquarters of an illicit jelly-baby-manufacturing gang. Spivs had been working in race-course gangs since the 1890s but the term was redefined in 1947 as 'one who earns his living by not working'. Their brand of ingenuity, often fairly amateurish by professional criminal standards, was, perhaps, no more than a prevailing native resourcefulness. American GIs famously 'over-paid, over-sexed and over here' had been open-handed with gifts of *nylon* stockings. Now that they had gone back Stateside, women had to make do with liquid make-up and a friend to draw a black mascara line up the back of their legs to mimic the nylon stocking's seam, unless, that is, they could get to the spiv hawking nylons from a suitcase parked on the kerbside before the police arrived. In some ways, the spivs were doing no more than continuing what had been deemed a fairly commonsense, pragmatic approach to supplying needs and perks in the services. My own father recalls a couple of sharp operators who worked a simple scam with an army-issue blanket as they travelled across North Africa on a troop train. One would sell the blanket to an unsuspecting native in the crowds which gathered round the servicemen at every stop the train made. His stooge, masquerading as a redcap, would then march up, confiscate the blanket and arrest his buddy. The pair of them flogged and redeemed that blanket countless times. In prisoner-of-war camps, the scrounger was a valued member of any escape team, his job being to get equipment that no amount of technical genius or resource could be made inside the camp – such as a camera for forging purposes – from malleable guards, by bribes of chocolate, cigarettes etc from Red Cross parcels.

During the War, very few houses had been built. The widespread havoc wrought by the Luftwaffe made the shortage of housing acute. (James Hilton's 1942 novel *Random Harvest* took its title from a German misunderstanding of a newspaper headline 'Germans drop bombs at Random'. Infuriatingly, one of their maps showed this town called Random, but *their* newspaper claimed to have flattened it in a daring raid.) The bombed-out basements of buildings destroyed during the Blitz had been painted with tar and used as water basins to supply the fire engines; kids used them as swimming pools. Drained, now, they became curious urban flowerpots for London Pride, fireweed and loosestrife. The sides of the broken buildings showed the wallpaper of the rooms that had been pounded into rubble by high explosives, the outline of the staircase that had gone with the rest, the bright patch where the picture had hung, the blackened gap of the empty hearth. Bombsites littered townscapes across the kingdom. It was estimated that almost half a million dwellings were destroyed or rendered completely uninhabitable and another quarter of a million badly damaged, largely in the main towns, centres of industry and dockyards: Birmingham, Coventry, Manchester, Liverpool, Plymouth, Bristol, Newcastle. London had been singled out for moral rather than strategic reasons. The famous photograph of the dome of St Paul's cathedral surrounded by billowing clouds of smoke from explosions, picked out by the illumination of fires and searchlights all round, was a powerful image of defiance.

The war scarred every aspect of life, and would, for years to come. Even the fortnight's break from the long grind of work in the cheap and cheerful vacational stalags built by Billy Butlin had a militarised tone. His first holiday camp, at Skegness, had been opened on Easter Sunday 1936 by Amy Johnson of Hull, the first woman to fly solo from

England to Australia. The post-war Butlins' day, from Skegness to Clacton, reminded the 'happy campers' of life in the services: jocular cries over a tannoy wakened the camp population in the mornings and urged them to pre-breakfast exercises outside the chalets. They handed over their ration books to the Butlin's caterers at the beginning of their week's stay and ate communally in a huge dining hall reminiscent of a NAAFI canteen if not an army cookhouse. One cheery visitor in 1946 reported 'eggs and bacon for breakfast and fresh peaches for lunch. It was an absolute dream' – and they were guided (kept an eye on) by redcoats, a name uncomfortably close to redcaps, as the much-feared Military Police were known.

The Navy, Army and Air Force Institute was set up in 1939 to cater to forces personnel who expected higher standards of off-duty provision than the conscripts of 1916. Every military camp had a NAAFI canteen with clubroom, bar, hot food counter, a shop for the purchase of tobacco, sweets and toiletries and, very often, a piano for a sing-song or background strumming. 'In large base areas like the Middle East, the NAAFI provided splendid leave camps, complete with gardens, swimming pools, shops, restaurants, dance-halls and bars. In service clubs in cities like Cairo, soldiers enjoyed the comfort and facilities of a good hotel.' [6]

The underlying problem of the early approach to the reconstruction of Britain was that it was being conducted in the image of the war effort, 'even if the home front ran on without a war effort to sustain it' (Paul Addison *Now the War is Over*). John Stuart Mill (1806-73) opined that 'When society requires to be rebuilt, there is no use attempting to rebuild it on the old plan'. The practical errors were compounded by an ingrained and dangerously outmoded imperialism. As Sir Henry Tizzard, chairman of the Advisory Council on Research Policy, warned: 'We are a great nation, but if we continue to behave like a Great Power we shall soon cease to be a great power.' He thus anticipated Dean Acheson's remark in a speech at West Point in December 1962, that Britain had lost an Empire and had not yet found a role. Churchill, whose bull-dogged pertinacity

---

[6] Corelli Barnett, *Britain and her Army 1509 – 1970*.

had done so much to stir the nation against what he called 'the Nazzies', was soon exposed as being hopelessly stuck in the view of Britain as still a Great Power. In a speech to a Conservative meeting in October 1948, he spoke of Britain as being uniquely involved in three great circles among the free nations and democracies: the British Empire and Commonwealth, with all that comprised; the English-speaking world, in which Britain, with Canada, the other British Dominions (principally Australia, New Zealand, South Africa) and the United States 'play so important a part' [ah, the condescension]; and United Europe. 'Now, if you think of the three inter-linked circles' he summarised 'you will see that we are the only country which has a great part in every one of them.' So retarded a view would bedevil much about Britain's drive to pursue the revolution without tears. The Treaty of Versailles had dismantled one of the last great existing empires, that of Austro-Hungary. VE and VJ Days heralded the imminent disintegration of the last great anachronism, the British Empire, even if schoolchildren continued to celebrate a day off every 24 May (Queen Victoria's birthday) as Empire Day until 1958, when it was renamed Commonwealth Day. As an instance of how the world viewed Britain in the immediate post-war period, consider Suez, her final essay in gunboat diplomacy, that imperial tactic sanctioned by Lord Palmerston when, as he said, a man's proudest boast was *'Civis Britannicus sum'* (I am a British citizen), just as, in the ancient world, it had been *'Civis Romanus sum'* – as St Paul could claim when arrested – because it guaranteed protection under Roman law.

When the Egyptian Prime Minister, Colonel Gamal Abdel el Nasser, nationalised the Suez Canal in July 1956, the British Prime Minister Anthony Eden sent in troops, as did the French to protect the Canal as a free and open conduit for their shipping. The USSR, approving the Egyptian action against the old imperialists, backed her and partly because of a massive build-up of Soviet troops, but largely because the USA refused to support them, British and French forces were compelled, ignominiously, to withdraw. Yet when Russian tanks rumbled into Hungary to crush a popular uprising in October of that year, the international community did nothing.

In 1947, Bob's father, William Chicken, became ill. Bob suggested that if he were to leave Clarke, Hunt & Co., his father might pay him while he learnt the business in readiness to taking over. William Chicken had, in truth, little choice in the matter but he did not accept the transfer gracefully. Impatient and acutely critical of almost anything Bob did, he was forever reproving him: 'That's not right . . . you shouldn't have done that . . . ' So, former matelot Bob, not a little practised in the art of eluding authority and dealing with irascible jacks-in-office, did not argue: he employed cunning and took to disguising what he'd done, confident in his own instincts, giving vent to his own growing flair for conducting sales, and thus, while apparently agreeing with everything the old man said, side-stepping his querulous carping. The onset of what proved to be a terminal malady cannot have improved his father's temper, of course, and relations between the frail and ailing boss and the man he treated rather as his upstart son made the partnership fraught.

On 6 November 1947, Bob writes to Naassan:

> *Dear George*
>
> *. . . Up to date I have had little aid from my Father, but he has now made it known that he wishes me in his business, one that is sound in its establishment, its name connections and agencies, and from which the future may provide us with sound healthy business relations.*

. . . I have pleasure in enclosing a brochure from one of Britain's best cycle manufacturers, relating to a new line of theirs – The Gresham Flyer Juvenile Tricycle, a most modern, well-built and pleasing cycle for children, which may find a ready market in your hands. This cycle, manufactured by the Aberdale Cycle Co., has already found overseas markets, and I am led to believe that an interest for the same has been found in the Lebanon. Perhaps you can enlighten me if this is so, or not . . . I would be pleased also to hear whether you are still interested in the importing of Ladies and Gentlemens' cycles, together with allied items in popular demand.

However, (as Naassan wrote) the Gresham Flyer Juvenile Tricycle had already been marketed in the Lebanon. If Bob could come up with a better price, 'rock-bottom quotations', A.B.C. might be able to do something. Besides no manufacturer would be willing to give sole agency to one firm without a guarantee of a yearly turnover. Neither A.B.C. nor Bob was in a position to challenge this and their hopes of introducing the Gresham Flyer to the Levant were, for the moment at least, grounded. As to the demand for Ladies' bicycles in the Lebanon, there was none, and for mens' bikes 'what the market requires here is the double bar structure . . . Another point of particular interest to me [writes Naassan] is Cycle Accessories in which I believe your father specialises. Could you make me an offer for 200 Handle bars including of course brakes, Chromium plated or Nickel, flat, PHILLIPS Model "Celtia".'

Bob explained that

Cycles with double-bar frames are most difficult to obtain, in so far as they are mostly made for special requirements, which in turn are few – in this matter I must apologise for being unable to help you. The same applies to Handlebars and Brakes. The only course I can suggest is for you to approach Phillips direct regarding same. Unfortunately, neither my Father nor myself has any connection with Phillips and these goods, like Cycle Chains, Freewheels and Pedals etc are still very scarce even for Export orders, manufacturers having already far more orders on their books than they can cope with.

Perversely, a reputable German cycle manufacturer had contacted the Chicken enterprise with regard to Export. This seemed to open the prospect of 'a sound and good turn of business' as Bob put it, enclosing a price list for frames and miscellaneous items. He also suggested that Naassan might well have a fair chance of getting sole agency and using his own transfers instead of the brand name 'Bismarck', the Iron Chancellor of a militaristic Prussia closely identified with the early burgeoning of German expansionist foreign policy, hardly an attractive selling point in 1947.

Bob adds: 'To date I haven't as yet joined my Father – I intend doing so shortly, but this business is nevertheless regarded as mine and will aid in my own establishment.'

Nassan replied on 20 January 1948.

> *Dear Bob,*
>
> *I have just received your letter dated December 18 enclosing quotations and illustrations for German Cycles for which please accept my thanks.*
>
> *Your offer has been thoroughly studied but regret that prices were not found competitive. I submitted same to a number of bicycle dealers and all of them showed me invoices in respect of English cycles that they imported from England recently and you will be surprised to note that the price of a complete British cycle <u>double tube</u> was quoted at £6 / 15/- Gent's Fob British port.[i.e. the price as shipped.] Supposing that your people in Germany would reduce the price to that much, dealers here would not even buy at this price for the main reasons that they not only prefer English cycles but also they do not know what the freight would amount to from German ports to Beirut. Furthermore, the question of delivery is not encouraging. To wait for some 5 to 6 months, our dealers would not wait as long as that when British Manufacturers can deliver within a month or so. As things stand at present, I wonder whether we will be able to do some business with the German Manufacturers and I suggest, Bob, that we mark time until the economic situation in Germany alleviates itself at which time we may hope to open up business relationship.*

William Chicken's health was declining, and with it sales turnover. Plainly this was a crisis and something urgent had to be done. In the winter of 1948, Bob took a week's holiday from his work at Clarke, Hunt and spent it at the William Chicken office in Goswell Road to ascertain the overall position of the company's affairs. They were in poor shape. Much to the regret of the people at Clarke, Hunt, not least because he was the only white-collar man to play for the firm's football team in the Enfield and District Football League, Bob handed in his notice and more or less took over in Goswell Road. Some 12 months later, in December 1949, his father died, leaving him in sole control.

CHAPTER SIX
COCK-EYED OPTIMISTS
AND SOUR GRAPES

Soon after the War, the British cycle industry resumed full production. It was still the world leader of the existing market and overweeningly confident in its capacity to remain so. But, that market was changing and new forces were on the rise, challenges which the British manufacturers failed either to register or adequately match. As for the authorities governing cycling – both the sport and the pastime – lamentably, they continued to indulge their brattish petulance and self-interest, like the spoilt kid who breaks up the scratch cricket game with his pals because it's *his* bat and *his* ball and therefore he can say who's in and who is out.

The cycle industry post-war; consolidation and decline

In 1943, Raleigh had bought out Rudge-Whitworth, a company with an illustrious pedigree. Dan Rudge, of Wolverhampton, made his first boneshaker in 1869 but should best be remembered for the exceptional Rudge racing Ordinary of 1884 which he had with a front wheel five feet in diameter and weighed a mere 21½ pounds. Flying along on this machine, someone said, delivered 'an enjoyment which was positively intense'. Rudge amalgamated with Whitworth soon thereafter and a Rudge-Whitworth advertisement of 1895 trumpeted the bicycling ' fashion set by Royalty, the Aristocracy and Society'. This upperclass cachet bestowed on the two-wheeler didn't last.

Sensible of the Rudge-Whitworth pedigree, Raleigh retained the name for some of its machines, but the writing was already on the wall for the smaller operators in the cycle industry. One such was a Mr Sibbit who hand-built frames in the kitchen of his bike shop in Manchester. Britain has a noble tradition of such one-man bands, producing a small number of machines for the sheer love of the craft, putting details on the frames which mark out the Sibbit, the Ellis-Briggs, the Roberts . . . and of them, more later. Sibbit had made a track bike for perhaps the greatest speed man this country has ever produced: Reg Harris. Harris, born in 1920, had served in the Tank Corps in North Africa for three years, been blown up and invalided out of the army, but not before he had won three events in the British track Championships of 1944. He had gone to Sibbit because Raleigh, caught up in the wartime production of fuses, lacked spare capacity.

Harris had been given his first free bicycle – a Humber racer – in recognition of his sponsorship value before the War. After he was demobbed he signed a contract with Claude Butler and won the 1947 Worlds Amateur Sprint title in Paris on a Butler machine. Butler, who had built radar equipment during the war and was now struggling to revive his cycle-building enterprise, withdrew temporarily from sponsorship.

A Raleigh representative met Harris in the Isle of Man when Harris was racing there, suggested to him that a second approach to the company might bear fruit and Harris, although recently injured in a car crash, took two silver medals (individual and tandem sprint) at the 1948 London Olympics on a Raleigh machine – a disappointing haul by his standards, although he added a Worlds bronze later that year.

The track events were held at Herne Hill, the oldest cycle track in England. Harris contested the final against the Italian Mario Guella and the Dane Schandorff, under floodlights. Harris had matters well in hand when suddenly the lights failed. Guella, in his dark blue strip, pounced. Harris, quite visible in his white GB vest, couldn't see his rival flash past in the murk. Darkly, Guella took gold.

The following year Harris signed as a professional for Raleigh and, in their colours, won a string of victories. He wrested the1949 World Sprint title from the holder, Van Vliet, in August (the first-ever British professional World champion in any discipline) and the following October, on an outdoor track in Milan, beat the ten-year-old 1,000 metre record in atrocious conditions. Afterwards he said: 'Never was I so exhausted. I couldn't stand up, my knees gave way under me . . . but it was worth it.' Thirty-six hours later he beat his own world record for the flying quarter mile on rollers, having wound up to a speed of 81.9 mph. The 1950 Worlds were held in Liège and, well in advance, Raleigh, confident that their golden goose was going to lay another lucrative publicity egg, had over 7,000 posters made: *Raleigh wins the World Championship for the second year in succession, ridden by Reg Harris* displaying an over-imperious, almost imperialist, arrogance. Worse, some boorish clown plastered Harris's changing room with this brash temptation of Fate. Luckily, the phlegmatic Lancastrian from Bury was not one jot discombobulated and he beat Van Vliet again by half a wheel. When he returned to Raleigh HQ in Nottingham, the Mayor and a complement of town hall and local dignitaries gave him a full civic welcome.

At the 1951 Worlds in Milan, he was beaten by an Italian, Bergomi, in the quarter finals but came through the rêpechage against Guella, and won the final easily – sweet revenge for Herne Hill's power cut. He missed out in 1952, took bronze in 1953, but came back to win a fourth World title, his last, in 1954. That same year, another Raleigh sprinter, Cyril Peacock, the first Englishman to win the Champion of Champions trophy (an open international race) at Herne Hill on Good Friday 1952, took the Worlds Amateur title. Harris took silver in 1956 before retiring.

In 1946, Raleigh produced nearly 400,000 bicycles; in 1951 production was up to 1,010, 077. How much Harris contributed to this boom is impossible to calculate, of course, but his international celebrity had given the company name vital recognition, worldwide.

As Raleigh's fortunes soared, so those of smaller concerns plummeted. Raleigh swept them up.

Triumph was founded by Siegfried Bettman who came to Britain from Nürnberg in 1883, aged 20. He worked for a while in the White Sewing Machine company and in 1884 set up an import/export agency selling imported German sewing machines and bicycles made in Birmingham under his own name. In 1886, he cannily changed that trading name to something less evocative of his Germanic roots and more consonant with the confident, late nineteenth century British mood: thus the Triumph Cycle

Company was born. In 1887, another Nürnberger, an engineer, Johann Schulte, joined Bettman and persuaded him that instead of selling other firms' machines he should make his own. They moved the operation to that hub of the cycle manufacturing industry, Coventry, and went into production of bicycles. In 1902, using a 2.25 bhp Minerva engine from Belgium, the first Triumph motorbicycle left the production line. The company took as its motto *Nulli Secundus* (Second to None) also that of the Coldstream Guards, and in 1913, Bettman became Mayor of Coventry. Their motorbikes continued to sell well, but Triumph sold off their cycle division to Associated Cycle Manufacturers of Coventry on the eve of war and, in 1954, Raleigh acquired their manufacturing rights, a curious arrangement which meant that for a time both the Coventry factory and the giant Raleigh works were producing Triumph bicycles. Triumph at Coventry subsequently went under.

The Birmingham Small Arms Company was set up by a group of munitions manufacturers in 1861 in competition with the government ordnance factory in Enfield which had invested in American machine tools for mass production. Towards the close of the century, as the armies of the British Empire imposed the Pax Britannica more emphatically and the demand for guns dropped, the BSA company switched to the manufacture of bicycle components – chains, hubs and brake parts. In 1888, in urgent response to the Boer War and various other new outbreaks of violence in Africa and elsewhere, BSA reverted to the manufacture of weapons. The survivors of the men who had marched off singing 'Goodbye Dolly I must leave you' came home in 1902 and in 1903, the BSA factory produced its first complete bicycle. The management had been sceptical, the work force enthusiastic. Management relented but insisted that the first effort must be built of scrap. Plebeian ingenuity triumphed over executive-class dithering and the factory produced 1,000 bicycles modelled on their prototype that first year. The workers were in full cry, now, and pushed for a motorcycle. Once more, the men in the top office hummed and hahed. The workers pushed on willy- nilly, fitted an engine – another Minerva – into a bicycle frame and by 1911, after successive refinements, the first BSA motorbike went on sale and was an instant hit. The company still produced bicycles but it was as a motorcycle marque that BSA became best known, as did Triumph. BSA, which had acquired Sunbeam and New Hudson in 1943, was bought by Raleigh in 1957 and was principally responsible for staving off what might have been a disaster. At the close of 1958, George Wilson, the Raleigh managing director, reported 'a further serious fall of 50% in our profits'. This he imputed to 'a sharp and unforeseeable recession both in our home and export markets'. A four-day week in the Nottingham factories ensued, turnover dropped by some 5 per cent 'and would have dropped much more severely but for the contribution made by the BSA cycle interests'. Thus ample proof of just how vital is an excellent brand name in the commercial world – a lesson that Raleigh would later ignore to its huge detriment.

There were two main factors affecting the slump in the cycle trade: cheaper cars bought on hire purchase and unimaginative bicycle design and marketing. The *Westminster Gazette* of January 1889 reports that a 'Mr Moore . . . was the inventor of the now widely adopted hire-purchase system' but who he was I do not know. Buying 'on the never', that is on credit often interminably extended, had an insalubrious image. First used in the military from around 1915 as slang for wangling, deferring payment, 'on the never' or (as later) 'on the never-never' seemed to many upright citizens who could afford to buy outright, not much better than legalised theft. Others were less niminy piminy about what looked like a good deal and conservative estimates reckon that from 1925 on, some 70 per cent of automobiles bought in the USA were paid for on instalment plans. Certain sections of the British population were also keen to buy on the HP: cars, furniture, jewellery, farm implements, factory equipment, office machinery, bicycles, even clothes, bibles and books. The post-war austerity encouraged hire purchase, not least because the entire nation was in hock to foreign loans in order to repay the massive war debt. What the government had visited upon the people in the wider scheme of things it could hardly deny them in the smaller. The most obvious boom in hire-purchase agreements was in the buying of cars, although the boom in sales of televisions provides a further indication of growing consumer affluence. In March 1955, 4½ million TV licences were issued; by March 1958, the number was 8 million.

As the country gradually recovered from the ravages of wartime, the home motor industry produced more and more vehicles for a populace keen to buy them. Many of the men – and women: social norms had been rarely shaken up – who had served in the war and would never have dreamed of being able to own a car before they joined up, had been taught to drive in the forces and got thoroughly accustomed to travelling about in military lorries or jeeps. Now that cars were more numerous and cheaper and available on the never-never, a newly liberated spending public wanted the freedom of the road behind a steering wheel once more and sucks to snotty middle-class disapproval of taking full possession ahead of full payment. 'Neither a borrower nor a lender be' Polonius gloomily advises his son Laertes as he sets off for university 'For loan oft loses both itself and friend /And borrowing blunts the edge of husbandry.' Husbanding resources, staying out of debt, cutting one's coat according to one's cloth, these were the salients of thrift. A jar or a pot for the week's money and savings, spend only what there is to spend and never spend over and wait in each Saturday morning for The Man from the Pru to call for the insurance instalment. That is prudence, anything else prodigality. As Mr Micawber puts it *in David Copperfield*: 'Annual income twenty pounds, annual expenditure nineteen nineteen six, result happiness. Annual income twenty pounds, annual expenditure twenty pounds ought and six, result misery.'

Between 1945 and 1955 the sale of cars in Britain tripled, parking at the kerbside *anywhere* was free, increased motor traffic in towns made cycling to work more hazardous and in 1960, the newly appointed Conservative Transport Minister Ernest Marples said that cities must be reshaped so as to accommodate the demands of motorists. Within five years, Richard (later Baron) Beeching, chairman of British Railways had 'reorganised' – in reality, butchered - the entire railway network with a swingeing closure programme of what he deemed to be unprofitable lines and stations – wielding what was acidly called 'the Beeching axe'. In many country districts, where local buses ran infrequently, ownership of a car became a necessity not a luxury. Nor was the cycle manufacturing industry addressing itself to a problem of image and demand. On the continent, manufacturers were producing bikes similar to those ridden by professional cyclists – sleek, lightweight machines with state-of-the-art components and the added kudos of the very best in bicycle engineering precision. In Britain, specialist hand-builders apart, manufacturers continued to produce the solid, boring, unlovely sit-up-and-beg roadsters that had been the staple for a public which pedalled its way, at work and at leisure. But whilst the desire of the potential cyclist was for more sporty bikes to suit leisure use, the trade resolutely refused to move on. But the bicycle continued to draw young people to the dream of freewheeling independence. Phil Liggett's experience of this was probably repeated across the country. Fishing expeditions on the bike with a friend led to his joining the Cyslist's Touring Club and longer excursions away from the anonymous back streets of Bebbington on the Wirral round the estuary into the paradise of open country in north Wales – Rainbow Pass, the Old Horseshoe, Moel Fammau mountain. And from the CTC progression to the local Merseyside cycling club. The passion was born and another customer for a racing bike arrived outside the specialist shop.

The British Cycle Corporation, Raleigh's chief competitor, was the bicycle division of Tube Investments, formerly TI-Reynolds, from the old firm. BCC held the brand names of Phillips, Hercules, Norman and Sun yet bought a large proportion of its components from Raleigh which, in turn, bought much of its tubing from TI. As both BCC and Raleigh struggled, the conclusion was obvious. Jim Boustridge, a Director of BCC. George Wilson, Managing Director of Raleigh, was an old friend of Sir Francis de Guingand, formerly Montgomery's Chief of Staff, now in charge of TI at Springs, outside Johannesburg, some 80km north-east of the Raleigh plant at Vereeniging. It was painfully clear that both companies were struggling to corner the same, dwindling market and this conflict was destroying each of them, not only in South Africa but elsewhere in the global market. One of them must surely go under. Wilson and de Guingand discussed a merger and agreed that they should unite. The Raleigh plant in

South Africa was shut down in 1959 in exchange for the acquisition of an interest in the operation at Springs. The following year, TI bought all shares in Raleigh and handed over the entire BCC operation to Raleigh management on condition that they assimilate BCC into Raleigh Industries. Further, TI decided that it would be far better for the new cycle manufacturer to discard all the surviving brand names of defunct companies and trade under one alone: Raleigh. In reality, this proved impracticable; the market simply would not accept the disappearance of such a famous marque as Hercules, for instance. And there was the matter of celebrity marketing. The old Sturmey-Archer factory had been relocated on the huge Raleigh site in Nottingham, so huge, in fact, that it took more than a day just to walk round it. Even before TI and Raleigh merged, the Raleigh people had called in Reg Harris to discuss the setting up of a small operation – Reg Harris Cycles – in the vacant Sturmey-Archer premises for the production of hand-built specialist racing bikes. Harris was keen, the idea astute; it would keep Raleigh in touch with the élite requirements of sporting cyclists. Yet the TI diktat on reducing the number of brand names did not countenance adding another. But, if Raleigh were to secure any kind of sales on the continent, it was quite apparent that they needed to make bikes of the highest quality to appeal to people who wanted to ride a machine similar to that ridden by the best cycling professionals. Equally clear was the impracticality of trying to combine small-scale hand-built workmanship with mass production. Accordingly, Harris proposed taking over a company that was already making specialist machines, Carlton Cycles in Worksop, owned and run by the O'Donovan brothers, Kevin and Gerald. The bicycles they made – around two per week – were of superb quality; with Raleigh marketing and distribution, Carlton bikes could sell well and widely, albeit the limited production of so specialised an outfit could not hope to redeem Raleigh's immediate shortfall in sales. Gerald continued to supervise the making of racing frames whilst Kevin went off to South Africa to work at the Spring plant. Donovan contributed enormously to the success of the Raleigh professional cyclists and the silverware they accumulated was kept on display not at the Raleigh works in Ilkeston but at Donovan's local pub just down the road from where he applied his own superior design skills and the engineering expertise of his craftsmen to the manganese-molybdenum alloy steel tubing.

The story of the merger has a dark side. When Wilson made the approach to BCC, Jim Boustridge, the chairman of BCC, advised TI not to accept. Raleigh was in wretched straits, that much was obvious. Boustridge said all that BCC needed do was to wait for a year and then pick up the ailing giant for a song. The MD ignored Boustridge's advice and bought at once at what Boustridge knew to be an inflated price for which Raleigh had no commercial support. Boustridge, overruled, resigned. The amalgamation was therefore, in effect, a reverse take-over: since TI already owned several highly reputable marques, in buying Raleigh they were, more or less, buying a single name at the reprehensible expense of ditching all those they already owned.

For years, the Raleigh operation had been massively top heavy and overweight. The main factory on Lenton Boulevard covered about 14½ acres. In fact the company, it might be said, *was* Nottingham. There were some twenty draughtsmen working at any one time in the drawing office. The buying department, a little empire of its own, boasted a buying director, a buying manager, four assistant buyers with different responsibilities – tyres and tubes, brakes etc. – each with one or two personal assistants. This was absurd and costly over-staffing. And, for some time after the new combine began trading, it lost money year upon year. The old-style advertising campaigns that were lavish, untimely and over-extravagant, the drain on resources from financing the TI-Raleigh pro cycling team for very little commercial return, and an ingrained habit of uncontrolled spending were separately untenable and, in combination, quite ruinous. There was, too, a stilted, blinkered approach to their way of doing business, inculcated over years of either crushing competitors or not acknowledging their existence.

In the 60s, Ron Webb, an Australian track professional racing cyclist based in Belgium, was approached by a group of German dealers who needed a supply of children's bicycles. Webb agreed to make the introduction to Raleigh and travelled with the Germans to Nottingham. They asked to see the Sales Director. The Sales Director sent word that he was too busy – they should apply to his junior assistant.

Admitted to the junior Assistant Sales Director's office, the deputation said they wanted 250 small-size bicycles with a single freewheel on the rear hub. The junior Assistant Sales Director told them that the order would be impossible to fill because, amongst all the many and various bicycles that Raleigh *did* produce, there was no small-size bicycle with a single freewheel on the rear hub nor, regrettably, did there exist any specification for such a machine. Webb and the Germans traipsed back south from Nottingham. An opportunity offered . . . an opportunity neglected.

Who will regulate the regulators?

In early 1978, Keith Bingham, of *Cycling Weekly*, was travelling home from a TI Raleigh pro team press launch in Holland with the late Jock Wadley, doyen of British cycle journalists. Wadley had introduced Bingham to a bunch of track riders who'd done the Six-Day race circuit in the 1930s. 'I'll introduce you to the old guys' he said 'and you can introduce me to the new men, okay?'

They were in high spirits – the buzz of the cycling scene in Holland was so invigorating, the enthusiasm for the sport, the history, the tradition, the pervasive energy and vitality, the feeling that cycling was a big deal. Walking down into a District Line underground station, Wadley said, wryly: 'Well, Keith, forget all that – here we are, welcome back to *British* cycling.'

Wadley was a mild-mannered civil man, passionate about cycling, friendly, charming, and of unstinting generosity. Leaving the train he looked at Bingham, shook his hand and said: 'You know what we need to do to sort out cycle racing in this country? Get all the top men in the B.C.F., the R.T.T.C. and the C.T.C. together in one room and shoot them. Cheerio.'

The sentiment is shared by many even today, the best advice to any young rider nursing ambitions in the sport being to leave Britain as soon as possible.

The Bicycle Union, forerunner of cycle sport administration in Britain, was formed in 1878 to organise amateur championships. That same year it also lobbied successfully against an Amendment of the Highways Act which would have outlawed cycling from the roads altogether. But, if bicycling was the new craze and cycle racing but one manifestation of it, there were other enthusiasts steadfastly opposed to the two-wheeled machine: the tricyclists. A number of the three-wheel devotees founded the Tricycle Association in late 1880, but succumbed to pressure two years later and joined the Bicycle Union to form the National Cyclists Union. The tricycle (decidedly not the slangy 'trike' which was reprehensibly vulgar, as was 'bike') fought back. Sometime in late 1882 or early 1883, tricycling members of the Bicycle Touring Club (founded in Harrogate in 1878, metamorphosed into the Cycle Touring Club in 1883), received a circular:

> *It is desired by most Tricyclists to separate themselves entirely from*
> *Bicyclists, who are a disgrace to the pastime, while Tricyling includes*
> *Princes, Princesses, Dukes, Earls etc. There are none of the upper*
> *circle*
> *who ride Bicycles. This is easily seen, and it is plain that the Tricyclists*
> *are altogether a better class than the Bicyclists, and require better*
> *accommodation on tours, etc. A new Tricycling Union has been formed,*
> *and could not that body make itself a Tricycle Touring Club as well?*

This Tricycle Union started up in December 1882, lasted two years, re-emerged as the Society of Cyclists and lasted hardly at all. One would like to think its decline was hastened by the snobbery it promoted: smooth, blue-blood tricyclist in coronet looking down on bloody cyclists, bloody nuisances in cloth-caps.

In 1885, the NCU, asserting its own sole interest in the nation's cycle sport, took over the regulation of track racing which, until then, had been overseen by the Amateur Athletic Association. Three years later, the NCU took a step which has bedevilled cycle sport ever since: it repudiated road racing and turned, instead, to what purists called the true measure of excellence, the only way of deciding superiority – time trials. The Road Records Association became the regulatory body.

The state of the roads in late nineteenth century Britain was not conducive to any sort of cycling. A *Text Book for Riders* published in 1874 describes various stretches of highway:

> *Liverpool to Prescot, 8 miles good road . . . within 6 miles of Newcastle-under-Lyme a very bad bit full of holes . . . Mansfield to Doncaster stiff clay, very rutty and uneven. Tadcaster to York . . . quite impassable..York to Knaresborough . . . in some places three inches deep in mud . . . Peterborough to Market Deeping . . . very bad . . . Rivesby to Horncastle nearly all loose flint; after this the road degenerates into two wheel ruts and a horse track, riding . . . sometimes impossible . . . roads after Herne Hill very pasty, very indifferent to Bromley and worse to Farnborough . . . Shrewsbury to Nantwich is simply execrable and for 45 miles further.*

Between Birmingham and Wolverhampton the road is 'very wearying . . . full of holes and tramway ruts. The bicyclist had better train this.'

For the repair of road surfaces and the infill of holes, McAdam had advised using stones no bigger than a man could put in his mouth. Under the compression of traffic wheels, a layer of such small stones would become compacted and form a more or less stable granular surface. However, the job of compacting was often done hastily, larger stones frequently employed and the road surface rendered treacherous to the cyclist. The law, in the case of accident, was against two-wheelers as well. If the work carried out by a highway authority could be proved to have been done negligently, without due attention to safety, this was classed as *mis*feasance and the authority was liable to pay damages to anyone injured in a resulting fall. If the authority was bound, by legislation soon to come into force, to repair the roads within its mandate and did not do so, this was *non*feasance and they were not liable to compensate any injured party. (Feasance comes from French *'faire'* to do.) Byelaws, for a long time not uniform across the country, were eventually standardised through the intervention of the NCU, but mishaps involving cyclists evoked shrill protest. During a 50-mile race on the infamous North Road in 1894, some 60 years before the manic time-trialler Alf Engers routinely terrorised lorries from his preferred position on the central line of the A1, a woman driving a horse and cart took fright when she saw three cyclist approaching at speed. She lost her head, pulled across in front of them and sent the trio flying off the left-hand verge. Riders badly bruised. Bikes trashed. Woman screaming blue murder to the investigating police who subsequently banned racing along that road.

As we have seen, in the early years the British ruling body wielded enormous power over cycle sport, even on the continent, but when the Union Cycliste Internationale was set up in 1900 the British regulators lost their influence at a stroke and were not admitted to the new set-up for another two years, just in time for the signing of the Entente Cordiale. Moreover, the tight grip of the Road Records Association on time-trialling events effectively marginalized them further. The two organisations refused to cooperate and the poisonous seeds of politicking in the matter of overseeing cycle racing in Britain had been sown. A proliferating number of local county cycling associations, each exercising control over their own patch, further jeopardised any possibility of cohesion or general agreement. British cycling took on the parochial nature and that fragmenting disunity, which has dogged it to this day. It is a less agreeable aspect of the small-club mentality.

A Road Racing Council was formed by a group of clubs in 1922 in an effort to impose some uniformity on time-trialling, but an attempt by the Road Racing Council to set up a single organisation with overall power to regulate the sport nationally was bitterly opposed and the idea foundered. Part of the trouble stemmed from the outlawing of any form of racing on the roads. Time trials had to be conducted in secret. Even for some twenty-five years after the setting up of the Road Time Trials Council in 1938, both time-trial courses and dates of events were given code numbers, post-event ups were expressly vague and pre-event publicity was completely banned. Furthermore, until the beginning of the 1970s as many as 700 time-trial courses were still code-numbered. As if to emphasise the furtive, hugger-mugger nature of hoodwinking the police, participating riders had to wear black alpaca tops and black tights, like pantomime cat burglars, to render them anonymous and were each responsible for making sure the name of their machine did not appear in any newspaper photographs. To avoid ordinary traffic, the trials had to start as early as 4am in the summer months. Of course, opinions about time-trialling are divided; from being considered as the worst sort of preparation for any ambitions to exercise a real talent in the only true test of a cyclist's ability, namely road-racing, as opposed to a lingering belief that racing against the clock – which the French call 'the race of truth' – is the purest form of competition.

Thus, on the track, the pursuit is the blue riband of events, the sovereign test of sheer speed and class. Sean Yates, still crushing the opposition in time trials long after his retirement from pro racing, went to the Olympics as a pursuiter, but his ambition and talent outstripped the limited confines of the Frant and the Ashdown Forest circuits in East Sussex where he did his early racing. There has never been a great road-racer who could not also excel against the clock, for it is as much a matter of temperament and focus as of athletic ability. However, the reverse is very far from being true, and the obsessive, solo nature of time-trialling, especially as it was – and still is – practised in Britain, is positively detrimental to the nurture of a cyclist with aspirations to excel on the road. That opinion was emphatically not shared by the governing bodies of the sport in Britain, the NCU and the RTTC who, some time in the late 30s issued a joint ban on 'massed road racing [in this country] except where the authorities had specifically closed the roads'. Has not racing, though, been a fundamental of human competition from earliest times, man pitched against man, a mirror of life, a metaphor of human striving? So Milton uses the image in *Paradise Lost*, of the Apostles:

Their ministry performed, and race well run,

Their doctrine and their story written left,

They die.   *(bk xii, 505)*

It was Milton who said, too, 'I cannot praise a fugitive and cloistered virtue, unexercised and unbreathed, that never sallies out and sees her adversary, but slinks out of the race, where that immortal garland is to be run for, not without dust or heat'.(*Areopagitica*) The solitary recluse . . . the introspective time triallist.

In December 1941, Percy Stallard, a prominent Wolverhampton club racer who had raced on the continent – he had been chosen with two others to ride in the Worlds Amateur Road Race in France, 1933 – wrote to the secretary of the NCU:

I have raced in France (3 times), Germany, Belgium, Denmark and should have competed in Italy in 1939, but unfortunately this event was cancelled owing to the commencement of hostilities. It is heartbreaking to come back to this country to see the apathy displayed by the authorities towards sport. In Belgium I was honoured to compete in a road race that was witnessed by an estimated crowd of 250,000 spectators.

It is amazing to think that this is the only country in Europe where this form of sport is not permitted. We even have road racing in Ireland, the Isle of Man and the Empire. The massed-start cycle race of the Empire Games was held in Sydney, Australia in 1938.

There seems to be a mistaken idea that it would be necessary to close the roads. This, of course, is entirely wrong. The roads are only closed in other countries when a very important event is being held, such as the Worlds Championships.[7]

Stallard concluded:

'There would be no better time than now to introduce this form of racing to the roads, what with decreased amounts of motor traffic and the important part that the cycle is playing in war-time transport.'

A.P. Chamberlin, the secretary, replied a month later: 'Mr Stallard and all massed-start enthusiasts throughout the country are assured that no effort will be spared to stage war-time massed start racing if circuits can be found.' It was not 'no' but neither was it 'yes'. Stallard went ahead with plans for a massed-start race from Llangollen, in the heart of the North Wales training grounds – home-from-home for Liverpudlian club men, in particular – 59 miles through the picturesque Dee Valley into Shropshire and the upper Severn valley to Wolverhampton, one of the Midland clubs' strongholds.

He limited the entry to "forty riders with massed-start experience: start for 1pm experience with the start set for 1pm on Sunday 7 June 1942. That same day, Bob Chicken, aboard HMS *Cleopatra* on station in the Mediterranean, noted in his diary:

Cleaned up last time as Mess Deck Dodger [ie sweeper and excused other duties.] New arrivals on station, Birmingham & Arethusa & destroyers. C.C.O. in afternoon and last dog.[Dog watch: the watch from 4-8pm is divided into two half or 'dog' watches.]
Slept on deck.

---

[7]When the NCU hosted the World's Amateur Road Race in 1922 – the professional road race did not begin until 1927 – they asked the outlawed Anfield Bicycle Club of Liverpool to organise it, as a *time trial* over 100 miles (160km). British riders took gold, silver and bronze, the last medal in the race till Les West took silver at the Nurburgring in 1966, since when . . . nothing.

A week later, the fleet was in the thick of action on convoy duty, under heavy bombardment by Ju 87s and 88s of the Luftwaffe.

Both the NCU and the RTTC condemned the event, despite Stallard's plea that to suspend competing riders 'was liable to raise controversy that was detrimental to the sport'. A *Cycling* editorial backed the authorities and denounced the race as 'a threat not only to time-trial sport but to organised cycling as a whole . . . no rider who has the very best interests of the sport at heart would wish the police to play such a part [that is in holding up other traffic to allow the passage of 40 racing cyclists on the public highway].This race must not be held and Mr Stallard is rightly warned that his thoughtless enthusiasm might lead to serious trouble.'

It did lead to serious trouble, but not the sort that the editor was thinking of, perhaps. Stallard was suspended *sine die,* the race went ahead, A.E. Price of Wolverhampton sprinted clear by a single second to win in 2 hours 25 minutes 41 seconds, fifteen riders finished and, within a week, all riders and officials named on the programme were suspended pending an enquiry. RTTC riders were warned not to compete against suspended riders at risk of their own suspension. However, on 12 July, at a meeting of the Wolverhampton Racing Cycle Club, members agreed to set up a new organisation 'to control cycling sport in all its branches'. This was, indeed, serious trouble, secession, no less, and the Midland League of Racing Cyclists came into being. Massed-start races proliferated along with official suspensions, of riders and entire clubs, but the banned rebels brushed off the pronouncements of the NCU and RTTC as mere sabre-rattling and got on with organising road races. At a special meeting in Buxton, the High Peak region of Derbyshire on Sunday 15 November, 1942, in a show of solidarity that shamed the mincing of the existing regulators, the three racing Leagues already established, in London, the Midlands and the North amalgamated to form the British League of Racing Cyclists. Of the twenty-two men and two women present at the meeting, none voted against. The author of a 'Personally Speaking' column in *The*

Bicycle expressed the fond hope that, having observed the determination of the League and the depth of the support it had won, it might settle down 'as a parallel body to the existing organisations, that is, the NCU controlling track racing, the RTTC controlling time trials and the BLRC controlling road racing and *all three working in harmony*.' [my italics.]

The history of the BLRC has been written in much greater detail than is appropriate here [8] but a summary of its activities is germane because all future sponsorship of cycle sport in the UK, as well as opposition to it, harks back to the pioneering work of the League.

The BLRC organised the First National Road Race Championship for 5 September 1943, a 65½-mile loop out of Harrogate and back. Ron Kitching, (later a major dealer in bicycle parts, of whom more later), had recently left the Yorkshire Racing Club for the Bradford Cycle Club and the League. Entered for the race he arrived late, having forgotten his shoes. As the field disappeared up the Ripon Road, watched by a crowd of a thousand or more, Kitching rode down Parliament Street and gave chase. Eight days later, the Home Secretary, Herbert Morrison, issued a statement:

> *The Home Secretary, after consultation with the Minister of War Transport, has circularised Chief Officers of Police calling their attention to the growing practice of holding massed-start cycle races on the highway. The official view is that these races are likely not only to cause an obstruction to traffic but to be a source of danger both to the public and the racers, particularly over roads containing dangerous hills or difficult bends and this danger will be considerably increased when normal road conditions return. A further objection to these races in present conditions is the considerable waste of police time involved.*

---

[8] Chas Messenger, *Ride and be Damned*

There speaks a non-cyclist. As to the involvement of the police, the organiser of the race, Chas Fox, had received a letter on 8 September from the West Riding Constabulary thanking him for his letter of the day before and expressing himself 'glad that the assistance of the police was appreciated . . . No complaints were received whatever and I shall be ready to assist on future occasions.'

From its inception, the BLRC did two things well and with gusto: it organised road races and thereby took on the combined hostility of NCU, RTTC and government; it also ripped itself to bits in committee rooms and carried the hurly-burly shunting and elbowing of the continental road-racing to which it aspired into all its internal dealings. Percy Stallard, perhaps jealous of his crusading success in getting the League going at all, had been lambasting the incompetence of some of the League's promoters. Their supporters hit back and moved his expulsion from the League on the grounds of 'conduct detrimental to the League's interests'. The London section took Stallard's side, Stallard chipped in volubly as often as he could and, after just over 3½ hours wrangling, the vote went against Stallard. He was removed from the committee (though still allowed to race) and his name expunged from the infant League's records. He gave the best riposte he could by winning the League's Road Race Championship in 1944. Having sent a letter to all League members outlining his own vision for the League's future – unlikely to be warmly received in the committee rooms – he announced his retirement.

The first stage race ever held in this country, a three-day event over a circuit of roads in Kent close to where I live and write these words, the Southern Grand Prix (1944) paved the way for the 1945 Brighton-Glasgow race. Thousands of spectators lined Madeira Drive along the front in Brighton on 6 August as some 90 riders (including the recently unretired Stallard, an eleven-strong French team, two men from the Belgian army, one from the Polish Air Force and three representatives of the Vegetarian RCC) headed north; the sole back-up van was provided by Ron Kitching and manned by his best mechanic. Claude Butler, the hand-builder of frames, put his name to the programme as a sponsor, with a slogan boasting 'Champion's Choice'. Brighton–

London (Putney Heath), 52 miles; Bignell's Corner on the A1 –Wolverhampton, 130 miles; Wolverhampton–Bradford, 98 miles; Bradford–Newcastle, 103 miles; Newcastle–Glasgow, 149 miles. Robert Batot of France won the overall and the Mountains prize and the French the team prize. Four English riders had presented a Loyal Address to the king at Buckingham Palace en route and the rejection by the RTTC, earlier that year, of any possibility of union between it and the League, albeit disappointing, must have seemed suddenly of no account.

Internecine power struggles continued in the committee rooms, however, and perhaps contributed to the disavowal of the League's 1946 programme by the UCI. The Brighton – Glasgow lasted until 1952, expanded to first six then seven and back to six stages, but by then it had spawned other major stage races, notably the Daily Express Tour of Britain, begun in Festival of Britain year, 1951: twelve stages from Brighton west along the coast and round to Weston-super-Mare, north to Glasgow and back down the east side of the country via Newcastle, Scarborough, Nottingham, Norwich and into London.

Most of the riders in the early League races rode as clubmen; a few had the nominal backing of bike makers or shops. Hickman Cycles and Dayton Cycles (which funded the support vehicle, a small removal lorry, for the 1946 Brighton-Glasgow – 'All British Cycles, *Supreme on Road and Track*') led the way. Hickman was the League treasurer. In 1947, there was, by regular British amateur standards, a positive bonanza of sponsorship, to the consternation of the League secretary, Jimmy Kain, who bridled at the intrusion of 'commercial interest'. Ernie Clements Cycles had six riders, Dayton Cycles five, Evelyn Hamilton Cycles five, Paris Cycles five and the International Totalisator Pools seven. The following year, nearly every rider entered in League events was sponsored by a bike shop or manufacturer. One of them, Bob Thom, destined to travel as mechanic with the first Great Britain team to the Tour de France in 1955, sported a famous name in cycle manufacturing on his jersey: Viking of Wolverhampton. '*You're behind the Times if you're not Riding Viking*'. Other riders of that first Tour team also began to show: Ian Steel, Viking, winner of the Daily Express Tour of Britain,

1951, and the Peace Race 1952; Bevis Wood, Pennine; Bob Maitland, B.S.A.; Dave Bedwell, Hercules, Mountains Prize Tour of Britain 1953; Brian Robinson, Ellis-Briggs (cycle-maker), 4th in that same Tour.

The Peace Race, Warsaw – Berlin – Prague, initiated in 1952, was a gesture of solidarity with three East European countries which had come under Communist rule after the war: Poland, East Germany and Czechoslovakia. The roads were in a shocking state but the reception the riders got en route was passionate, joyous and wonderfully hospitable. A Polish woman of my acquaintance remembers, as a child of 9 in the early 60s, watching the race come through her hometown of Gliwice in Silesia. It was 15 May and her mother Zofia's name day; her father had made a special cake decorated with confectionery cyclists, lemon-zest *maillot jaune*. From the balcony in their two-roomed apartment, they beamed with delight and cheered exuberantly as the peloton went by in the street below, her father waving a Peace Race silk scarf, red, white, navy blue, yellow and black, evoking the colours of the three national flags of the countries the race visited.

The success of the British League men in the inaugural race, first overall and the team prize, gave an undoubted boost to the image of road-racing in Britain but to any rider hungry for a real test of his ambition, there could be no question about where he had to go: across the Channel. Track racing, like athletics, offered international competition as a matter of course and, as such, did not disturb the governing body, the NCU, out of its antipathy for the pesky, vociferous, unruly loose cannons of massed-start road racing. For the members of the League, which had been born in revolt, seemed bent on fostering its pertinacious spirit willy-nilly. Freddie Durman, a rebellious former chairman, actually defected to the NCU and at the League AGM in 1950 censured the League's plans to hold one fifteen-day and two seven-day races. Such a programme flouted the advice of the Minister of Transport and it was, he said, a fact that the League was 'acting in the worst interests of cyclists as a whole.' I'm not sure where he got the curious notion of 'cyclists as a whole' but it is clear that the shouting matches in the League meetings did nothing to serve their greater purpose and were symptomatic of the very obstructions to cycle sport which they lambasted in the other bodies so stoutly opposed to them.

Of those other bodies, the NCU could happily rest on its laurels. Their amateur track men did not make nearly so much trouble and they consistently came home with the spoils.

Raleigh had not yet branched into sponsorship of road racing. Of the other large manufacturers, B.S.A., Viking and Hercules (Britain's second-largest manufacturer of bicycles) were paying riders to race hard and promote their brand names. Dave Bedwell received around £ 1,000 per year from Hercules, just under £ 20 per week at a time (the early 1950s) when Kerry's distributors advertised a sports bike for £13 6s 6d (£6.32). Fiscal equivalents are notoriously hard to pin down, but this comparison gives an indication that Bedwell was certainly being looked after in some comfort. For the rest, the deal was not much more than the basic *à la musette* payment, namely use of a bike and the chance of a bonus for a win.

Brian Robinson, the pioneer of the still tiny contingent of British riders to have cut the mustard in the continental peloton, began his working life as a carpenter in the family building firm. Born in 1930, by the late 40s he was showing enormous class as a road-racer. He was a formidable climber – his record for Holme Moss still stands: from the shepherd's hut at the bottom to the base of the radio mast, 6 minutes 10 seconds in a 1951 hill climb. But he already felt confined by the domestic scene and was eager to be blooded on the continent. His temperament was cool, his approach down-to-earth. He argued on the pragmatic, even bloody-minded, principle to which all the best riders I have ever talked to cleave. Undaunted by the ferocity of competition in the professional peloton, ill-disposed to listen to the Jeremiahs who warned him off mixing it with the continental riders, hardened heirs to a long tradition of no-quarter racing , Robinson said, simply: 'If they can do it, so can I.' They were bike riders, so was he. Even Fausto Coppi had been dismissive of aerated talk about superiority. 'We all have but two legs,' he said.

Robinson was 18 when he bought his first purpose-built racing bike, from Johnny Bury of Manchester, the favoured frame-builder of the moment. Brian followed his brother Des to be taken on by Ellis-Briggs of Shipley, a small firm of bike makers, and, though the gift of a bike for advertising purposes to an amateur rider was not strictly countenanced, the practice was well established and winked at. Robinson was still working full-time in the family building firm until he joined the army on National Service on 3 January 1952. He had already been selected as a possible for that summer's Olympics in Helsinki and was therefore, by government ruling, ineligible for overseas posting. Since British forces were engaged in the bloody conflict in Korea, (1950-53) this exemption was a considerable relief. He raced for the Army Cycling Union against the RAF, rode the Route du Sud in the South of France in army colours, and had the support of what was, effectively, a professional team organisation. He left the army at Christmas time in 1953 and spent the next season racing for Ellis-Briggs alongside Ken Russell, much of the time in races against the professionals of the ten-man Hercules team or the equally strong BSA mob and getting constantly hammered by both. On a flattish course, there was no chance of the two Ellis-Briggs men getting clear in a break: either the BSA or the Hercules pack would chase them down every time. The only chance he ever had of worsting them was on the testing uphill slopes of the Peak district or Yorkshire Moors where gradient made the combat necessarily one to one and Robinson's exceptional climbing ability gave him a prime advantage. Nevertheless, at the close of the season he had more or less had enough of the non-stop pasting from the big boys' gangs. Flogging himself to death with no real hope of a win had little attraction and he was ready to quit, saying to himself that unless he got into a team he was 'done with this business'.

But Hercules approached him with an offer of £50 per month, all his kit, staying in the best hotels when they travelled to races – a first-rate deal. He signed. Almost immediately the manager of the rival BSA team, Sid Cozens, a pre-war track rider, rang to offer him a deal with BSA. When Robinson said he was too late, he'd just joined Hercules, Cozens lost his rag and slagged him off. 'Why didn't you wait to hear from me, you bugger?' A fortnight later, Cozens packed it in at BSA to become manager of the Hercules team. Between him and Robinson there was mutual respect but not much liking. Joining Hercules was a much better bet for a man of Robinson's ambition. BSA, whose team enjoyed scarce a tenth the budget of Hercules, had neither the interest nor the resources to fund a shot at the Tour de France. Viking, another big manufacturer, was also a longstanding sponsor, but offered only a bike and bonuses for a win. Their team was co-sponsored by GB Milremo brakes, which were imported by Ron Kitching of Harrogate, who took over the team when Viking went under.

In 1953, Coronation Year, as Britain was still emerging from a long period of post-war doldrums, Dave Bedwell headed for the continent with the (unexpected) blessing of the NCU. For, on 7 March the UCI had voted at a meeting in San Sebastian to give temporary recognition to the BLRC. The NCU had been scolded very publicly and, in April, its officers signed a tripartite agreement between League, Union and RTTC, granting 'control of massed-start racing on open roads by Professionals, Independents, Aspirants and Amateurs'; the number of events was limited to 750 a year. Bedwell rode the Route du Calvados in Hercules colours, won the first stage, came 3rd on stage 2 and 4th overall at the finish. On 30 August, he competed in the Worlds Road Race at Lugano, just across the Italian border in Switzerland. Riding the last 6km on a flat tyre, he became one of very few British riders ever to have finished the World's road race course. Fausto Coppi won by over seven minutes. That evening, some members of the Hercules Road and Track-racing team sat round a table in Nino's café near Lugano. It was a sun-soaked, hot summer evening, the wine flowed and with it animated talk about the recurring dream of building a team to compete in the Tour de France. Others joined the group, and past midnight two of them, Peter Bryan, a journalist with *Cycling Weekly*, and D.D. 'Mac' McLachlan, the Hercules PR manager, ambled round to the hotel where Jock Wadley, reporting on the event for the *Daily Telegraph*, was in bed, fast asleep. They rang his room, called him down to reception, said it couldn't wait; he stumbled down and they told him the whole Hercules outfit was in agreement: a team for the Tour de France, now or never, worth a crack even if they knew they'd be up against it, but what do you think, Jock? Wadley hadn't even had time to put his teeth in.

Unimpressed by this brilliant showing against some of the best riders on the continent, the NCU suffered a fit of petulance. In early 1954, they retrieved their control over track *and* road races at a UCI congress and issued a diktat by which any British rider who wished to race abroad was required to hold an NCU licence. The League countered: they would issue their own international licences. With who-knows-what collusion from the NCU, the Minister of Transport weighed in behind them, severely restricting the permission for road racing in Britain and when the League sent six men to ride two of the great spring classics, the Liège–Bastogne–Liège and the Flêche Wallonne, the Belgian racing authorities refused them entry. Domestic politics had nullified the UCI ruling. The NCU and the RTTC served further notice on the League that, because of its pugnacious refusal to honour the spirit of the three-way agreement, any future application for international licences would have to go through the NCU. In the December issue of *The Leaguer* a committee member, Chas Fearnley, wrote: 'There is a malignant ulcer prevalent in the cycling world and common to all three racing bodies in this country. It is the taint of vanity and culminates in clashes of personalities.' It was a brave, honest assessment of a very disagreeable truth. The fellowship of two wheels had been poisoned by the jealousy of definition. Cycling itself had wilfully split into rival camps, each determined to maintain its own self-serving sovereignty and to hell with the rest. Touring cyclist . . . time-trialler . . . track rider . . . road-racer . . . and *vive la difference*, even if it kills the ideal. Unity had come to mean surrender and all discussion was compromised from the offset by a fiery distaste for acquiescence . . . shades of those disgruntled egomaniacs of ancient Athens, Hippias and Alcibiades, stomping off to Persia to side with the enemy rather than have any truck with their fellow citizens, the worthless creatures.

In the 13-stage 1954 Tour of Britain sponsored by the Daily Express, five future Tour riders made a good showing. Brian Robinson, still riding as an amateur for Ellis-Briggs, came second both in the mountains prize contest and overall; Dave Bedwell

(Hercules) was third overall and won four stages; Ian Steel, 9th overall; Bob Maitland 10th and Fred Krebs (Hercules), winner of a stage, 11th. The Hercules men took second in the team prize behind the French team, whose Eugène Tamburlini won overall. None appeared in a rival 8-stage Circuit of Britain sponsored by Quaker Oats that August, but Robinson competed in the Tour of Europe and won the Schwenningen to Augsburg stage. (He got no prize money, nor did anyone else, the race organiser being something of a fly-by-night who made off with the cash.) It was quite clear that any British team formed to ride the Tour de France must build itself round this exceptional rider.

Early in 1955, Chas Messenger, international racing secretary of the League, who had had some experience of continental racing himself, asked a friend to get him a list of race organisers' names and addresses in France. A bit of smooth talking at the Paris offices of *L'Equipe*, the sports paper which sponsored the Tour de France, and, *hop-là*, the precious information winged its way across La Manche.

Robinson, having by now signed for Hercules, was already at their training camp in Saint-Raphaël on the coast of the French Riviera, where Napoleon had landed in 1799 after the ill-fated Egyptian campaign. He was raring to go, bubbling with enthusiasm for the fully professional life, determined to make a go of it. The other members of the Hercules team were not so happy. Over the four years that the team had been in existence, the luxury of a large budget with plenty of back-up in a cozy domestic racing season which they dominated had made them lazy and complacent. Besides, several were married with children: the move to continental racing disrupted their altogether comfortable life-style back home. For a man like Robinson, 'more or less a bachelor at the time' as he put it, whatever *that* means, there was no such reluctance. His mind was made up: he wanted a life in pro cycling and here was the great opportunity to learn and adapt. He got on well with the boss, Mac McClachlan, who splashed money around as if there were no tomorrow and drank as if today didn't count. And money there was: from every Hercules bike sold, the coffers of the racing team received 6d (2.5p), probably around .015% of the sum.

The Hercules newcomers met their neighbours on training runs, among them Louison and Jean Bobet, riding under the colours of *L. Bobet-Hutchinson* part sponsored by Hutchinson, the tyre-makers.[9] The elder Bobet, Louison, a man of prickly temperament, had won the last two Tours and had a marked tendency to play the *grand seigneur*. His brother Jean, who could speak English, was friendly from the start and the British tyros mixed in with the French veterans without being made to feel that they were not welcome, crashing the scene.

They rode the Milan–Sanremo, (Jean Bobet came 3rd), the Tour of Belgium, Flêche Wallonne (won by the great Belgian Stan Ockers, Robinson an astonishing 4th) Dauphiné–Libéré (a race which Robinson later won overall, in 1961), its 7th stage over the dreaded Mont Ventoux – and the Grand Prix de Cannes, in which Robinson took the Mountains prize. He was also 5th in the Grand Prix du Moulin, 10th in the Grand Prix du Havre and took a stage and, briefly, the leader's jersey, in the 8-stage Tour du Sud-ouest which started from Albi. These were remarkable results for a débutant.

Thanks largely to him but with support from the rest, the men of the Hercules team had announced themselves in style and the dream came true: they were invited to ride the Tour de France. Mac McLachlan was cock-a-hoop. The commercial possibilities were enormous, the publicity accruing simply from an appearance in the Tour incalculable. The manufacturer of the Tour winner's bike could more or less close their order book for a year. McLachlan said: 'This will be the greatest ever test of British bicycles. A British win in the Tour, although only a dream at the moment, would have a terrific repercussion on the sales of British cycles throughout the world.' The Hercules investment in cycle racing was already substantial. Now, surely, they must reap the dividend manifold.

---

[9] Hutchinson had been established by an American, Hiram Hutchinson, in a former royal paper factory at Montargis, south-east of Paris in 1853. The company was bought by French investors in 1898 and had been sponsoring cycle teams more or less ever since. The 1910 Tour de France winner, Octave Lapize, was a member of the *La Française-Hutchinson* team which made its Tour début in 1913.

I have told the story of the first Brits in the Tour elsewhere.[10] Of the ten-man team, eight were out by stage 11. Stan Jones, the consummate *domestique*, had worked himself into the ground to keep the tailenders going and, when he rode back to pace Bedwell and Bevis Wood back into the bunch on stage 3, they told him they'd packed.

'You can't' he said. 'This is the Tour de France.'

'Well, we have.'

Jones himself abandoned on stage 7 in the Alps and only Robinson and Tony Hoar made it to Paris. Hoar finished as *lanterne rouge* as the back marker of the race is traditionally called and won huge popularity with the French – strictly he should have been disqualified on time limit – but Robinson, who came a highly creditable 29th overall, drew more telling praise from the great André Leduc, winner in 1930 and '32.

'Well done,' said Leduc. 'You climbed splendidly and descended like a devil. With your class and a good team to support you, you could finish in the top 15 next year.'

Robinson, so tired he could hardly speak, replied, laconically: 'I've learnt how to descend in this race.'

After the Tour, Robinson landed contracts to ride in twenty-five of the thirty post-Tour one-day exhibition races for appearance money and primes (prizes) known as criteriums on offer in small towns across France, a significant bounty for a first-time rider. Until the recent years of big team contracts, professional riders depended on a good enough showing in the Tour de France to secure cash-paid rides on the town circuits where spectators lined the local roads to see their Tour heroes flash by. It was a hard round of one-day events – drive across country, ride the race, as often as not drive straight off to the next engagement, grab some sleep and so on, relentlessly. But, the money riders earned at these criteriums, even dented by travel and hotel expenses, made up a substantial portion of their year's earnings of which the team contract made up probably no more than half. Robinson rode these races with a will, picking up every

---

[10] *Inside the Peloton*. Mainstream Publishing, 2001.

prime he could, not only for the money but to show his paces in front of team managers on the hunt for talent. On one occasion, he was racing against Bobet, who had just won his third Tour and, happy to let the English upstart bag as many primes as he had energy to go for, nevertheless needed to remind him of the sacred protocol of the yellow jersey. He rode up alongside Robinson and hissed: '*C'est moi qui gagne*' – *I* win this. There could be no doubting the weight of the seigneurial interdiction.

At the end of his first pro season, Robinson rode the Worlds in September and returned home, completely worn out. He attended the autumn Cycle Show as a Hercules rider and it may well have been that the contract to ride for them was still in place for the following season, but his sights were on France and, in the upshot, Hercules withdrew from sponsorship of cycling. They had shelled out huge amounts year by year anyway, but the exorbitant, unwonted outlay on the publicity for the Tour de France alone, had probably given the company accountants a fright, if not the screaming habdabs. The whole home bicycle manufacturing industry was tumbling into a slump and the Hercules board was advised that the firm simply could not sustain – or justify – continued lavish spending on the racing team. The comparative failure of the team as a whole in the Tour de France, after such high hopes and apparent long-term commitment to finding its way in the continental peloton, cannot have reassured the weaker spirits, certainly not anyone who had been opposed from the beginning. So, despite McLachlan's jubilant claim that Hercules had 'broken through the Tour de France barrier', there was no Hercules-Great Britain team in 1956 nor ever again. In Britain, sponsorship of cycle racing dwindled as the cycle manufacturing industry went into a heavy downturn. I asked Robinson whether Hercules bikes had sold in France after their showing in the Tour. He paused, laughed. 'They sold a hell of a lot in Egypt,' he said. (The RAF held a series of championship races in Egypt at the time.)

For Robinson, as his solid début performance, largely unsupported, in the toughest bike race on the calendar proved handsomely, the die was cast. At the beginning of the new year he set off back to France, aware that it was going to be a tough call, but ready to see the job through.

He had, of course, come to the notice of the racing fraternity in France. After a bit of a struggle in the early months down in the south-east, where most of the early season races are held because of the temperate climate, he was taken on by the Saint-Raphaël-Cilo team on a basic *à la musette* contract. With them he got a ride in the Vuelta a España (in those days held in May) and came 8th overall; he was then entered in the Tour de Suisse to ride for Ferdi Kubler who in the upshot, distracted by an affair with a movie star and the usual argy-bargy with the tax men (salting away cash paid out at criteriums for example), did not ride.

A word of explanation about Saint-Raphaël-Cilo. Until 1954, professional cycling teams could be sponsored only by manufacturers of bicycles or bicycle parts and components. However, Raphaël Géminiani, Le Grand Fusil, 'Big Shot', a stalwart of the French team and later directeur sportif of Jacques Anquetil, put it to the Tour organisation that extra-sportif sponsorship could only be beneficial. There followed a big injection of cash from industry outside the bike trade and a splendid fillip to cycle racing. Cilo made bikes and Saint-Raphaël, for whom Robinson continued to ride, produced the famous aperitif.[11] Within a few years, breweries, makers of ice-cream, fizzy drinks, salami, cigarettes, motor oil, cars as well as bicycles, and so on had joined the growing throng.

Robinson did ride the 1956 Tour de France in a Luxembourg combine led by Charly Gaul, (who repeated his 1955 victory in the mountains competition) and came 14th, thereby honouring Leduc's prediction.

Within a year of its appearance in the Tour de France, Hercules had axed even its domestic racing team and been bought by the British Bicycle Corporation, the bicycle division of Tube Investments which in 1960 merged with Raleigh. By then, the BLRC

---

[11] Wine of unfermented grape juice blended with alcohol is aged for two years in casks and then cut with red (or white) wine and spiced with bark of quinine, zest of lemon and bitter orange, columba root (a mild tonic and stomachic from Mozambique) and aromatic berries and plants.

was also defunct. League teams crossed the Channel occasionally – the Four Days in West Berlin 1956, the Peace Race, Tour of Poland, Tour of Austria 1957 (Bill Bradley set a record for the passage of the Grossglockner, 3,000+m, 56 minutes 53 seconds – the first time he'd ridden it) but the general view of what went on across the water, on the continong, the 'foreign over there' may be encapsulated in the story of Norman Taylor meeting his three team-mates at Victoria station en route to Austria. Messenger asked each of them to check that he had his passport. Taylor looked blank. 'What's a passport, mun ?' he said.

In 1957, the UCI announced that the only road-racing body it recognised in future would be the NCU. In late March, 1958, NCU, RTTC and BLRC signed another tripartite agreement and a sort of peace reigned over the inaugural Milk Race (Tour of Britain) over 12 stages that May/June. Although a national executive meeting of the League rejected a proposal to amalgamate with the NCU just after the Milk Race ended, a special general meeting in October reversed the decision and League and Union were merged in what was to be called the British Cycling Federation.

Tommy Simpson, Olympic bronze medal team pursuit 1956, individual silver, Commonwealth Games 1958, winner national Hill Climb 1958, turned professional in 1960, inspired by Robinson's determination to succeed in the real world of road racing. They rode in the peloton together. At the top of a steep descent, the by now very experienced Robinson told Simpson to take his wheel and follow his line. Simpson did so, but in the agitation, the tension of trying too hard, came off. Robinson pulled up and waited for him. Simpson remounted, but a bit further on came off into the verge again. Robinson nursed him back. At such times the shock of the new, the outlandish, demands of merely keeping abreast can bruise, if not finish off, a beginner. All riders say it: going into the professional peloton can be a cruel, lowering experience. All the class they've shown before counts for nothing. The pace is ferocious, the conditions of racing merciless. Simpson admitted that if Robinson had not taken care of him that day, he might well have given up – not just that race but the whole idea of riding as a pro. With what riches he repaid the older man's thoughtfulness.

1948. With Christina in Paris, guests of Guillane Vahe, Export Manager of the Yellorex cycle chains company – Bob's first foreign agency. (Yellorex became SEDIS in 1953.)

Jimmy Savile, OBE, riding in the first Tour of Britain, 1951

Brian Robinson taking the Holme Moss prime (prize) on Stage 3, Tour of Britain, 1953

With Milton Fisher, Baycliffe's American agent at the New York Cycle Show, 1962

Bob and the members of the Centenary Club – all prominent names in the British cycle industry – on the Club's first overseas weekend jaunt, as guests of the Vredestein Tyres company at Hummelo in Holland, 1974

1979. Sid Barras signing his RJC-WEINMANN PRO RACING contract,
witnessed by Albert Hichen and Bob

1979. Keith Lambert signing for the RJC-WEINMANN team,
witnessed by Cedric (left) and Bob

Cedric with the RJC-WEINMANN publicity girls
and the race support vehicle, Milk Race,1979

Milk Race, 1979. Stage start. Media and Secretariat coach, a communication and
computer nerve centre attending the start and finish of every stage,
provided and equipped by the Vredestein Tyres company

Sid Barras, winner of the National Criterium Championship, 1980

With Christina (far right) and Mr and Mrs Hooley, of Raleigh Industries,
at the Vredestein plant in Holland, 1980,
to celebrate the two hundred million tyres manufactured there since 1934

Cedric and Robert Chicken with guests Phil Liggett (left centre), doyen of cycle commentators and former race director of the Milk Race and Alan Lloyd (right) at the opening of the 'Penguin and Fishbowl' 1980. Alan Lloyd, a wholesaler of lightweight components, drove the Rover supplied by RJC as support vehicle in the Milk Race

Bob, Keith and Sid, British Road Race Champions in successive years – 1980 and 1981 - with RJC racing team bikes

Bob discussing finances with a Director (left) and Area Sales Manager (right)
of the Royal Bank of Scotland prior to extensive rebuilding
of the Bisley Works at Dunstable, 1981

The President of the Union Cycliste Internationale and his committee, with Eileen Gray,
President of the British Cycling Federation, guests of Bob, Cedric and Robert Chicken at
a buffet luncheon in the Bisley Works, during the World Cycling Championships
at Goodwood, Sussex, in 1982

At the 1986 Milk Race finish in London. Bob with his friend Lord Jack Dormand, MP for Easington, County Durham, and former Chairman of the Parliamentary Labour Party, died December 2003

Phil Liggett signs copies of his book about the Tour de France on the Chicken stand at the National Cycle Show, 1988

David Duffield (second from right) with Cedric and other guests at the Chicken and Sons annual Harrogate Show dinner, 1988

2002. On the *procycling* stand at Cycle 2002 in the Business Design Centre, Islington. Bob chats with the great cycling champion Sean Kelly – 'King of the Classics', one-day races, and four times winner of the green Points jersey in the Tour de France

With Jack Morris, Chairman of the Business Design Centre, at the inauguration of Cycle 2002

28th February 2002

Bob Chicken
Glenwood
31 Broadwalk
London
N21 3BU

Dear Bob

It seems I am always thanking you at the moment.

Can I first of all thank you for your recent gesture of wishing to assign the trademark in IBEX to Business Design Centre Limited. I realise how much this means to you and am touched by the thought that you should choose to entrust it into our hands. I think you know by now how much I value our relationship and look forward to making your dream come true when we launch Cycle this September.

Secondly, can I also thank you for Susan's bicycle saddle. Although she will reap the benefits of this more than I, I do appreciate having received the advice of the 'Father of the Industry' on this most important matter, not to mention your subsequent generosity.

With warmest wishes.

Yours sincerely

Jack Morris
Chairman

Directors
J A Morris, D R Jones, S D Fisher, Company Secretary D I Price
Registered Number 1593648 England. A City Industrial Ltd Group Company

INVESTOR IN PEOPLE

Business Design Centre Ltd
52 Upper Street, Islington
London N1 0QH
Telephone +44 (0)20 7359 3535
Facsimile +44 (0)20 7226 0590
www.businessdesigncentre.co.uk

With Jon Snow, (second left) presenter of Channel 4 News and a keen cyclist, and Monty Young (far right) and his son, Grant, (far left) on their Condor stand at Cycle 2003

DECADES LONG PAST I

1869: Front Wheel Brake Stirrup and Brake Arm

1869: Front Wheel Sprung Fork Suspension

DECADES LONG PAST II

1895: Bamboo Frame & Fork Bicycle

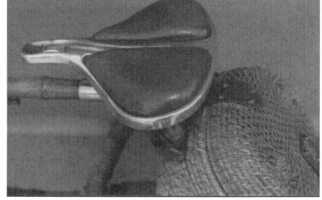

1895: Fashion Saddle on Bamboo Frame Cycle

1905: Derailleur Gear and Chain Wheel

1905: Derailleur Gear Improvement

CHAPTER SEVEN
CHICKEN ENTERPRISE

The scarcity of petrol for private use both during and immediately after the war led to a widespread revival of interest in cycling, not only as a social activity but also as a convenient and cheap mode of transport. One June Kilbey joined a club formed by a man who worked for the London Electricity Board. She later married him, testimony to the powerful kinship that bowling along on two wheels in cheerful company can instil.

'We considered ourselves proper cyclists,' she said, which somewhat begs the question as to what 'improper' cyclists might be. The club was affiliated to the National Cyclist's Union, members wore all the right clothing and abided by cycle club rules.

A club run would be members getting together and they would say 'We'll go Sunday' and arrange places to meet and eat. We'd all meet up early in the morning, perhaps there would be half a dozen of us, perhaps there would be fifty of us . . . and we'd just cycle off and it would be really lovely because the roads would be quiet, there was no traffic in those days you see; and you'd be going through villages and they were so unspoilt, no traffic, nothing parked by the side of the road and people would come out and see you go through, especially if you was a large club. They'd just sort of come out and, you know, wave to you, and you'd wave back, and if you had a puncture they'd come out and ask you if you wanted a cup of tea.

Something there of the wartime 'all mucking in together' spirit and, when in doubt or dilemma, brew up a nice cuppa (cup of) tea.[12]

The revived craze for sociable and serviceable cycling was not confined to the UK where it had begun. In 1948, the Phillips cycle manufacturing company appointed Ken Collins as overseas sales representative. His first mission was to India. He sailed

---

[12] British cups of tea were always 'nice' although the stock epithet first joined the cup in Australia.

on a passenger liner into the Mediterranean, through the Suez Canal and across the Indian Ocean to Bombay where he booked in at the Taj Mahal hotel. He reports:

> *To the best of my knowledge no dealer knew I'd arrived although they knew I would be coming to India. And so the next morning my intention was to go down to the Bazaar, but I was awoken by banging on the door. Went to the door in my pyjamas and there's a manager of the hotel requesting that I leave the hotel, the hotel was crowded by cycle dealers wanting to see me. I looked out the door and there, far as the corridor went, there was possibly 200 or more of these Indian dealers.*

Collins' experience in India reflected how dealers, particularly in Africa, the Middle East and the Indian sub-continent, were crying out for bicycles, indeed for a wide range of goods, as Naassan's letters from Beirut confirm. But British companies were struggling to cope with the demand. Order books were full, and while manufacturing industry had made enormous progress in efficiency and technology to service the war effort, materials were in desperately short supply. Industry needed more steel and more coal. The government instigated a campaign to encourage higher production – 'A Fair Day's Work for a Fair Day's Pay'. Miners, now on a five-day week for a wage of £6 10s (£6.50), were asked to dig harder and steel workers to roll the stuff out faster. The latter did so – from 12.7 million tons of steel in 1946 to 16.3 in 1950. A government poster promoting the export drive showed three Liberty ships, cargo ships mass-produced in America during the war. They represent Import. Two are black, 'PAID FOR BY EXPORTS 2/3; the third is grey: 'ON TICK 1/3'.[13]

The legend over the image is:

---

[13] ON TICK meant bought on credit, originally from a ticket, an IOU, given by buyer to seller acknowledging the debt.

WE NEED

more imports from abroad

(cotton, rubber, tea and the like)

than our exports now pay for.

The subscript is:

This can't go on. We must export one third more this year **or get less and fare worse.**

We're up against it! WE WORK OR WANT

But, to save the hopeless imbalance in trade deficit, Britain needed to export more. In November 1945, Cripps had told guests at a dinner of the Society of Motor Manufacturers and Traders that they should be exporting at least 50 per cent of their output. British drivers would have to wait. The diners greeted that with cries of 'Tripe . . . No!' The Secretary of the Rover motor company, Sir George Farmer, explains the dilemma:

> *The two major preoccupations were on the one hand exports and on the other hand shortages of materials. The two were linked together because [the] government, rightly or wrongly – wrongly in my view – decided that they were only going to allocate scarce materials to those motor manufacturers who could produce exports. So much so that the number of cars one was allowed to sell into the home market was a strictly limited and very small number, and those cars were sold only to people who were able to obtain special certificates of need, by doctors and people of that sort. We'd virtually no exports before the war. We were a very small manufacturer making about 10,000 or 11,000 high quality, luxury cars a year aimed at the home market. We did have a few exports but they were virtually negligible, so we found ourselves in a highly dangerous situation. Had we not been able to find some way of getting exports quickly we were virtually going to get no steel.*

As France and Germany struggled to rebuild their manufacturing industry, the export of British cars demanded by the government went almost unchallenged. However, they were too underpowered for the long roads of America, unsuited to the dust and heat of Africa or South America and insufficiently sprung to ride the cobbled surfaces of the old network of northern European roads in any comfort. When the continental industrial machine revived and more adaptable French and German cars began to appear on the market, the British export trade slumped.

At an exhibition called *Britain Can Make It* put on at the Victoria and Albert Museum in September 1946, 1,300 exhibiting firms showed a dazzling display of 6,000 products, all, as yet, unavailable for purchase. One of the items was a futuristic streamlined monococque steel bicycle. It looked more like a piece of sculpture than a practicable machine, and that is what it remained.

Karl Koppel, Chicken senior's main supplier of tubing, had been taken over by Kronprinz AG, a large manufacturer of tubing together with automotive and bicycle rims who, during William Chicken's time with them, expanded into the manufacture of chemical tubing. Their export manager, Max Küper, a tall, dark-haired man with bushy eyebrows, had visited the Chicken household a number of times, even before the War, and when the old man died he renewed the original agency contract with Bob. Within 18 months of Bob's assuming a leading role in the business, Kronprinz itself was taken over by Mannesmann, a bigger concern with a much wider industrial base. Such successions were worrying. There was never any guarantee that the new operation would maintain the existing agency links it had acquired. However, the Mannesmann director responsible for tubing, Doktor Menke, came to England, met Bob and renewed the contract. By this time, Bob was also dealing with Sen-Raleigh, one of the big conglomerate's overseas operations factory at Vereeniging in South Africa.

From the 1890s to the end of the War, Raleigh's exports to Europe had been handled by the firm of Baker and Strasse in Birmingham. In 1946 Eric Baker, son of one of the founders, was appointed export director of the company. He assessed the current situation thus: 'In 1946 people began to pour into Nottingham from all over the world anxiously wanting bicycles. As a result there had to be rationing but rationing with an eye to the future.' But, the War had pronounced doom on the British Empire. Nation states began to flex their independent ambitions. The dissolution of the old order ushered in a new attitude to trade and world markets. The Commonwealth had supplied forces loyally to help the mother nation. Now they sought redress. Many foreign governments, besides, resisted what had been the pattern before the War: they baulked at importing finished goods from a far-distant manufacturing base at prices, moreover, often dictated by a country claiming sovereignty over them. Exclusive importation of manufactured goods disadvantaged their own labour forces as well as their balance of payments. Raleigh, having opened an assembly plant in Dublin in 1936, the Irish Raleigh Cycle Company, and under pressure to stimulate local manufacturing as a return for reducing imports, set up a factory at Vereeniging **in** South Africa in the autumn of 1951. The plant was fully equipped for frame and wheel building as well as enamelling and finishing components shipped out from England. A few months later, they opened a plant at Asansol in India in partnership with their distributor on the sub-continent, S.K. Sen, under the name of Sen-Raleigh Industries of India. The site, about 140 miles from Calcutta, was close to good supplies of coal and steel as well as being a road and railway hub for communication with the rest of India. Sudir Kumarsen, who managed the project, was also a keen cyclist, and a former champion of the University of Calcutta. Sen-Raleigh had an office in London but not in Germany, from where Bob, as sole agent for Mannesmann, supplied them with tubing.

Sources for tubing in the UK were very limited. The Patent Butted Tube Company, set up in 1898 by J.T. Hewitt and Alfred Reynolds, a grandson of John Reynolds, founder of a family nail-making business in Birmingham, patented a process for making butted tubes with thin walls and ends, and thickened internally where the stress load was greatest.

In 1935, the Reynolds engineers produced their famous 531 tubing, made of manganese and molybdenum alloyed with steel. (The 531 refers to the proportions of the main ingredients.) During the First World War, the Reynolds expertise with light tubing of high tensile strength was diverted into the construction of aircraft and from there on, much of their manufacturing concentrated on supplying the booming aviation industry, both civil and military. Within the vast diversity of their manufacturing interests, the division producing bicycle tubing was small indeed. Given the huge demand for bicycles in the late 40s to mid-50s, home production of tubing was wholly inadequate.

Bob's entrepreneurial energies and spirit, allied to a powerful belief in the European manufacturing base, made him intent on diversifying the Chicken interests. His first priority, after the death of his father, was to secure agency agreements under his own name whilst continuing to trade as William Chicken, his father's *known* title, with both The Humber Oil Company, based in Marfleet, a suburb of Hull, and Baycliff of Halifax, both in Yorkshire. In succession to his father, he became agent for the Baycliff Company Ltd., Akroyd Place, Halifax ('From Hell, Hull and Halifax may the Lord protect me') a manufacturer of Bicycle and Sports bags – leather and leather cloth goods, cycle touring bags, straps, toe-straps, saddle covers, travel, shopping and sports bags; motoring and cycling accessories, camera cases, school bags and picnic cases. The company had been founded by Fred Sutcliffe and Ernest Bayley (the conflation of their names gave the company its name) in the mid-30s though Bayley was killed just before the War, knocked off his bicycle by a rogue car. He was replaced by Arthur Milner.

Having negotiated a new agreement on his own behalf to represent both companies in Greater London and the Home counties north of London as well as the whole of South-East England, Bob made it his absolute priority to drum up a substantial increase in the market for both manufacturers. To this end, he concentrated all his efforts on dealing with and winning the confidence of Brown Brothers, a major distributor of bicycle components and the largest wholesaling company in Britain. Their headquarters was situated in Great Eastern Street, London EC1, home, also, to two other wholesalers of bicycles, accessories and component parts: Hobday Brothers and the Runwell Cycle Company. The relationship with Brown Brothers proved to be particularly fortunate.

From their head office they controlled every aspect of the company's buying as well as the operations of a chain of some fifty branches in every main city and town in both the United Kingdom and Eire, the Irish Republic.[14] They accounted for fully 30 per cent of sales to retailers up and down the land of cycle and electrical products as well as complete bicycles. Bob was, indeed, dealing at the very hub of the vast Brown Brothers network and in his contact with one Browns' employee he was singularly fortunate.

Early in his contact with the company, he had met Alfred Priest, an assistant buyer who in July took over as chief buyer when his superior retired. Priest, known by everyone as 'Mick', had served his first 15 years as a warehouseman before joining the buying staff. He and Bob had an instant rapport. They shared a passion for football and their friendship and business association lasted over 30 years till Mick retired at the age of 65. It continued even afterwards, the two of them meeting regularly at White Hart Lane to watch Spurs, until Mick found the journey from his home in Rayleigh in Essex just too much. As Bob said of his old friend: 'I was blessed in meeting Mick.' Every time he arrived to see Priest at the Brown Brothers HQ, the General Manager, George Tiffen, told his chief buyer to make sure to bring Bob to the office to say hello.

It wasn't long before Bob's natural conviviality led to a regular invitation to join Tiffen and a small elite of other important buyers for a lunchtime indaba – social and business   – at The Coach and Horses pub on Curtain Road, about three minutes walk from Brown Brothers. Here were to be found such luminaries of the industry as K.J. Davis, of the Phillips company, Jim Harrisson of Raleigh, Eric Williams of Lucas, Clem Holland of Wright Saddles, and Gordon Miller and Tom Vickery of Middlemores. These contacts were top notch and Bob, along with the MDs of or? Sales Managers of these big concerns, would be invited – indeed almost summoned, and extremely glad **so to be** – to George's famous lunches at the pub. Tiffen was a man of steady wisdom and warm instinct and became something of a father figure to the younger man just starting out.

---

[14] Southern Ireland (the Irish Freet State) officially left the British Commonwealth in 1948 and, in 1949, became the Republic of Ireland, or Eire in Gaelic.

Bob's other main outlet, The Humber Oil Company, manufactured Excelene cycle lubricant, bicycle repair outfits, calcium carbide lights [15] and a bright black paint for cast-iron ovens (the domestic norm at the time) and so on. Brite Black enamel paint had an interesting genesis. The Humber Company bought up the thick black sludge left in oil tankers after their cargo of crude oil had been discharged. This gunk was then strained and refined and a pigment added to make a highly concentrated oil-based black paint with a remarkable coverage capacity. From the basic tone (reminiscent of Ford' 'you can have any colour so long as it's black') they later developed a range of fast-drying coloured enamels.

The Humber Oil's Governing Director and Founder, Douglas S. Barton came to London periodically. Part of Bob's duty as agent was to meet him off the train from Hull at King's Cross Station and accompany him to the headquarters of F.W. Woolworth Company, a major client. The sale of cycle oil and repair outfits represented 40 per cent of the Humber business and F.W. Woolworth was one of their main customers. In those days, no large office was complete without a commissioner in braided cap, white gloves and uniform frock coat in the foyer of the main entrance, supervising the ingress and egress of visitors. Whenever Barton walked into the Woolworth building, he handed the commissioner a white five-pound note, a substantial sum at the time, the big white fiver with its handsome copperplate legend being a hangover from days before cheques when notes instructing a bank to 'Pay the bearer . . .' could be handwritten and issued on a private account.

On 7 December 1954 Bob was elected a member of the oldest bicycle club in existence, founded in June 1870, days after the death of the man who inspired it, Charles Dickens. In accordance with the tradition of the Pickwick, Bob received a Dickensian sobriquet. He was dubbed Angelo Cyrus Bantam, the elegant Master of Ceremonies at

---

[15] On contact with water, calcium carbide produces acetylene and the calcium carbide lamp allowed the chemical to drip onto a small sump filled with water; the resulting acetylene could then be ignited and the flame reflected by a small silvered mirror at the back of the lamp's interior.

Bath, who makes his first appearance in an inn where Samuel Pickwick is taking a break on a journey to the spa city:

> [he] . . .was a charming young man of not much more than fifty, dressed in a very bright blue coat with resplendent buttons, black trousers, and the thinnest possible pair of highly-polished boots. A gold eye-glass was suspended from his neck by a short, broad, black ribbon; a gold snuff-box was lightly clasped in his left hand; gold rings innumerable glittered on his fingers; and a large diamond pin set in gold glistened in his shirt frill. He had a gold watch, and a gold curb chain large gold seals; and he carried a pliant ebony cane with a gold top. His linen was of the very whitest, finest, and stiffest; his wig of the glossiest, blackest, and curliest. His snuff was princes' mixture; his scent BOUQUET DU ROI. His features were contracted into a perpetual smile; and his teeth were in such perfect order that it was difficult at a small distance to tell the real from the false.
>
> "Mr. Pickwick," said Mr. Dowler; "my friend, Angelo Cyrus Bantam, Esquire, M.C.; Bantam; Mr. Pickwick. Know each other."
>
> Charles Dickens *The Pickwick Papers* ch.35

When Douglas Barton died in 1955, his son Gerald took over as head of Humber Oil and invited Bob to continue his selling contract with Woolworth. And now Bob pushed sales of the Humber enamel paint further. The company manufactured tiny pots for the purveying of the thick enamel with the mammoth spreading capacity and Bob christened them 'tinlets'. Brown Brothers and other leading bicycle manufacturers took readily to the idea and it was the sale and popularity of the tinlets of what was now called Humbrol enamel, (another Chicken neologism) which proved pivotal in the vast increase of sales of Humber Oil products.

Around this time, there was a huge boom in the sale of plastic model kits, aircraft and battleships in particular, trading on the images of wartime seen in comic strips, war hero story books and magazine-style publications, and at the cinema. The great virtue of the quick-drying Humbrol enamel was that it adhered perfectly to plastic. Soon Airfix, Frog, Revell, Lindberg and Aurora (these latter three came from USA) were all the rage. Hitherto, model-making kits had largely been made of balsa wood. Gerald Barton was a keen model-maker and used proprietary glue with the brand name Oh My manufactured by a firm in London. Barton decided that Humber Oil could surely produce something as good and he researched and developed his own glue. Bob persuaded Barton to market the new fixative in tubes similar to toothpaste tubes. They called in expert opinion on it the efficacy of what they called 'Britfix Cement' and Herny Nicholls, the manufacturer of Mercury model aircraft pronounced it superior both to Oh My and another rival which had just appeared, Joy Plane. When plastic models superseded balsa wood, Humber Oil deployed their undoubtedly superior research and development skills to produce the very best plastic moulding adhesive on the market, Humbrol Polystyrene Cement. Plastic model kits soon dominated the toy industry. When Bob imported the first kits of models of horror film characters from America, Frankenstein's grotesque, Dracula and Godzilla – this last based on the Japanese cult movie – he was labelled a sadist by the *Daily Mail* for purveying such horrific items to unsuspecting children. 'Chicken becomes a monster.'

During this rich period of product development by the Hull-based company, the board rewarded Bob's close involvement by asking him to join the company as Sales and Marketing Director. Bob accepted but insisted on maintaining his own identity as an agent. He took on responsibility for worldwide sales of all Britfix and Humbrol small-pack consumer products on a remuneration of 0.5 per cent against his previous commission of 5 per cent for the UK area for which he was currently responsible. In the time during which he worked for and within Humbrol, their trading increased tenfold.

Woolworth was a major client for the Baycliff products, principally sports and travel holdalls which Bob had introduced to the range; these included such novelties as the compact Ladies' twin-handle shopper, soon selling up to 300 and even 500 dozen per month, depending on the season.

This kind of entrepreneurial reading of the market made Bob's management of the basic agency requirement so much more valuable to his clients, as demonstrated in the case of the child's school satchel, which he suggested. In the first year of trading, the satchel not only reaped Woolworth an extra 30 per cent of profitable turnover but stimulated enlargement of the core stock to include cycle saddle and pannier bags, several different-sized holdalls, and sales to a subsidiary distribution company, Denewood Distributors based near Jesmond Dene, Newcastle-upon-Tyne. Denewood was also responsible for production of the Embassy Cigarette Gift Catalogue in which were featured eleven items from the Baycliff range. As a result of Bob's prolific work in boosting Baycliff's sales volume, he was invited to join the company as Sales Director whilst retaining his independence. When Fred Sutcliff, the company's major shareholder, died suddenly, his widow Dorothy asked Bob to consider buying her late husband's shares 'at a fair price'. This he did. Within a year of Sutcliff's death, his junior Director and partner Alfred Milner (actually his senior in age) also died and it was natural for Bob to buy his shares, too, and thus take control of the company. More of Baycliff later.

In 1958, George Tompkins founded The Green Shield trading stamps company in small premises near Highbury Corner, Islington. The idea of offering trading stamps as a small dividend on each purchase of, for example, petrol, with the incentive of accumulating enough stamps to trade back in for a free gift, originated in America, (where they were *yellow*) although cigarette cards had been established in the UK long before that. Packets of cigarettes might contain cards from a set, say, of different makes of bicycle, motorcar and motorbike, or of leading football or cricket players. From this developed cigarette coupons, which could be exchanged in sufficient number for gifts from a catalogue. Embassy cigarettes were early dispensers of coupons.

Seeing what a good opportunity a link with Green Shield afforded to promote Baycliff products, Bob contacted their buyer, Michael Goldsmid, and soon the Green Shield catalogue of gifts for happy customers featured a range of nine Baycliff shopping, sports and travel bags. At the height of the Green Shield stamp craze, nine out of ten motorists used garages which offered them, but it was when the new supermarket chain Tesco took on Green Shield that the business soared *and* gave the shops a tremendous boost in the winning of customers from the established giant, Sainsbury.

Within three years, however, Tesco announced that they would be withdrawing from the scheme on grounds of cost; besides, their own growth was, by now, so strong they didn't need the lure of trading stamps. The loss of Tesco was fatal and in 1974, Green Shield closed down. Tompkins then founded Argos, the cut-price catalogue seller, and Baycliff bags continued to sell through that outlet.

'Mick' Priest was a member of the Centenary Club, founded by the executives of the Cycle Industry in 1939. Frank Urry, a cycling journalist, had founded the club because no one else had. He scolded a bunch of cycling manufacturers one day: 'All you buggers manufacture bikes but you never get together to *ride* bikes. Well? How about it?' The upshot was the club named for the centenary of Kirkpatrick Macmillan's early bicycle of 1839: an annual dinner in February or March and two celebration bicycle rides, in spring and autumn. Priest introduced Bob and secured him an invitation to join.

Priest and another man of huge importance to Bob, Leo Rotger, Governing Director of The General Fittings Co. of Farringdon Road and later Kentish Town, were, truly, the architects of his rise. As he has acknowledged, 'I would never have achieved so much in my early business life without the full encouragement and support of Mick Priest and Leo Rotger.'

Rotger, whose father was German, had served as a major in the Royal Artillery during the War, and he sold cycle and electrical goods wholesale. He'd known Bob's father from before the War and became almost like an older brother to Bob from the time of their first meeting till Rotger's death in 1984. In 1951 Bob went with Leo to the <u>RAI</u> Fair near Arnhem in Holland. It was quite a small set-up, but Vredestein, the Dutch manufacturer of bicycle tyres based in nearby Doetinchem, had a stand and Bob called by to talk. Vredestein already had an agent in the UK – the Levy Brothers, Joe and Lesley, of Edmonton under an agreement renewable annually. However, Levy Bros. also dealt exclusively with the Aberdale Company, makers of Bob's first bike, which had changed its name to Trusty Manufacturing Co. Ltd. after the war. This narrowed the opportunity of sales considerably, so surely the broader sales programme which Bob now proposed must be infinitely more desirable to the Dutch firm? For the moment, they stuck with Levy Bros, and when in 1952, at the Cologne Fair, Bob approached Vredestein again, Wim Oorlog, the Vredestein representative on the stand, told him that, sorry, they had already agreed another year with Levy Bros. In spite of this their conversation continued and there was something about this tall, handsome Englishman, of high intelligence, who talked straight and with complete assurance which prompted Wim to suggest that Bob come back next day and meet his father Geert, the senior partner. Geert took to Bob immediately and told him that they might well be interested in working with him. To that end, he said, Wim would come to the UK where he could meet Bob's customers and assess the possibility of appointing him agent when the annual agreement with Levy Bros. next lapsed.

Wim arrived. Bob took him to Brown Brothers of Great Eastern Street to meet Mick Priest. Priest, conscious how important a deal this could be, but fully confident in Bob Chicken as a man with flair and nous, assured the young Dutchman: 'Wim, if you give Bob the agency,' he said 'you are absolutely assured of our support.' Since Browns had one of the largest distribution operations in Britain, such warranty was of enormous value.

Wim, aware that much hung on this decision, sensibly asked to see as many other of Bob's customers as possible. Off they went to the Runwell Cycle Company and Hobday Bros, along from Brown's on Great Eastern St; thence to Southern Trading and Kerry's of Stratford, down the Mile End Road. Very encouraged, Wim went back to Holland and told his father that Vredestein had a splendid opportunity on hand to increase their sales in the UK many times over. Bob Chicken offered a much broader spread of customers than the Aberdale-only arrangement. Geert and Bob met, discussed terms and shook hands. Making the deal, Geert said to Bob: 'Mr Schicken, my agreement is my handshake.'

As some indication of the new confidence that this strong link with the UK market bred in Vredestein, soon after after Bob joined them, Vrededstein bought four other tyre-manufacturing companies in Holland.

Thus, in January 1954, Bob assumed the agency for Vredestein in the UK leaving Levy Bros. with what had hitherto been Vredestein's only UK outlet – Trusty Manufacturing. Bob introduced Vredestein tyres and tubes not as Vredestein but under their registered name of Paragon. The name Vredestein sounded too foreign, too German. Even as Paragons the name could not be entirely disguised and the Vredestein tyres were popularly dubbed 'Freddy tyres', 'Freddy', like 'Fritz', being First World War slang for a German, especially a German soldier, (Freddy from Friedrich).

Even as Paragon the Vredestein tyres and tubes couldn't compete in Britain with the long-established Michelin and Dunlop's which enjoyed such cachet in the British market, their high prices commensurate with their high standing in the public perception. Competition from them was intense. The other French tyre company, Hutchinson, originally represented in the UK by Holdsworthy, was an also-ran: the company did not, in truth, find Britain interesting commercially.

The breakthrough for Bob and Vredestein in the UK came when the chairman of Dunlop looked into the accounts of the main company and concluded that it was absurd for them to continue to make bicycle tyres – the division incurred massive annual losses.

Fort Dunlop near Birmingham had been making tyres for bicycles for a long time but the slump in the bike trade in the early 50s persuaded them that there was no profit to be had from that market. Moreover, Raleigh bought much of their dwindled production of tyres, having had a long-standing supply deal with Dunlop, but at a fixed price way below the current market average negotiated on the basis of a discount price for bulk purchase. This meant that, even when Dunlop's profit had become a significant loss, Raleigh were still obtaining an essential commodity on the cheap. The Dunlop directors had no choice but to order the immediate cessation of manufacture of bicycle tyres.

Raleigh went to Michelin. Michelin made tyres for cars and trucks and most of their profit on the manufacture of the 1 million tyres they did make for bicycles was was not from new bikes, but in the replacement market for worn tyres. An important selling point was the look of the Michelins, each tyre individually wrapped, a very traditional, stylish touch. Michelin, which made nothing else for bicycles except tyres, asked Raleigh how many tyres they would need per annum. Raleigh said: 'Two million.' But, used to the artificially low price they had demanded from Dunlop for so long and sheltered from true market values, the price they quoted was far below what Michelin could accept. Besides, the quantity they were sought hardly warranted much interest from Michelin when the French firm's existing replacement sales were so comfortably won. Anyway, the small number of tyres Michelin sold to cycle manufacturers meant they had little interest in Raleigh's raison d'être – the bicycle market per se.

Impasse.

Bob saw the opportunity. Raleigh was in a fix. Discussing the matter with Wim, Bob persuaded him that they could sell tyres to Raleigh at a price far higher than Raleigh had been paying to Dunlop. The Nottinghamshire monolith would now have to confront the cold reality of real market prices. Because they all but monopolised British cycle manufacturing, their long-term policy of bleeding British manufacturers and suppliers of components and accessories down to the lowest possible profit margins worked badly against them when those suppliers pulled out. Suddenly unprepared, Raleigh faced much higher prices from other far less malleable sources. The smaller fry had been squealing for a long time: now the leviathan itself would squeal. At the time, Raleigh were paying 10½ pence per tube and 3 shillings 8 pence per tyre (just under 5p and 24p respectively). So Bob, knowing that Raleigh must contact him as an importer of the only bicycle tyres comparable to Dunlop's, would put the asking price for Vredestein's at 7s 10d (39p) for tube and tyre combined.

Wim objected: Raleigh wouldn't want to pay Bob's price and if they held out for what Raleigh would dismiss as a vastly inflated figure, other suppliers would move in to exploit the gap left by Dunlop's withdrawal from the market. Bob held firm. *Tenez ferme.*

Wim pressed him: 'Come on, Bob, we'll never get that.'

'No, we won't, but it's the starting line.' Bob replied:

Now Charles Fellows, purchasing director at Raleigh, phoned Bob, as Bob knew he would. Raleigh were in trouble, said Fellows, in desperate need of tyres. Bob told him to phone Wim and at once rang Wim himself telling him to expect a call from Fellows and, for sure, a request to visit the Vredestein factory.

The deal was eventually struck at 5s 7d per tyre(28p) which meant a net profit of 15% on manufacturing costs. The Vredestein tyres were made of Indonesian rubber, grown in their former colonial possessions which remained a Dutch vested interest.

In 1954, Vrededestein were producing approximately 8 million tyres a year, mostly for the European market and, after 18 years hard commercial graft from Bob as agent, added an annual 2.7 million for the UK market alone, the great bulk of that sum down to Raleigh.

During the negotiations on the Vredestein deal with Raleigh, Bob was called in to speak to Philip Cheatle, their chief buyer. Bob sat down facing Cheatle across the big desk. Cheatle opened a drawer, took out a book and placed it on the desk in front of Bob.

'What's this?' asked Bob.

'It's a bible. I'd like you to swear on it that everything that is said between us will be taken on absolute trust.'

'It will be.'

Cheatle tapped the bible. 'Nevertheless, I'd like you to swear.'

Bob was dumbfounded. 'You want me to swear an oath on holy scripture?'

'That's right.'

Bob eyed him. There was a long pause. Then he said: 'Listen, you will get no lies or flannel from me. Put the bible away.'

Wim Oorlog, about the same age as Bob, was a very forceful character, somewhat of a paradox – an essential bonhomie coupled with an inclination, on occasion, to be brusque and offhand. (Christina never took to him.) He was also an enthusiastic party animal. In the early 50s, when he made his first trips to UK, he brought with him the managing directors of Sparta and Gazelle, the Dutch bike manufacturers. Bob entertained them royally at the Embassy Club. He had very little money at the time, but he did know that entertaining foreign contacts generously was an essential part of business dealing. Hospitality counted for much and what dividends that early generosity in straitened circumstances paid in the long run. The strain wasn't just financial either. Sessions at the bar of the Embassy frequently went on to the small hours.

One time, at 3am, Bob, drooping, told Wim he was done: 'I have got to go home, Wim, I'm tired out.'

But Wim was in full flow, certainly not ready for bed yet – he needed company, so he rang the Vredestein US agent staying at the Mayfair Hotel. 'George? You've got to come now.'

Bob clung on to whatever shreds of compos mentis he could still find for another 40 minutes until George arrived and he got his release.

'Okay Bob' said Wim 'off you go.'

Not everything went smoothly. Soon after his father died, Bob took up with Pieter Brüninghaus, director of Präzision Werker,[PWB] a firm in Bielefeld which made freewheels, hubs and steel ball bearings. For firms involved in the bike trade, Bielefeld was a sort of Coventry in Germany It was his first overseas agency for bicycle components and he arranged an appointment with Arthur Fidkin, chief buyer for Hercules Cycles in Rockey Lane, Aston, to persuade him to look at samples of the high-grade steel ware from Bielefeld. He showed Fidkin PWB steel ball and roller bearings and steel small-flanged hubs. Fidkin, a very canny man, expressed interest but said Bob would have to do better on the prices. Bob negotiated a lower price with the PWB boss, Peter Bruninghaus, and went back to see Fidkin, confident of securing a good order. Once again Fidkin told him the prices were not competitive; he needed a further drop of 6 per cent. Bob asked to see invoices from Hercules' present supplier. Fidkin refused.

'You gave me the price yourself when I was here last time and I agreed it with PWB.' Bob remonstrated:

Fidkin wouldn't budge. 'You'll have to lower your prices,' he said

Stubbornly Bob said a curt 'Good afternoon, you're a crook,' turned on his heel and walked out, slamming the door behind him.

Furious, frustrated, badly let down in an issue he saw as trust over a gentleman's agreement, he took Fidkin's shifty behaviour not to heart, which was pointless, but to mind. Wise up, don't give up. As Mark Twain put it: 'After a setback a man has no place to get disappointed, he ought to be making up his mind to get even.' For, here was an important lesson: know your man, watch out for being side-stepped, pin the agreement. He also reflected: were not Hercules making the cheapest bicycles in the UK, a million plus of them per annum? Before the war they had been asking £4 19s 10d (£4.99) for a whole bike. They had a reputation for price as well as quality to maintain. It became clear why Fidkin was cheap-skating, trying to squeeze out a price from Bob that would be commercially unviable. No thank you.

He extended his overseas commitment by contacting the Peugeot Company which manufactured Sedis bicycle chains at their factory in Saint Siméon, east of Paris.

The Sedis chain had originally been named Yellorex, as used and made famous by the great Rik van Steenberghen. [16]

As Coppi's name gave huge impetus to the sales of Campagnolo, so Van Steenbergen lent considerable cachet to Yellerex and now Sedis. A chain, the invention which made the bicycle possible in the first place, is a vital part of the transmission and a complex and often neglected item. It must combine lightness with strength, be resistant to clogging and the friction of cog teeth, sufficiently flexible to afford smooth movement over chain and free wheels and, after the advent of the derailleur, through the serpentine flow of the jockey wheels. The extreme thrust put on the chain in the acceleration towards the finishing line exerts huge force on a chain: a slipped cog, a jumping chain, a

---

[16] 'The thing about Rik Van Steenbergen was that he never really trained,' said Brian Robinson. 'He just rode races all the time, *kermesses* (as criteriums arfe known in Belgium) all over the place. He'd park his car at 100km and climb off before the race finished but it was the best preparation you could have. They ride those one-dayers in Belgium so fast.' One of the speediest finishers of his day, Van Steenbergen's professional career at the front of the bunch spanned an incredible 23 years. In 1943, aged 19, he rode the championship of Belgium, first time he had ridden more than 200km in a race. Discouraged by two punctures he nearly abandoned 100km from the finish but, persuaded not to, caught the bunch at astonishing speed and outsprinted them. Not till Jacques Anquetil won his first Grand Prix des Nations at the same age was there another such exuberant début.

He held the title the following year, (and won it a third time 1954). In 1946 he took the Tour des Flandres and came third in the Worlds. Never a solid climber, Van Steenbergen honed his exceptional finishing power on the track, riding Six Days through the winter – madisons and omniums, i.e. medleys of sprints, devils, (mixed-event races) 25-lap points races. Immersion in such competition made him fast, chancey and cunning, even sly, a bit of a burglar. Born into a very poor family, he acquired his survival skills early.

In his first Tour de France, 1949, Van Steenbergen won two stages and came second in the newly-inaugurated points prize behind another great Belgian sprinter, frequently his Six Day partner, twice World road race champion, Stan Ockers.

That autumn at the Worlds in Copenhagen, Van Steenbergen himself pulled on his first rainbow jersey. In 1951 he took six stages and the points prize in the Vuelta and was second overall in the Giro d'Italia, the first Belgian to get a sniff of the leader's *maglia rosa*, pink jersey, since Demuysere, second in 1932/33. He accumulated 15 stage wins in the Giro in several participations.

He showed no signs of tiring. His third Worlds title came in 1957 and the year after that his second Flèche. This astonishing longevity reinforces what made Van Steenbergen so special. He was still capable of second in Paris-Roubaix 1957 and Milan-San Remo in 1959.

Van Steenbergen retired, sort of, after the last meeting at the Palais des Sports in Brussels, 15 November 1966. He was 42 years old. He actually rode one final race a month later at the Palais des Sports in Anvers where, on the boards he'd graced with such dazzling speed and tactical nous, before a home crowd cheering on the last of one of the greats, he outsprinted three ex-Worlds champions Jean Stablinski (1962), Beheyt (1963) and Jan Janssen (1964).

wobble in the derailleur cage are disaster. A properly maintained chain will lose only 1.5 per cent of its transmission power to friction. So, there are chains and chains, and the Sedis was a winner.

There was still a great shortage of cycle parts available for the replacement market in the UK, including chains, saddles and tyres. Bob saw an opening and rang Peugeot to suggest a meeting to discuss a British agency. The market for chains was dominated by the German-made Union, imported to the UK under strict licence since 1947 by Leonard Newman of Birmingham, and the Reynold Chain Company of Coventry, major supplier of chains to all the many UK bicycle manufacturers in production at the time. Peugeot contacted their International Marketing Coordinator, M. Dumonde, who phoned Bob to propose that he come to the main Peugeot Paris office to meet the export manager, Guillaume Vahe.

Bob duly arrived in the residential district of Passy between the Bois de Boulogne and the Seine, where the Peugeot HQ was sited near a house rented by Benjamin Franklin between 1777 and 1785, on which he erected the first lightning conductor seen in France. Vahe introduced Bob to a Monsieur Barbier, the managing director of the bicycle and motorcycle division which made all the chains for the Peugeot vehicles and transmission systems and Bob signed a contract as agent for the import and distribution of Sedis bicycle chains throughout the UK. He had now added two major import agencies to the small existing portfolio built up by his father.

CHAPTER EIGHT
BRAKES OFF

In late November 2004, I visited Robert Chicken, younger of Bob's two sons, and his wife, Christine, at the hotel where they were staying, close by the Botanical Gardens in Puerto de la Cruz, Tenerife. We talked about his, indeed their, involvement in the family business which Robert joined when he was 23. Not knowing that she *had* been involved, I put the question. She gave a complex, wry smile, slow to unfold, which was pure eloquence. It told a long, a very long story.

In the course of our conversation, as my mind became periodically saturated with detail and I needed to take a break from scribbling notes, anecdotes about Pa tumbled out. One I note here, because it has something of the spirit of the remarkable man who is the subject of this book.

Bob and Christina used to own a magnificent villa in the north of the island in the Orotava valley overlooking Puerto de la Cruz near where, during a night-time landing on the beach in 1797, Horatio Nelson received the wound which led to the loss of his arm. As they drove down the steep, steep mountainside after a visit to the island's main peak, the extinct volcano Mount Teide, Christina in the front and Bob's brother Harry and his wife Babs (out on holiday) in the back, Bob touched the brake pedal. It went straight to the floor . . . total brake failure. Unwilling to alarm his passengers with news of their plight, he decided that evasive manoeuvres were in order and, heaving at the hand brake – only partially effective – he began to crunch the side of the car with glancing blows into the rock face bordering the road. Each successive collision slowed the car but heightened his passengers' not unnatural fright and stark realisation that their driver had quite clearly taken leave of his senses and was, it appeared, trying to kill them all. He persisted in the deceleration tactic, despite the mounting frenzy beside and behind him, until, by huge good luck, he saw a lorry trap ahead – a ramp deviating off the road into a long sump of gravel which brought the car to a dead halt with the four of them still alive. How Bob explained this extraordinary turn of events to Christina and the others in the immediate aftermath of their survival, and their total distraction, is not recorded.

By his own admission something of a carefree spirit (read under-achieving drifter . . . expelled from school, one sole A level) Robert had worked in advertising and was a trained salesman but had yet to show any interest in serious direction of his talents or energies. He spent some time as a sales representative for the Imperial Tobacco company but the area he covered – Suffolk and Norfolk – was dead: towns scattered broadly over wide open farmland under a big sky, miles and miles of driving between the scant few customers he supplied. It was hard work, not very rewarding, but good training. Alas, one day in early summer, 1973, after a generous lunch with a big retailer, he was followed home by the police and arrived to find another police car waiting for him. The tail had phoned ahead. He blew into the bag: over the limit, banned from driving and sacked. What was he to do? Bob suggested he join the company. Bob's elder brother Harry was running the Industrial Chain Supply Co. Ltd. based on Tyneside. Sedis supplied them with motorcycle and automobile chains and, when they went into receivership, Sedis asked Bob, agent for their bicycle chains, to take the company over; this he did, for a modest sum. He then employed Harry, who had been involved in medical printing, to run the company with the two of them as directors. However Reynolds Chains had an unshakeable grip on the market, and as the Industrial Chain stock could hardly even be given away, the company more or less melted away.

Cedric, Bob's older son, had spent a year with Sedis at their plant in Saint Siméon-de-Bressieux, near Lyon, consolidating his knowledge of the language and learning the business. He had been offered a university place to study Modern Languages but declined it. From France he went to Nürnberg to spend a year with the Schreiber family, the original German agents for Humber Oil, whom Bob had taken over, once more for language and business experience. However, after his year in Germany, Cedric had had enough of the business and in 1969 he emigrated to South Africa to work for The National Carpet Company at their office in Cape Town. The climate was wonderful, the opportunities to play sport plentiful (he had played for the English Public Schools' football team) and for a while life was good. The company then transferred him to the Johannesburg office. He hated the place. It was enough to drive him to phone home and say that he was coming back to England in search of other employment.

Bob had been asked by the Peugeot company to act as agent for importing their bicycles to the UK but declined because of conflicting interests with British companies. However, there was no reason why Cedric should not act for them. An agreement was reached via Bob's contact, Henri Lasardier (on the proviso that when Bob needed Cedric he would be permitted to leave) and Cedric became Managing Director of Peugeot UK after spending some preparatory time at the Peugeot Cycle Company factory in Sochaux, Alsace, and other installations in Holland and Germany. He stayed with Peugeot for three years.

Meantime there was an urgent need to rationalise the various disparate operations of the Chicken enterprise. Since brother Harry was not doing much in the way of importing, Bob put it to Robert that here was a chance to knuckle down by injecting a much-needed impetus into the company on the sales side. In the reorganisation, Harry took over the Kronprinz agency alongside control of Industrial Chain and, on the very day that brother Cedric set up as importer of Peugeot bikes in Bedford, Robert began work out of one of two outsize lock-up garages in Winchmore Hill which Bob had taken over as warehouse storage for the stock of chains from Industrial Chain. Originally built in the late nineteenth century as the depot of the local fire brigade, the arches with their cobbled floor still stand on the green in the north London suburb. Bob rented an office on the green opposite the lock-ups and Robert set about building up sales and imports on an existing but very limited customer base. He brought in tubular steel luggage carriers from Steco in Holland; the now-famous chromoplastic mudguards from ESGE of Bielefeld which, in time, monopolised the UK mudguard market, as well as bicycle kickstands (standard fittings on bicycles at the time); rims from Schothorst; Sedis chains in batches of 1 or 2,000 at a time, (some indication of the popularity – and usefulness – of the item); and Videc bicycle bells from Germany, which the Chickens christened 'Shamrock' bells from the tiny seal on the dome of the bell.[17] Annual turnover was £30,000.

Robert inherited what may fairly be called an unstructured outfit supplying a number of independent wholesalers, notably Brown Brothers and Kerry's of Stratford, east London, and Affiliated Factors. Furnished with a wage and a car, he set off to see what he could make of the Industrial Chain Supply Co. Ltd. from the cobblestones underneath the arches on Winchmore Hill green. He worked through the list of existing customers and to them swiftly added other wholesalers. To the first wholesaler he visited, a man called Rutter, he showed a sample of the Videc 'Shamrock' bell. Rutter took hold of it and twanged the lever. The bell didn't work. He looked at Robert. 'Okay' he said 'we'll take 2 gross.' (Rutter's later went bankrupt though it would constitute a scandalous lack of taste, at the very least, even to frame the suspicion that Robert Chicken sold them 288 identical models of their own passing bell.) The Chicken name was well established in the bicycle wholesale world and it was not hard to double

---

[17] When bells were a standard fitting on bikes, most of the population had rung a bicycle bell at one time or another and knew what one sounded like. No more. Recent legislation has made compulsory the fitting of a bell to every new bicycle on grounds of safety. As well try to get pedestrians to yodel. Amid the roar of traffic, the blast of car sound systems, the thump of loud music in personal stereos and the beep-beep-beep of reversing delivery lorries, the bicycle bell has as much chance of registering in the urban maelstrom as the mew of a cat in steel foundry. Besides, who among the milling crowd on pavements or in the hermetically sealed interior of a motor vehicle knows what a bicycle bell sounds like any more, still less what it signals? Some while ago, a French friend brought me home a very grand bicycle bell from China and, optimistically, I chimed it as I pedalled through the flocks of shoppers and cars to warn the constant spillage across my path of jay-walkers and meandering Japanese tourists, clearly bent on acquiring a holiday souvenir of bruising or intermediate mutilation from honourable British (imported) tyre rubber or brake levers. Albeit my bell released a carillon worthy of a continental cathedral clock, the aimless flotsam of kerb-hoppers and the bewildered foreign tourist jetsam dumbly ignored it, deaf to its appeal, whereupon I chucked it to rely, as before and since, on constant qui vive – quick reactions, supple braking fingers and a parade-ground shout. So much for protection of the cyclist. To hell with bells, we need bicycle lanes, continuous bicycle lanes.

the turnover in the first year even from such a relatively small base and limited expenditure of time.

The interesting bit, as Robert put it, came in his second year of trading.

Otto Weinmann, a Swiss mechanical engineer, had become famous as a maker of superb quality cycle components, in particular rims and brakes. His side-pull brake was very popular during the 1930s and the Weinmann Carrera, developed as a challenge to Campagnolo's brakes, was acceptable as a good alternative at considerably lower cost. The Weinmann operation was superbly run, too. Their brakes and components came smartly wrapped in the glossy brown greaseproof paper used to keep moist the slick of oil on the best tools and packaged in handsome stout cardboard boxes. Weinmann brakes were sleek items lovingly presented, whereas Campagnolo was a shambles: for all the class of their manufacturing standards, the Italian company delivered its spare parts to their British agent, Holdsworthy, wrapped in newspaper, a muddle of them jumbled up higgledy-piggledy.

The Weinmann agent in the UK, Walter Flory, another Swiss, was coming up to retirement. Flory also dealt with Pallas chains from Germany, which put him in direct competition with Bob's Sedis interests. However, as early as 1971, Bob, being aware of Flory's pending withdrawal from the scene and, looking out for a wider involvement with European manufacturers, had asked Wim Oorlog of Vredestein for an introduction to the Weinmann people. Vredestein acted as agents for Weinmann in Holland.

At an exhibition in Milan in 1974, Wim arranged a meeting between Bob and Otto Weinmann to discuss the possibility of Bob's taking over from Flory when he retired. Otto, a tall, imposing man of immense charisma, was by then 70 and spoke no English but he and Bob clicked straight away, their relationship fired up from the start. The switch was agreed. Of course Bob knew Walter well from peripheral trade contacts, but when Otto told him that Bob would be taking on the agency, Walter, who could be a rather dour, cranky, uncooperative individual and cagey with it, advised Otto Weinmann that he was making a big mistake. 'Bob Chicken?' he said 'Don't even think about it. He's too erratic, a playboy.' This had more to do with cultural misunderstanding than personal animosity. Flory spoke only broken English; he had few friends outside the small Swiss community living in London and, although his English wife Phyll (Phyllis) was always a supporter of Bob, Walter didn't read him at all well to begin with. Furthermore he was undoubtedly a little wary of the man who was pressing to take over the agency which was the bedrock of his life's work, even if he was giving it up voluntarily.

Flory's adverse opinion might well have proved to be very damaging if not fatal to Bob's tender. Naturally plenty of other agents were keen to take over the Weinmann contract and Bob knew he had a fight on his hands, but Otto was adamant: he preferred the testimony of his own assessment and the clarity of understanding the two men shared. Wim confirmed his judgement. He told Otto that Walter didn't really know Bob and gave his view bluntly. 'You need Bob,' he said, 'he's the best.' Sure, he played hard – he enjoyed good living, it was part of his ebullient nature – but if he played hard, he worked hard too. That was the man, no bluff: a hundred per cent undivided effort and attention whether he was working *at* the business or entertaining on its behalf. . Mick Priest of Brown Bros. confirmed the assessment and spoke highly of Bob to Weinmann's. Over time, Bob and Walter actually became good friends, with Bob visiting Walter every Friday at his home in Southgate, not far from his own house.

Re-enter Robert.

Having agreed the agency deal with Weinmann, Bob suggested that Robert join Walter Flory at his Islington warehouse – a converted three-storey house on Duncan Terrace – to learn the business, acquaint himself closely with the Weinmann operation, and thereby make the eventual handover as smooth as possible. He could run the Industrial Chain business easily enough in his spare time and so began the work which transformed the Chicken enterprises. He knew the place well enough – often on Saturday mornings Bob had taken his two young sons with him to collect the post and left them to play mountaineers over the heaps of packing cases. Robert and Flory had their occasional contretemps. Flory phoned Bob to tell him he'd twice found the lad asleep, it was no good, he'd have to give him the bullet.

'Please don't, Walter, he's a good worker.'

'I know he's a good worker, but he's no kind of worker if he's having a kip on my time, is he?'

'He's only young. Be lenient.'

In addition to the Weinmann stock, Flory imported luggage carriers from Pletscher in Switzerland, gears from the French firm Huret, and freewheels, hubs and pedals from Maillard, also in France. He was a dear old man in some ways but he could also be cantankerous and prickly, capriciously disinclined to sell to a customer because he'd taken against him for reasons obscure. Because his faltering English and heavy accent made him sound gruff, often incomprehensible, on the phone, he put a lot of people off before they even started talking business. Furthermore he had frequent problems with his warehouse staff, and were it not for the benign and efficient Cockney, Mrs White from the East End, who virtually ran the business and smoothed ruffled feathers, Flory would probably have shed custom more quickly·than he acquired it. When Robert canvassed an order to supply Roy Roper, a wholesaler at Erith in Kent, with a batch of Maillard pedals, Flory looked at the order and scoffed: 'He'll never buy those' he said and tore it up. But, for all his quirks, Flory had a lot of charm, a twinkle in his eye, a glint of mischief which may have given rise to the (possibly apocryphal) story, that he had made his first big money during the First World War on the sale of contraceptives to randy soldiers.

Deliveries came by lorry to Duncan Terrace where every single box and packing case, some weighing in excess of 100kg, had to be manhandled through the narrow front door into the store rooms or else heaved bodily to the upper stories on an old-fashioned pulley hoist fixed to the outside wall. Whereas the Maillard 5-speed freewheels arrived in batches of 150 per ropey old wooden case, nailed and strapped, having been freighted across the Channel from the works outside Le Tréport by tramp steamer and then sent on by road, Weinmann sent (for example) batches of 54 cards of brakeblocks and shoes, or

50 pairs of brakes or 100 brake shoes, immaculately packaged in separate modular containers - tough cardboard cartons - all symmetrical, in a handsome wooden packing case which would then be used for delivering on to wholesalers.

Flory retired at the end of 1974, by which time Robert was fully conversant with the Weinmann business as well as engaged to be married to Christine, an international photographic model. Like his father, Robert enjoyed a good understanding with Otto Weinmann and the firm's export manager, an extremely likeable and dependable man with whom, naturally, he had most dealings. Good working relations and strong mutual esteem and liking underpinned a remarkable aspect of the Chicken-Weinmann agreement: it was clinched on that handshake between Bob and Otto. There was never a contract, no signature on paper, only a pure, gentleman's agreement. In today's harsh and unethical economic climate, dominated by faceless corporations and huge conglomerates where responsibility for mistakes is evaded, rarely admitted and seldom paid for by the culpable individual at the top or his immediate underlings, loyalty and trust might seem to be ill-affordable luxuries, and to base commercial agreement on anything so nebulous and unnegotiable reprehensibly cavalier and almost criminally stupid. However, a generation ago much of the cycle industry operated on that very basis of trust and mutual respect. It managed itself more in the manner of a cottage industry; everyone knew everyone else and agreements went on the nod over a drink. There were so many regional wholesalers at work that personal contact was an essential. Above all it was the underlying *trust*. In *The Magnificent Seven*, that seminal film (really a morality play) of the 1960s, when the seven gunmen are betrayed by the villagers who hired them, they face a moral dilemma: whether simply to ride on or else to continue to honour, somehow, the contract they agreed. Vin, the Steve McQueen character, says: 'Not a contract any court of law would uphold,' to which Yul Brynner replies: 'That's just the sort you have to keep.'

Otto Weinmann's great liking for him caused Bob some embarrassment. One day he visited him at his house in company with an old associate of the Weinmann enterprise, Tom Beyltjens. Beyltjens, a Belgian, somewhat anomalously, had long held the agency for both Campagnolo *and* Weinmann in Belgium and Luxemburg. He and Otto Weinmann had jointly established the Alesa company in Antwerp, Belgium, in 1946, manufacturing Weinmann alloy rims. Weinmann contributed 80 per cent to Beyltjens' 20 per cent on the agreement that whichever of the two died first, the other would take over his shares. (In fact, Weinmann, the younger man, died first, in 1986, leaving Beyltjens in sole ownership of what became Alesa-Weinmann.) Beyltjens and Bob arrived at Otto Weinmann's house, Otto opened the door and Beyltjens made to go into the house first, but asserting his own protocol of attachment Otto beckoned Bob in ahead, such was their mutual respect and affection. This highly personal affiliation was and remains the keystone of Bob Chicken's business practice. He believes that the friendship built through commercial agreement is quite as important as agreement on practical and financial matters because friendship is the basis and the root of loyalty, the essence of good business. The old Stock Exchange in London worked on a principle of mutual trust: no chits were signed, or even hands shaken on the floor of the Exchange. A deal was a deal, sealed on word of mouth alone: 'My word is my bond'. In his friendships as in his dealings, the bond has been the mainstay of Bob's ethic.

The Chicken agency for Weinmann got under way at the London Cycle Show at London Hilton on Park Lane in October, 1974. Weinmann loaned them a showboard. They set up a pokey little booth which Robert's wife Christine draped with cloth from a local haberdashery and stood amazed as queues of wholesalers trooped onto the stand to order Weinmann brakes and rims. They took orders to a total of over £9,000 for delivery in November. The Weinmann name, the efficiency of their supply system, the strictly fair dealings, were impressive, as impressive as the Schaffhausen factory Robert visited for three days that December – a model of Swiss efficiency. (To give some idea of relative monetary values, Robert was earning £139 per month and, for the visit to Schaffhausen he was allotted expenses of £40 to cover hotel, food and drink.) In 1974, some 90 per cent of the 1 million bikes per annum produced in the UK were fitted with their brakes, so the replacement market for the hitherto unavailable parts was more or less guaranteed. Customers with bikes fitted with Weinmann's would now be able to buy replacement brake blocks and shoes, levers, cables, stirrups, clamp bolts.

As in any business operation, the priorities now were to identify potential customers – in Bob's case by extending the customer base inherited from Flory, to set up a system of working practices to eliminate hiccups in the overall process of order, supply and delivery, to streamline the finances and, using that phrase which characterises hard work and endeavour, to 'get on yer bike'.

Weinmann, because of its prestige and high commercial competence, must be the lodestone of the business but the other accounts had their place. Pletscher decided they did not want to deal with Chicken: they had links with the German ESGE firm, for whom Robert already acted, and they went elsewhere. Huret, whom Flory did not represent, were a considerable force in the market for gears, mounting a fair challenge to the other leaders, Campagnolo and Simplex. However, as well as gears they produced speedometers which Flory was at liberty to deal in, but there simply was not enough room in Duncan Terrace to accommodate them.

From the outset, after he had taken over the business, Bob offered his buyers direct supply (but not delivery) from the companies for whom he acted as agent, thus cutting out the middleman and the middleman's percentage. (The Chicken deal with Weinmann on which Robert worked was for payment within 120 days from the date of the invoice or 2% discount for payment within 90 days.)

Walter Flory, an old-school intermediary, had always followed established practice: buy the stuff in as stock and sell it on, just as Bob's own father had done. By keeping a certain amount of stock and thereby keeping prices somewhat higher, the middleman hoped to make a bit of extra profit. For this reason, Raleigh were fitting Weinmann brakes, which apart from the very expensive Campagnolo alternatives were really the top of the range, on only 10 per cent of their bikes, including their best racing models, principally the Carlton, partly because the components were available only from the stock Flory held in the warehouse in Islington.

The rod brakes familiar to the old-style Raleigh came from A.E.Radnall of Birmingham but these were going out of fashion in favour of caliper brakes. Most of the caliper brakes Raleigh fitted came from GB, a major competitor on the home market. The GB owner, Gerry Burgess, had set up in business just before the War, buying in components from Germany – he manufactured none of his own forges or castings – and assembling the complete units at his works in Slough. Burgess also acted as an agent for a German metalworking company whose design for a stacking chair he copied and then marketed in the UK.

Bob's radically different approach of direct supply kept the Weinmann marketplace prices low, and above all competitive. On taking over the agency he persuaded Weinmann that this would do them both good. Because he was supplying direct, he could afford to add only 5 per cent commission on Weinmann's ex-works price, whereas hitherto the middleman was adding 25 per cent. At a stroke, therefore, Raleigh's purchasing price of Weinmann brakes, through the arrangement for buying direct set up by Bob Chicken, fell by 20 per cent. In fact, Bob had to work on an approximate source price because Flory never did disclose what he was charging. He also established direct invoicing of Raleigh from Weinmann itself, which offered further savings, and there were regular exchange visits to stimulate good contact and friendly business relations. Nowadays, incidentally, it is highly unusual for big companies to appoint a sole agent – the style of competition owes more to the ethos of the piranha pool than the quaint shake of hands – but in the mid-70s it was the norm, albeit some German firms preferred to sell through appointees from within their own ranks.

The transition from Flory to Chicken was pretty smooth. The Duncan Terrace premises were closed on the old man's retirement because it was clearly going to be hopelessly inadequate, both for storage and handling of the increased supplies which the Weinmann deal promised. In its placed, Bob offered Robert use of the basement in an old mill in Halifax, part of the Baycliff Company property holdings. It was dark, dank, cold, miserable and nasty *but* spacious and so began a bi-monthly routine of return trips to Halifax for Robert and Christine. He went up at the beginning of the week every fortnight to spend three days in Halifax sorting out orders before delivering on Thursday and Friday. Back in north London, Christine cycled over every day from their house to Bob and Christina's house, the registered office of the company, to type up invoices and sort out the rest of the paperwork – orders, checks on supply, contacts with customers. The manner of her being co-opted into the company deserves notice. The minimum wage of the time (not a statutory enforced amount) was £13. As a model she had never earned as measly a sum as £13 for half-an-hour's work, let alone per week, gross, no extras, no expenses. £13? Chicken feed. That being so, the Chicken offer – how could she refuse? – was for £13, with (of course) the irresistible added perks of working for the family, near home, separated from her husband one week in two . . . small sacrifices intermittently spiced with the rare fun of travelling up to Wakefield every other Friday to go through invoices in the hotel bar that evening and, all next day, help Robert pack orders in the damp and chilly dungeon of a basement, swathed in sheepskin jacket, scarf, gloves and hat, often going back on Sunday morning to finish the job before driving back south late that afternoon. Pure joy.

Sitting one day at the long table in Bob's office in the Southgate house, tapping out invoices on a crummy old black Remington typewriter probably bought from a job lot of used ex-services pre-war equipment, she observed Bob, seated at the other end, toying bemusedly with a calculator. He peered at it, shook it, knocked it on the table, prodded it, poked it, shook it again, then stood up, walked over to the wastepaper basket, dropped it into the rubbish and resumed his seat. She asked him what was wrong with the calculator.

'It doesn't work.'

'But you haven't had it long. '

'I know. The bloody thing has packed up.'

'Have you renewed the batteries?'

'Renewed the batteries?'

'The batteries have probably run out, that's all. Didn't you get any replacement batteries? That may be all it needs.'

'Oh.'

She got up, walked over to the wastepaper basket and retrieved the calculator. She rummaged in a drawer and produced some batteries, swapped them for the old. The calculator hummed back into life. Bob hummed and hawed back to work.

The début Weinmann consignment arrived in November 1974, as promised, at the dingy basement in Halifax. Most encouragingly, existing Chicken customers responded very favourably to the arrival of so highly respected an outfit as Weinmann on their books.

The bonanza at the Hilton continued, the sales graph shot up in a steady steep incline. The Chicken enterprise turnover went from over£18,000 in 1973 when Robert joined to £41,000 in 1974 and, in the first year of the Weinmann link, 1975, to £203,000; in 1976, £357,000.

They kept the Winchmore lock-ups for a while, at a rent of £19-50 per quarter, for emergency storage, such as the occasion when deliveries were late and came in just before Christmas. Robert hired a lorry to convey them south, the lorry broke down and had to be towed back. The archways housed the stock until it could be delivered after the brief holiday period – never more than Christmas Day and Boxing Day, certainly not New Year's Day, in that epoch.

By the end of his first year as agent for Weinmann in Britain, Raleigh were fitting the Swiss brakes to 90% of their machines. Some time previously, through a director at TI, Tom Barnsley, the company had agreed to pay Weinmann an annual consideration price were they to produce the brakes themselves, by buying in components from Switzerland and assembling the components in Nottingham. This they never did. At a stroke, therefore, Raleigh's purchasing price of Weinmann through Chicken fell by 20 per cent and Raleigh found themselves, by their own mismanagement, compelled to pay considerable sums to honour the indemnity agreement. This added financial strain was the more damaging because Raleigh had, for so long, not only luxuriated in such a strong command of the home industry but had kept their suppliers' prices pegged artificially low at large discount levels for bulk ordering, so that when they came up against real competition from Europe and soon from the Far East, they found themselves in dire trouble. False security gave way to a rude wake-up. Dealers across the UK who had been forced to buy from Raleigh, for lack of alternatives, turned against the Nottingham giant when those alternatives *did* finally offer. For example, the Austrian firm Puch launched an aggressive sales campaign in the UK during the late 60s and were warmly welcomed by dealers who had had enough of Raleigh's restrictive business practices. Puch made such cheap bikes that they were highly competitive from the outset. The UK end was run by a former salesman of the NSU company which manufactured scooters whom Bob had supplied, from Baycliff, with covers and panniers. Puch stepped up their sales campaign of the imported bikes and cut deep inroads into Raleigh's already failing share of the market.

Such was the Puch drive to win a big chunk of the market that they took to buying the full front cover of *Cycle Trader* for advertisements, calling on retailers:

> *If you're short of bicycles and doubtful about deliveries, trust Puch to put your mind at rest . . . Our offer is simple: order now, we'll deliver. And, just in case you don't know the Puch deal and the Puch range, get in touch with us or your local Puch distributor today. We'll tell you about the unique Puch guarantee, the rationalised range that makes every prospect a potential buyer. And one or two things not every bicycle manufacturer can say. After all, we don't want you to be left out in the cold at Christmas.' [This was in the early October issue, 1975; it was followed up by the same ad on 18 November.]*

A few months later, in March '76, a trader wrote a mordant letter, a rambling philippic, to the magazine complaining that 'British bikes are poor' and enumerating the counts against the UK cycle manufacturers and industry in general:

'1. Mail order cycles should be banned – bike shops who didn't sell them are expected to maintain them.

2. Poor paintwork (on British bikes), in many cases no paint at all, poor brazing and the welding especially poor.

3. Wheels generally of very sub-standard quality "necessitating hours of extra work".

4. Tyres – most foreign tyres fitted by the major concerns are, in my opinion, rubbish.

5. Poor assembly – lack of attention to detail.

6. Poor packing – this causes damage and, in some cases, loss of a sale.

7. Inclusion of carriage charges. This has already started and cannot be placed against the customer's account if they have already had price lists.'

The Penguin and Goldfish Bowl

The subterranean Baycliff oubliette simply could not cope with the exponential growth of the Chicken enterprise and a move was imperative. Baycliff itself was rapidly becoming a lost cause. It had already survived a receivership in 1970/71 and staggered on. But, sweatshops were opening in Manchester and the company could not match the competition. Bob was trying to run it from London and had the misfortune to land himself with some very bad directors – one with a morbid drink problem he appeared to be funding with the stock that went missing. Moreover, a new law imposed purchase tax on shopping bags with open tops such as those made by Baycliff. (Zippered bags already bore the tax.) This extra weight of tax added to cost and Woolworth were very unhappy about the sudden hike in prices. Bob kept the company going for some time out of unflinching loyalty to the employees and he was, naturally, unwilling to accept defeat in anything he attempted. Pride and a sense of honour were not infrequently more to the fore than hard-nosed commercial decision; he was, and many have said it, perhaps too much a gentleman for his own good sometimes, but such men will never have it any other way. He propped up Baycliff with money drawn from the cycle import business but eventually faced what had, perhaps, been inevitable for some time, and in March 1979, reluctantly, he closed it down.

Meantime, in 1975, Cedric found a 1, 500 square foot open warehouse in a straggling industrial estate near Watford. Robert, a shop-fitter whom he met socially in his local pub in Winchmore Hill charged £1,500 to partition the yawning space into more manageable units for the grossly expanding business. Christine was expanding too with their first child and could no longer squeeze behind the wheel of the car to drive out to help, so Robert spent much of the first year in the Watford premises on his own. The summer of 1976 was a scorcher – blazing sun day after day after day – and he sat under the glazed roof with sweat plop-plop-plopping onto the books. The shop-fitter friend came back to knock through to a further unit of the building shell.

That November, they took on their first employee, a secretary/typist. The following January Cedric quit Peugeot and joined Robert to manage the publicity side of the business, Robert, as ever, controlling finance and buying. Bob, who, because of his agency work, had little to do with the day-to-day nuts and bolts running of the operation, concerned himself with overall planning and, at this point, continued to hold 100% of the company's shares. This excited no contention: the family agreement was rooted in trust and it made little difference, in truth, who held what proportion of the assets and shares. Rows? Of course there were rows, disagreements, vigorous mental deck-clearing. Board meetings? In the pub, every day, after work.

In the autumn of 1976, Bob, Cedric and Robert, now trading as Chicken and Sons, went to a cycle show in Milan and came back with a galaxy of new agencies. Wim introduced them to Gianni Tagliabue, agent for a number of the top Italian brands of cycle components – 'Here, meet my friend Gianni' – and the whole deal, agency agreements and terms, for three exceptional Italian marques, Selle Italia (saddles) Ofmega (alloy and steel chainwheel sets, headsets, hubs, pedals, work tools) and BRT (toe straps and toe clips) was settled in an afternoon: copious quantities both of 100 per cent commercial good sense and 13 per cent alcohol by volume of good red wine.

Another wall in the Watford premises was knocked through to provide an additional 1,000 sq ft of space (this happened every year in succession as the business grew and grew), Bob moved his business south and, the Baycliff upset still nagging at him, decided to look for another outlet in luggage. Container lorries packed with bags from Dionite in Canada began to roll up but, unhappily, customers did not. The European importer in Belgium could not help. The two sides of the Chicken business were so different: most of the cycle components went to wholesalers, the luggage had to go to retailers and there simply were not the resources to drum up that market, despite all Bob's efforts. It was an expensive excursion. The distraction of the booming Chicken cycle enterprise was too consuming. They took on supplies of bike-locks from Trelock in Germany, then found out that the locks were going to be made in the Far East. Bob instantly and adamantly refused to have anything to do with them: the European manufacturing base had to be defended against all such incursions, particularly from the Far East where business practices and manufacturing methods were so utterly at odds with the traditional European ethos.[18]

1978 was a freak year: 40-foot containers full of mudguards were arriving at the warehouse and the contents, as soon offloaded were being sent out for delivery without even going inside the building. Everything they were dealing in was over-sold. Customers would phone and ask for '10,000 kick-stands'. They'd get 1,000, maybe 2,000 at a pinch and have to wait for the next flood of deliveries to come in. Another partition in the Watford works got knocked through.

In November 1980 Chicken and Sons moved to their Bisley Works near Dunstable.

An ammunition factory during the war, the site was sold by Imperial Metals

---

[18] For a while in the early 80s, I worked as business manager with my wife, Jane Wheeler, a knitwear designer. We sought to open contacts in Japan through an Englishwoman married to a Japanese. She introduced us to an agent who promptly copyrighted Jane's name so that *he* could trade as *her* in Japan and she could not. It took some doughty remonstration and pressure to force him to give up on what he saw as a perfectly natural and entirely *moral* commercial manoeuvre.

Industries, manufacturers of shotgun cartridges and clay pigeons, who wanted to centralise in Birmingham. Across the way from the main premises stood an outbuilding, about 30 feet by 12, with toilet facilities. Cedric and Robert designated this the works canteen. Then, the idea occurred to put a barrel of beer behind the counter. Bob came into the office, having been to the works canteen.

'There's a barrel of beer in the canteen' he said.

'That's right' said the brothers 'it's the company pub.'

'Company pub? You can't do that' said Bob.

'Bollocks,' they said.

Now, to contemplate the very notion of the Chicken triumvirate getting into a blazing altercation about the provision of alcohol on or off the works premises for the stimulation and encouragement of leisure-time unwinding and creative relaxation ranks with earnest mediaeval scholastic arguments as to how many angels could perch on the head of a pin. However, plonking a barrel on a table did not accord with Bob's sense either of decorum or of practicality. His forte had always been organisation, whether it be a double-decker bus for his friends and neighbours in Southgate for the jaunt to Epsom on Derby Day or an international import agency. So, the works canteen got properly fitted out as a company pub – interior design and decoration courtesy of Robert's Christine. There remained the vexed question as to what to call the place. Isn't there a cruel, sickening and frankly inhuman story behind that song The Pub with no Name? I believe there is. Thus it was that when the Chicken brothers met up with the Halford's people at an Italian show for an evening's light-hearted banter and mild imbibing of the local beverages, the conversation turned upon a name for the Chicken company pub. Now, I have sat in rooms with members of a band with whom I played and locked the door on pain of finding a name before anyone was allowed out even for a pee. Vagaries of title are amongst the most elusive of vagaries. However, the name-quest that evening found its target and, some while later, the Halford's men sent the Chickens a present: a handsomely painted wooded pub sign in black and white bearing the legend:

The Penguin and Fishbowl. For reasons entirely locked in the haze of failed memory and vinous exuberance, nobody now knows, or owns up to knowing, why that name was chosen, but chosen it was. The sign was hung outside the premises where it could be seen by all those to whom it mattered. That was Cedric. Cedric, also known in the business as Jeeves, for his urbane air, immaculate turnout, polished manners and accent did Publicity. So it was that The Penguin and Fishbowl became a sort of nerve centre, on and off duty, for many aspects of the Chicken enterprise – not least entertaining clients and staging product presentations. As Bob remarked when I went to the works (the Penguin and Fishhbowl gone, alas) 'They concluded a lot of business in there, team presentations, too.'

For, as the boom in bicycle sales continued, Bob had gone into sponsorship of cycle racing.

CHAPTER NINE
FULL CYCLE

It's not easy to say why British bicycle sales suddenly soared. Perhaps, a decade on from the last throes of post-war austerity, people were spending more and more money on inessentials. Had the health and fitness craze begun? Did the oil crisis of late 1973 which precipitated the three-day week *and* petrol rationing imposed by the Heath government on 2 January 1974 send people out to the garage to lift down the old bicycle hanging, neglected and cobwebby, from a hook? The Tour de France came to England for the first time in 1974 and may well have sparked new interest in the beautiful machine. Certainly, huge crowds came to the portable velodrome at Wembley designed by Ron Webb for the Six-Day races sponsored by Skol through the 70s. In the central bowl, Chicken and Sons entertained their customers amid the excited roar of the spectators and the rumbling thunder over the steep-raked wooden planking of thin track-bike tyres pumped hard with helium: the flash of the racing silks, the thrill of the high-speed chase within inches of the rails, the close calls in the jostling of the take-over when a rider handed over to his partner, grabbing his hand for the forward sling through into the pell-mell action. Cycle track-racing is one of the most exciting sports events on offer, but it is and can only ever be a specialist discipline within the broader context of cycle sport and the main event, road racing.

Through his close connexions with the Vredestein company, Bob got to know Wim Breukink, a very good cyclist and owner of Gazelle, the largest bicycle company in Holland, ahead of Batavus which Raleigh bought in1971, having previously bought out its Dutch distributor in 1967. (Wim's son, Erik, became a fine rider, eleven Tours de France, third overall and two stage victories in 1990.) Through Wim Breukink, Bob was introduced to the continental racing scene and was greatly affected by the excitement it generated, the passion it aroused and the huge popularity of road racing, particularly in the Benelux countries.

British cycle sport needed greater backing by major manufacturers and it was logical for Raleigh to add its considerable impetus to the domestic racing scene. In 1977, the year after he took over the Weinmann agency, Bob discussed the possibility of sponsoring a professional team in the UK with Gerald O'Donovan, Raleigh's hand-builder of frames in the small Ilkeston works. Raleigh had been sponsoring a pro team in Europe since 1974, the year in which the astonishing Reg Harris had come back at the age of 54 to win the British Sprint Championship, riding the 25-year-old Raleigh bike on which he'd won the World's Spring title twenty years earlier. Raleigh backed the team with an annual budget of around £1 million with Peter Post, an outstanding former track and six-day star as manager, and David Duffield as chairman of the organising committee. In a 16-year career, Post rode 165 Six-Day races, won 55 including four consecutive London Six Days (1968–71) partnered by Patrick Sercu (World Sprint champion 1967 and '69) and won World Pursuit silver and bronze as well a hatful of road races, notably the 1964 Classic Paris-Roubaix at a then prodigious record speed of 45kph. Retired from track and road, he became a brilliant directeur sportif. Nevertheless, Raleigh kept him on a very tight leash and prudently held back 10 per cent of the budget through the season as a rescue fund. Too many teams have overstretched expenditure and left riders unpaid. In the matter of sports sponsorship, it is important to set a budget, which needn't be vast, and spend it on PR and the riders, not fritter it on big advertising campaigns. The backing needs above all to be concentrated, interested and involved, coming from people who love the sport and want to give something back, as Bob did. Peter Post ran TI-Raleigh on very little money and the men at HQ checked the management of the team every month, keeping things very tight which was to be praised. However continental sales did not follow, and justification of team funding simply leached away.

To begin with, things went very well. In their first Tour de France, 1977, TI-Raleigh's Dietrich Thurau won the Prologue and 3 stages and came 5th overall, Gerrie Knetemann came 2nd in the Prologue and won a stage, Hennie Kuiper came 3rd overall and they won the team prize. (Sadly, Bill Nickson, the only Briton in the team, former winner of the Milk Race, didn't make it to Paris but neither did 46 others in the field.) It was a marvellous début, a splendid reward for Tom Barnsley, Raleigh's Managing Director at the time and an enthusiastic supporter of the continental venture from the start. Knetemann became a prolific winner for the team, Joop Zoetemelk won the Tour de France in 1980 in Raleigh colours, and Phil Anderson came 5th in 1985, when Raleigh were co-sponsoring with Panasonic before they pulled out of the sport.

Bob contacted Ken Collins, the Marketing Director in Nottingham, to put the idea of co-sponsorship of a team to race in the UK. The response was warm. Collins brought in George Shaw, an assembly plant manager allied to sales. Shaw had ridden in the BMB-Raleigh team (co-sponsored by British Manufactured Bearings and O'Donovan's Carlton bikes) formed in 1963 and then managed it from 1967 when it became Carlton-BMB. (From 1969, the Carlton name was used again, in co-sponsorship with Truwel, who made welded tubes, and Campagnolo.) Shaw, like many who've known at firsthand the unforgiving world of pro racing, was a likeable man, laid-back but enthusiastic. The Raleigh board passed the broad agreement reached between Bob, Shaw and Collins, and confirmed an opening budget of £15,000 of which they would contribute £10,000 to Bob's £5,000. The team would race as Carlton-Weinmann. Bob's share of the budget was his own money from his agency work, to be written off as a marketing expense in promoting his and Weinmann's particular interests.

Details were agreed, and in 1979 the Weinmann-Chicken and Sons team took to the road, managed by Albert Hitchen who had been National pro road race champion twice – 1963 and 1965 – 2nd in 1964 and 3rd in 1971, behind one of the team's first signings, Sid Barras.

It's Phil Liggett's opinion that Sid – 'Supersid' – Barras could have ridden in the top flight in the continental peloton. He was a rider of exceptional class, a gritty, intelligent, hard-working professional rider with a very powerful fast finish. Riding one of the hardest stage races on the calendar, the Tour de Suisse, in 1973, he won the first stage and took the leader's yellow jersey. Also riding was the great Eddy Merckx. 'Who is this guy?' he asked Liggett. Praise indeed.

Puzzled about the Barras fast finish, which obviously had a physiological as well as psychological basis, combined with deep stamina and the superior will to turn on an exceptional burst of power when you're as tired as everyone else – as the French say: 'Today, *I* win' – I e-mailed the question to Pat Liggett, one time directeur sportif of the British team on the Tour de France Feminin. Basking in the sun in South Africa just before Christmas, 2004, she very nobly dragged herself inside to the laptop to explain:

Sid was blessed with a high percentage of fast twitch muscles and an excellent heart, lungs and circulatory system which meant efficient production of aerobic energy and stores of glycogen. *(See Appendix I)*

I asked Sid how it all started, the moment when the bike entered his life. He grew up in Middlesborough.[19] His first bike, from when he was about 12 years old, was a heavy old Rudge, handy enough for getting to and from school but not a machine to inspire thoughts of competition. One day on a whim, or perhaps there was deeper purpose in it, his father, who'd been a racer before the War, mostly time trials, inevitably, suggested they go up into the loft in the family house. Up in the pitched space beneath the roof, Sid's father unwrapped a bicycle which he had laid up, fully swaddled in clean covers to keep it safe from rust, dust and must beneath the fust of the house: the lightweight hand-built E.F. Russ bike with chrome tips which he'd ridden in the 30s, a beautiful machine. One can imagine that simply exposing it once more to the light of day awakened a glimmer of that spirit with which we know the best bikes which have served their rider well are imbued; the sense that, given the chance again, they will turn on the power if the legs driving them are good legs. Was this uncovering of the treasure trove mere nostalgia, a retired racer drawn back to the source of his great pleasure and satisfaction on the bike and the bittersweet memory of battling through the hard times when the bike seemed a creature only of torment? Or was Barras senior handing the challenge on,

---

[19] One of the most terrifying rides of my life was round the Middlesborough ring-road, me and the snake-whip of a long tail-back of speeding artics out to get me.

giving his son the key to something but who could yet tell what? Probably a good deal of both. In any event, he built the bike up and, for a year or two, Sid rode it with friends, getting the feel of a responsive racing machine, before joining the amateur club he stayed with all through the first part of his career: The Teesside Cyclones, based in Middlesborough.

With them Sid Barras discovered racing and, unusually for one of our best riders, was never much enthused by time-trialling. He loved road racing, the play of tactics, reading the reactions of other riders, judging the moment when to go and when to hold back, keeping the nerve for the right opportunity to attack when other more fidgety riders are chancing their luck too early. In 1963, he won the schools Division Championship with a fine burst of speed in the closing yards and it was then, he says, that he realised he had a sharp finish, a killer punch he delivered time and again in the Teesside colours.

In early June 1967 he went to the Isle of Man with a few clubmates for the annual bike-fest. His hero, Tom Simpson, was riding in a starry bunch of continental pros alongside an entry of the best home-riders. An Olympic bronze team pursuiter in 1954, Simpson had worn the yellow jersey of the Tour de France, taken the rainbow jersey of World road-race champion and had a clutch of big wins in his *palmarès*. A month after his appearance in the Manx race, Simpson was dead. On Thursday 13 July, in suffocating heat, he collapsed off his bike on the climb up Mont Ventoux, stage 13 of the Tour de France. His body already weakened by lack of nourishment – he had been taking large glucose supplements which inhibited his appetite – he had also taken amphetamines and a large slug of brandy at the foot of the climb. His system gave out and, carried off the cruel mountain by helicopter, at 5.30pm he was pronounced dead.
 Simpson's death and the circumstances in which he died hit Sid Barras very hard and cast a big cloud over his ambitions, stiffening his attitude towards the sort of compromises that professional cycling on the continent imposed, his deep sense of propriety. Simpson, the affable joker off the bike, the dedicated pro on it, had

beaten short odds not merely to survive in the continental peloton but again and again to dominate it: 1961, Tour des Flandres; 1963, Bordeaux–Paris, 2nd Paris–Tours, 2nd Paris–Brussels, 2nd Gand–Wevelgem, 3rd Tour des Flandres; 1964, Milan–San Remo; 1965,Tour of Lombardy, 3rd Flèche Wallonne; 1967, Paris–Nice.

The shock of his demise and the ghoulish publicity which attached to it affected Barras deeply. His hero had run foul of a darker side of the sport he so loved. When Peter Post of Raleigh approached him about his ambitions to ride as a pro on the continent, Barras replied that if he did join a pro team, it would have to be on his terms. When I asked him if this was to do with drugs he answered, firmly, 'on my terms'.

.In 1968, Barras was picked for the England team riding the Milk Race. He won stage 4 between Paignton and Weston-Super-Mare and came 5th overall. The England team came second behind the USSR. The following year, he rode for Great Britain, took another stage win, and, when the rider/manager of the Bantel pro team, the great pursuiter Hugh Porter, (four World titles, two silvers, one bronze) offered him a contract, Barras accepted. From school he had served an apprenticeship as an electrician – time-served not serving time, he made that quite clear – and now became a full-time professional cyclist. These were buoyant times. Barras and the others in the British pro teams were on a mission to show that they were as good as anyone on the continent and they certainly proved that. In the Worlds Road Race at Gap in 1972, Barras was well up with the leaders but got two punctures in the closing miles and eventually came 21st. Given that it was unusual for British riders even to finish over much longer distances than they were used to racing, and at such leg-sapping speed, this was a fine result. Two other Worlds stick in his mind: the cruel hard circuit at Sallanches in 1980, won by Bernard Hinault, one half uphill the whole way, the second downhill. Barras packed at around 80 miles at the same time as the Dutchman Jan Raas (champion the year before) climbed off. Two years later, at Leicester, he was in the lead break, alongside Les West, his senior in the team, but was ordered to drop back – his presence in the break would compromise West. This was almost certainly a tactical error, because Barras had a much better finish than West who just missed out on a medal.

Barras rode the Tour de Suisse three times in all. 'A very hard race, that,' he said. His great showing in his début ride – having relinquished the leader's yellow, he then took the green points jersey – against riders of the class of Merckx and Francesco Moser might have prompted an approach from an Italian team, but none came. A disappointment, for sure; Barras felt that the Italian scene would have suited him. In fact there *was* an Englishman riding with Moser, Phil Edwards, but his mother was Italian, he spoke the language fluently and, as he explained to me once, 'Moser's saddle is only a millimetre higher than mine so it makes my bike an easy swap if he needs one'.

But, from the mid to late 70s, the home circuit thrived and Barras thrived in it. He raced against Merckx on the Eastway track and the famous TI-Raleigh tandem of Gerrie Knetemann (World Champion 1978) and Jan Raas at Crystal Palace. Sure to plan, this pair worked the old one-two to perfection, made the winning break, Moser with them, and, when Raas attacked, the Italian went too. Knetemann chased and kept going, Moser was cooked. 'If Moser had brought me back,' said 'De Kneet' as he was nicknamed, 'I wouldn't have been able to make another effort. When you go, it has to be 150 per cent or it doesn't succeed.'

For the first time in the UK, ample commercial sponsorship was ready to hand. Cycling and cycle sport were becoming more and more popular. Optimism, energy, confidence were abroad. Bantel, manufacturers of mudguards, notwithstanding that pro bikes are never fitted with mudguards, had been sponsoring the sport for about nine years, under the tutelage of the Managing Director, Barry Brandon. He was an out-and-out enthusiast and the Bantel operation reflected that: a good set-up, everything the riders needed to hand, unstinting encouragement and support. Barras joined a team of eight Bantel riders, where hitherto there had usually been no more than six. He raced for them 1970–73, spent a year with TI-Raleigh, which didn't work out, and returned to Bantel 1975–7. Why did he then leave? He said he felt he had done all he could with the team and that it was time for a change; he needed a move, a new challenge, breaking out of the comfort zone, even. He signed for Viking.

In 1977, Viking cycles, which had been revived and established and relocated to Northern Ireland, entered cycle sponsorship with a grant from the Northern Ireland Development Agency. The Viking set-up was lavish and well funded; the riders were decently treated to begin with, even if the driving force behind the venture was commercial rather than sporting. They were riding the bikes for one reason alone: to persuade others to buy them. The year with Viking, 1978, Barras described as a bit of a disaster. Based in Northern Ireland, the company had benefited hugely from government subsidy to encourage the establishment of industry in the province. But, although there was plenty of money around, it often didn't get to the riders. When Barras (whose wife was pregnant) and Keith Lambert spent six weeks in Majorca for early training before riding the Tour of Majorca as sole Viking representatives in the race, they got no financial recompense at all. Even after Barras won a stage and came 5th overall in a high-class field but there was still a long wait for any payment. Another miserable and all too familiar case of mismanagement. Barras and Lambert were due to ride the prestigious two-up time trial, The Barrachi Trophy, at the end of the season and were training hard for it, but at the last minute were told they wouldn't be riding. Lambert put his bike away and didn't take it out again until the second week of the following January.

A new manager arrived at Viking, offered Barras a cut in salary, which he politely refused, (Lambert stayed on) and, when Albert Hichen, ex-National champion and an independent or professional rider for 13 years, now manager of the Weinemann-Chicken team, made an approach early in 1979, he accepted. Barras had a great respect for the former road man. 'Albert instils a quiet confidence – he doesn't say much but when he does, you take notice.'

There was some muttering about Barras, that he had been too individualistic, too demanding as team leader, forever expecting other riders to sacrifice their chances for him. But this is the continental ethic and Barras retorted: 'If anyone in the team can't win themselves, they have to work for someone who can, that's all.' That certainly was the case with his teammate and still good friend Keith Lambert, albeit now a rival, and in the very first year with Chicken's Barras won the title had had eluded him since he first rode as a pro: the British Road Championship.

The race, at Telford, went 13 laps round a circuit of 12km, 156km in all, including a hard climb, The Rock, and 1½ mile of uphill to the finish. (The pro Worlds is generally around 256km.) It was a class field, including all the Brits who raced for continental teams – Phil Edwards, Graham Jones, Bill Nickson, Paul Sherwen. In the final sprint, Barras, riding 53 x14, beat the renowned fast man Barry Hoban, whose victories included, notably, eight stages of the Tour de France and the 1974 Ghent–Wevelgem, ahead of Merckx and Roger de Vlaeminck. There was quite a lot of needle between the two men – Hoban, a known figure in the continental peloton, and Barras, undoubtedly the best rider in the UK. And, when Barras and Lambert were riding for Viking, they took it in turns to give Hoban a hard time.

Almost inevitably, Hoban accused Barras of switching him in the sprint, that is changing his line across the opponent's wheel. In an interview with Keith Bingham of *Cycling Weekly* long after the race, Barras said: 'It rained all day, which suited me. I rode him clean and anyway, he'd sat on my wheel for the last 20 miles. If he'd led out, he'd have leaned on me just as I leaned on him.' (His comments at the time were, predictably, more neutral: 'I didn't switch him . . . the road was wide enough for everybody. . . ')

Across the line, Hoban protested immediately – standard continental practice. [20] Deliberations took about five minutes, Barras and Hoban waiting nervously for the decision and, when it came, Hoban grabbed his bike, went straight off to the changing rooms, to a chorus of boos and counter-boos, and refused to join Barras on the podium. The £250 prize money was doubled and Barras immediately donated half to the widow

---

[20] For example, when Eric Vanderaerden, a noted sprinter of the time, was disqualified after winning a sprint during the Tour de France, he swore innocence despite the fact that, seeing a rival about to fly past on the far side of the road, he'd gone across like a slingshot and blocked him. When Vanderaerden asked Sean Kelly, standing behind him, what *he'd* have done in similar circumstances, Kelly said 'The same,' without hesitation. That's the game, that's what they all did routinely and came away with bruised knuckles from the contusion of handlebars jostling in the mêlée.

of Dave Broadbent, a teammate who had died a few days earlier from injuries sustained in a heavy fall in a race on 10 June. Hoban, who never did win the national title, played hurt. 'It was a pity it had to be spoiled by this. [Not for Barras.] I've been up against all the best in the world – Esclassan, Karstens, Van Linden – there was bumping and boring but never anything vicious like this and it seems to happen here every week.'

Two weeks later, to celebrate his wearing of the champion's jersey, Barras won the inaugural Criterium Championship in Milton Keynes, a fairly straightforward mile circuit with few of those nasty corners to which cyclists refer blandly as 'technical' and a slight uphill finish which suited his closing power perfectly.

Barras said that of the 140-plus victories he had won over the past ten years, the national title win was the sweetest. Keith Lambert, who had only just recently won his first victory of the season, lost a spoke and had to change bikes, yet recovered and came 6th. Later that year, he was the only UK finisher in the Worlds road race (274.8km) in Valkenburg, won by Raas.

At the end of the season, the Carlton-Weinmann team had recorded a massive 24 wins from a total of some 36. Barras took 18, Reg Smith, the team captain, 5, and Trevor Bull 1. Barras also won a prize marking an overall superiority in home racing, the Prestige Pernod Trophy.[21]

That September, Patrick Sercu won the Skol Six-Day races at Wembley and so equalled his former partner Peter Post's record of 65 six-day wins. (He went on to beat it.)

In October, after their most successful season ever, Denis Hensby, Home Sales Director of Raleigh, came to the headquarters of Chicken and Sons in Watford, purportedly to discuss ways and means for the following year. Henbsy brought bad news. Much to his chagrin, he had been overridden at a meeting in Nottingham the very

---

[21] To give some idea of what his training schedule was like: in a typical week, Barras did 3½ hours on Saturday, 5 on Sunday, 2 ¼ (hilly) on Monday, 6 on Tuesday, and 3 hours each, Wednesday – Friday.

afternoon of the day before, with Collins telling him that Raleigh would not be putting any more money into the domestic team on the grounds of cost. They also confessed to a general disenchantment with the home professional scene, (perhaps in contrast with how things were done in Europe.)

A Raleigh spokesman told the cycling press that '. . . axing the team was just one of many harsh economies forced on the company as a direct result of the current national engineering dispute which is causing the company severe financial problems'. Losses for the first half of the year were put at £1¼ million and the protracted engineers' strike referred to was costing the company some £200–300,000 per week. Hensby himself said: 'When the team was launched three years ago, cycle sport in the UK looked to be on the verge of a breakthrough in terms of popularity and support; however, the sport's growth did not materialise as hoped for, nor looks like developing to any great extent in the near future.' The promotions director of the British Professional Cycling Association (BPCA), Benny Foster, was unequivocal: 'In my opinion, the leading bicycle company in the world should be seen supporting professional bike racing in this country.' Given that they continued to sponsor a team on the continent of Europe where their bikes didn't sell, he had a singular point.

Bob's reaction was of disbelief. By comparison with the money they were spending on the continent, £10,000 was very small beer, peanuts. For the sake of saving such a trivial outlay they would be letting down cycle sport in the UK badly needing the boost of a Raleigh commitment. But it was too late; the Lenton Road moneymen were intransigent. Bob contacted Otto Weinmann: would he be prepared to take up the shortfall so as to keep the team going? Otto said he would and the Weinmann-Chicken team was launched in 1980, with some input from Ofmega of Italy and Carlton, whose bikes the team continued to ride. Because money was tight, they opted for three of the best rather than a full sextet: Sid Barras, Reg Smith and a new signing Keith Lambert. The Barras-Lambert one-two was back in business.

I met Keith Lambert in 2001, on the first annual Phil and Friends ride in the High Peak district of Derbyshire and Yorkshire. After a good pounding over the various bits of geological mischief between the Slynes, Wigtwizzle, Holme Moss and Mam Tor, a small pack of us were heading nicely past the placid waters of Ladybower Reservoir towards the closing miles.

Elbow to elbow with Phil Liggett, bowling along this rare flatter bit of road, I said to him: 'This is all right, Phil, isn't it?' He sniffed. 'It isn't round the corner,' he said shiftily, 'you'd better go to the front.' I went to the front, saw the road backing off my front wheel and dutifully got stuck in, up what turned out to be one of those long drags that doesn't really look bad enough to be hard work but gradually squeezes all your pips out.

Nearing what looked like the top but wasn't, Lambert rode up alongside me looking disgracefully fresh and said: 'I thought I'd better have a look at what you were riding.' Typical old pro trick, that: sidle up and drain the last bit of oxygen you've got with an invitation to idle chitchat.

' um I. Gladter. Seeyou' I gasped in reply and, having neither the heart (nor lungs) to spurn the man's hospitality, we rode on companionably at the head of the bunch. *He* rode, *I* dredged up some semblance of composure. Thus it was that, deep in conversation about aluminium and anaerobics, we swung off the drag at the next left turn, closely tagged by Brian Robinson, Brian's son-in-law Martin and Della from the CTC. It was one left turn too early. Oh, the folly. That left turn too early was going to heap on us seven extra miles and several extra extremely disgusting steep climbs, any one of which would have been enough to make me wince.

Liggett, tucked away nicely in the bunch we'd dropped, watched us – the break – go, thought 'Oops, they've gone the wrong way, better shout,' paused, reflected, thought 'Why waste breath?' muttered to himself 'Ah, bugger it,' and rode on to the right - left - turn.

When Keith Lambert, born in 1947, started riding a bike the English club scene was buoyant. His parents bought him his first bike in 1959, a Ken Russell machine. There had been a stipulation: before he got the bicycle he had to pass his piano exams. He passed the exams. Ken Russell had been a prominent racer in the 50s, riding for the ITP (International Totalisator Pools) team alongside another noted rider, a big rival, Ken Jowett and it was Jowett who propelled Lambert into racing. Almost literally.

Shortly after he got the bike, Lambert's parents moved from Bradford to Bingley, from the heart of urban industrial Yorkshire to a quieter West Riding town in Airedale, on the southern fringe of Rombalds Moor. Keen to ride the new bike in company, Lambert was advised to go along to Leicester Park where the Bradford Elite met: they'd look after him. Aged just 13, he rode with the Elite regularly – up to Kettlesing and back, then club events, mostly time trials. Curiously, the Bradford Club had been one of the founder members of the British League of Racing Cyclists dedicated to road racing, but time trialling had gradually taken over and, as he grew older and stronger, Lambert concentrated on time trialling to a degree which, he said, was detrimental to his later career. Indeed, he didn't start racing proper until he was about 20.

On one chain gang – an activity used by club nutters to kick the pretensions out of anyone with the temerity to imagine he's stronger than anyone else, to the general collapse of their physical and mental coherence – Lambert and the others were joined by Ken Jowett, who, having retired as a pro at the early age of 28, had started riding seriously again. Pushing the pace hard, rider after rider came through for a spell at the front. Lambert was moving up the order, as riders slipped off and back down the line. Then Jowett scorched up and piled on even more speed, Lambert on his wheel. 'Those guys never really lose it, you know,' Lambert told me. Class will out.

Suddenly Jowett turned round, gave Lambert a good hard look and said: 'Come through, boy.' Times like that. . . you wonder how you hold it together when everything – body, brain, common sense all coming to bits – at the same time knowing that if you don't you'll never hear the last of it, not least from yourself.

Lambert, working for an insurance company, taking technical exams to shape a career in underwriting, rode a few races on the road, and it was Jowett who saw the potential in the 20 year old and encouraged him to race more. At the time Lambert, having just met his future wife, was thinking of steady employment and going to night school, so riding the bike competitively was no more than an aside in his life. But in 1972, Jowett, the reigning national Veterans' champion, pushed him to turn pro. Albert Hitchen, who'd won the British Cycle Federation professional road race championship in 1963 and 1965, (second in 1964) was still riding for Falcon as well as managing the team. He'd come third in the 1971 national Championship behind Sid Barras, (the Falcons won the team prize) and offered Lambert a contract.

Lambert was by no means an outstanding rider in terms of results, very far from the top of the tree, but in the two years he'd been racing, he had made huge progress and it was quite obvious that he was going to be a first-rate racer. Lambert went round to Jowett's house to ask him what he thought he should do. Jowett said something on the lines of 'What are you waiting for? Get on with it.'

Lambert signed for £35 a month. He kept the insurance job and raced every week on the Falcon machine, the first brand new bike he'd had, apart from the boyhood machine which started it all. (At the time, my full-time salary as a young schoolmaster was around £60 per month.) The firm was generous with time off whenever necessary, but for the most part Lambert used up holiday time to cover his absences during the week for a stage race like the Tour of the West – five stages, Bristol, Barnstaple, Penzance, Plymouth, Bournemouth, Weston-super-Mare, sponsored by W.D. & H.O. Wills, the tobacco manufacturers. That first season he rode races just about every week of the season and the odd race abroad; it was always a big highlight to mix it with the continental racers. He enjoyed putting something back into cycling, being part of the whole scene, riding for a big manufacturer at a time when the entire industry was geared to producing top range racing bikes. Overseeing the Falcon team was another man who'd been a formidable racer in the early years of the BLRC, Ernie Clements, winner of the first National Road Race championship in 1943. The team of six riders was well looked after, the organisation was, by and large, excellent. The Falcon mechanics did a good job, but the operation was, even by British standards, quite limited. In his first year with Falcon and co-sponsor Tighe, Lambert came 4th in the nationals and the following year 5th.

In 1973 he joined what was, apart from TI-Raleigh, the largest and best-funded home team, Holdsworth-Campagnolo, and rode with three of the best racers of the time, Les West, Colin Lewis and Gary Crewe. The contract was more lucrative; Lambert rode with Holdsworth for four years and steadily became one of England's foremost professional riders.

At the end of 1977, Lambert signed for Viking. The money was substantial and Lambert quit his job in the insurance business. The office was in the middle of Leeds, which he hated, the travel as much as the environment, and he'd grown disenchanted with the work, the cynical attitude, the grasping nature of the insurance companies. At the end of the year he had set up in business with a bike shop, which his brother-in-law ran for him.

He did well with the team, especially when he and Barras were riding together, but in 1980 he joined the team which gave him most pleasure in all his time as a professional: Chicken & Sons. A big incentive was the fact that Albert Hitchen had joined the team just as Lambert left Viking and Lambert admitted to a new surge of excitement. 'I've got almost junior-like enthusiasm,' he said.

Benny Foster from the BPCA had been collaring town councils and drumming up sponsorship for races across the country; in January 1980, he announced that there was already a guaranteed £50,000 in prize money available to the upwards of 40 registered professionals in 49 races between March and October, plus 6 mixed races for pros and amateurs. However, by 1 March there were only 34 sponsored pros and only 20 of them signed for the Elswick Centenary Tour at Easter. Amateur teams had to be drafted in to make up the field. The signs were ominous.

When the season did get going, once again the Chicken boys were in dominant form. At the National Championships in June, Lambert was in a break with Bill

Nickson. They caught, and dropped, the Scot Robert Millar, (later to ride on the continent as Britain's most successful Tour de France rider – King of the Mountains prize and 4th overall in 1984) and Lambert, knowing that he had a much better finishing burst than Nickson, was confident that he'd have the edge in a two-up race for the line. In the approach to the finish, Nickson stayed glued to Lambert's wheel. Lambert, banking on having the better finish, thought 'he's not going to come round, I'm clear here.' Dangerous conclusion. Nickson knew about Lambert's finish. He was ready to neutralise it.

A left-hand corner took them onto the 700 yards finishing straight. Lambert immediately took the right-hand gutter to leave the final tussle as late as possible. The rider who takes the crown of the road almost always lays down the challenge and leaves himself vulnerable to attack from the man who can take his wheel from behind and pounce at will. Suddenly, Lambert saw Nickson flash past: he'd hit the bend and immediately gone flat out for home, turning a 15, ideal for an explosive burst of speed at high revs. Lambert kicked on 14, too high. The road was wet, his back wheel spun and could get no purchase on the slippery surface as he frantically tried to work the small sprocket. But maddened and seized with a manic determination, he heaved the bike up to pace, accelerating and accelerating until he'd chased Nickson down and was on his wheel. Nickson slammed his gear into 13, a last desperate bid for added speed but hugely taxing on the legs. The revs went down. The closing 50 yards. Nickson faltered an instant, no more than a small check of the body, a nod of the head, a barely perceptible slump in the back, but sign enough that the effort is waning. Both riders lunged, arms full out, pushing for the finish, but Lambert was past and took the line by an inch.

'I nearly fluffed it' he said afterwards. 'Had the line come a yard earlier, I don't think I'd have done it . . . this one's for my little boy.' As for Nickson, he rued that change to a higher gear. 'If I'd kept it on 14 or 15 I might've been able to keep it revving.' (He won the title the following year.)

At the end of the season, Barras had accumulated 9 wins and 4 seconds, Lambert 5 wins and 1 third out of the 36 on offer.

It was all about to go badly wrong.

On 25 October 1980, Viking announced that 'because of the economic climate, we have decided to change the emphasis of our publicity and support'. They were pulling out of sponsorship and the four riders in the MAN VW-Viking team were now without a contract. Then, after 13 years of sponsoring the Wembley Six Days, Skol called time. The promoter Ron Webb said that 'marketing strategy now demands that funds be directed to other projects'. Skol had decided that by now their name was sufficiently established to allow them to switch sponsorship from national (expensive) events to more local (cheaper) ones. 'I'd love to continue promoting in Britain' Webb added, 'but for the last 3 years the Skol just wasn't a feasible proposition. It was a hard slog to build up until 1974–5 when we reckoned it would be viable. But this last three years the rent has been going up and the audience has not.'

On the continent Jones and Sherwen were joined in the peloton by two Irishmen destined for great things, Sean Kelly and Stephen Roche, while in England a rider who would soon be crossing the Channel himself, Sean Yates, the National 25-mile time-trial champion, was turning in some prodigious times against the clock. But at home, the sponsors were melting away. Only Moducel and KP Crisps-Viscount had teams, while WCK remained undecided. Speaking for Chicken and Sons, Cedric Chicken said that they had planned to take on more riders but they were having to reconsider. The fact was that the Chicken trio had so cleaned up in 1980, that the competition was fading and, Cedric said: 'There's no point in being in if there are no pros to race against. There are other ways of getting our name across. But we'd be sorry to pull out – pro racing has proved to be a very good publicity vehicle for us.'

Sadly, there *was* virtually no one to race against, so pull out they did. Perhaps the dominance of the Chicken trio soured their enthusiasm; perhaps, too, the entire lack of interest from any media other than the cycling press – no coverage of races on television and scarcely in national papers – made the venture non-viable so that accountants waved the failing balance sheets pointedly. Yet behind all this the whole bicycle industry was about to hit the rocks.

Barras voiced the kind of melancholy they must all have felt. Having tried dozens of possible backers he had had no luck. 'I just hope something turns up before the season starts.' (He eventually found a backer in a new Coventry Eagle-Campagnolo combine as various other teams emerged: Falcon-Campagnolo, Sugino-Harry Quinn, Liverpool Mercury, all racing together with a number of unsponsored pros. However, for both Barras and Lambert the Chicken years were a real joy: the sheer ebullience of the support from Bob and his sons added to the impeccable management and fair dealing made life as good as it could be for a pro rider. The Chicken-Weinemann trio packed a big punch on the road, certainly, but what made the time special, says Lambert, was the passionate interest Bob, Cedric and Robert Chicken took in them, the care they evinced. Their pleasure at seeing them do well, winning races in their colours far exceeded any mere concerns about commercial advantage. Quite simply they were concerned heart and soul with the whole adventure. They made their riders feel great and it was even better when they won. The money side was almost incidental and, in a sport known for its hard-nosed commercial stringencies, this approach was almost unique and very welcome.

The history of sponsorship of cycle sport in the UK is chequered, for many reasons, not least the vicissitudes of the cycle industry, the obvious source of commercial funding.

But the lack both of a national tour and any enthusiasm from television as well as the resistance of the BCF to the vagaries, as they see them, of road racing, all contribute to a lack of interest in a sport which, whenever it *does* get a public showing gets massive popular support, as in the recent hugely successful inaugural Tour of Britain.

Barras rode the Milk Race twice as a pro, after the regulations allowed a mixed field, first in 1983, when he won the first stage, once again from Paignton and on to Bristol. The roads were closed, the field was full of class, the public cheered. But he had a hard time. His second son was born with Downs' syndrome at the beginning of the year and it was touch and go whether he would survive. Barras lost all January and February and after six days of the big race, working hard for a young Sean Yates and Tony Doyle, he had nothing left in his legs. He rode the 1986 Milk Race but acknowledges that he was past his best. Training had become more and more of a grind, and towards the end of his career – he was 39 nearing 40 – he had to drive himself to get out and put the hours in. He still loved the racing and reckons that, had he taken a year out to refresh his mind, he might have returned with the old verve and raced on for another three years. (Malcolm Elliott quit when he was 36, took four years out to recharge and is once again racing on top form.) Barras did race as an amateur again when he was 47, won eight races and still rides the bike – he's just told me over the phone this wet Friday morning that he'd been out for 5 hours on Saturday with his son Tom (who's been racing in Belgium for 4 years) and Jeremy Hunt. 2 hours on Monday, 3½ on Tuesday, 2 on Wednesday and 4 yesterday; not a bad pabulum. The three keep company on the flats and the young men sprint the climbs and come back for Sid. I asked him what reflections he has on the coming of the pro-am era. It was, he believes, the beginning of the end for road racing in this country. [22]

Lambert raced on, too, and shared with Barras the domestique work for Yates and Doyle in '83. The hiatus at the end of 1980 had been a blow, of course. But there were other issues, too. He had two young children and was beginning to feel mildly uncomfortable about 'just riding the bike', which had been so attractive to begin with. He believed he ought to be thinking more closely about the future. However, a month after Bob had pulled out of sponsorship, Falcon approached Lambert to offer him a new contract at around half what he had been getting from Chicken & Sons. He signed, to supplement the income from the shop's trading.

---

[22] Jeremy Hunt, now 30, rode through the fag end of the golden age and, after a listless period when he felt a bit adrift, has, as Sid put it, got the bit between his teeth. Training with the brilliant young rider Roger Hammond, (the 2004 National Champion) in Belgium inspired him. Hunt took 4th place in the international classic, Paris–Brussels, autumn 2004.

Within a very short time, Kelloggs began to sponsor their series of city-centre criteriums which drew television coverage, so Lambert's decision to continue in racing was a good one though, at the time, it had seemed a mite quixotic. The 80s were good for him; he did well and in his last season, 1987, aged 40 and riding for the six-man Watertech-Dawes team, he was on the verge of what he was thinking would surely be the biggest win of his career on a circuit in the city centre of Cork in Ireland. He had broken away with Stephen Roche, who that year had already won the grand pink/yellow/rainbow triple – Giro d'Italia, Tour de France and Worlds Road Race. A mere half-mile from the finish the two of them were caught. It was a course full of horribly tight corners and on the final bend there was a huge stack-up; about twenty riders went down and Lambert with them. As he put it, he 'broke all sorts' and was out for good, a sorry way to finish his racing career. He went into management and was in the following car for the Linda McCartney team at the Giro d'Italia in 2000 when David McKenzie made his astonishing long break 11 miles from the start and rode an epic solo 102 miles to victory in Teramo. The team management said there couldn't have been a better guy than Lambert; the quiet strength of the man as he handed out drinks and offered words of encouragement.

The demise of the McCartney team has been chronicled elsewhere,[23] but it was a miserable day for cycling, both for the image of the sport and for the riders and others who had put so much into the team; they had mostly gone unpaid for months and were dumped, without any redress or comensation, from the man under whose name they raced. Was the team doomed from the start, funded to ride in Europe by a company that did not sell its products in Europe?

How must it have tainted any ambition other potential sponsors had of putting money into cycling? That has always been the problem. In January 1979, Barry Hoban told *Cycling* that in his opinion:

---

[23] John Deering, *Team on the Run* Mainstream Publishing 2002

Cycling is in the situation that they should either put the money into improving it or forget about it. They cannot continue as they are, playing at it while other countries are putting so much in. The basic ingredients for successful sport is champions and money will instigate them. We've got the raw materials but when also-rans are allowed to stay at the top, then the ones below have nothing to aim at.

There were a number of factors militating against success on the professional scene in the UK. The relatively small band of pro riders – never more than around forty – didn't get enough racing on the continent, but their home-based sponsors had little interest in spending money where their goods didn't sell. Barras' first sponsor, Bantel, manufacturers of toys as well as cycle accessories, *did* export and backed their man in the Tour of Switzerland, for example, but this was an exception. Further complication: the Swiss tour clashed with the domestic Rediffusion series of races which could ill afford the loss of the six-man Bantel team. Moreover, whilst the BCF financed the amateurs to race in the Worlds, the pros were expected to pay for themselves or to be paid for by their sponsors, who were, understandably, reluctant to cough up for what the BCF should have been covering. When the Worlds were held in Britain, Les West just missed a medal. When they were held in Belgium, the journey was manageable, but in Venezuela? Montreal? Even the 2,576 mile round trip to Ostuni, near the heel of Italy on the Adriatic, for the 1976 Worlds meant that British pros would not be able to go, unless (as with the Bantel men) they were already in Europe at another race. Roy Thame, team manager of Holdsworth, said publicly that it would be a waste of time to send his riders. And, where organisers of big international races held in the UK were not permitted to charge entry to spectators, the organiser of the 1975 Worlds professional road race at Yvoir in Belgium made something like £1,600,000 on gate receipts alone, against overall costs of £114,000.

Underlying these practical obstructions was the ingrained prejudice against the mercenaries. In 1974 the Wool Mark event for amateurs in Bradford had a kitty of

£250 in prizes for amateurs, but only 21 riders entered. Maurice Cumberworth, the promotions director and general manager of the BPCA suggested to the organisers that they make the race professional – the pros were free that day. The organisers got their committee together and emerged from the huddle a while later: 'Well, we're prepared to do that. We'll give the professionals £50 in cash as prizes and keep the other £200 the Wool Mark has given us and probably run a good classic amateur race at the end of the season.' (At the time, the average weekly wage of a manual worker in the UK was £55-70.)

When the racing scene was dominated by the richest teams, what new sponsor would be particularly interested in a similar commitment to such a small number of professional riders. In 1975, Bantel and Holdsworth-Campagnolo riders won 41 of the 53 races. In one whole season, a total of some £80,000 was spent on the professional riders. For the two weeks of The [amateur] Milk Race alone, the Milk Marketing Board spent *over* £80,000 but it had taken 19 years to build up to that investment.

The Milk Race

Phil Liggett moved south from the Wirral in 1967 to work at *Cycle and Mopeds* (later *Cycling*) and one of his first assignments was to interview Cedric Chicken, then sole concessionary for the importing of Peugeot bikes to the UK. The Peugeot professional cycling team was one of the best in the peloton. Roger Pingeon of Peugeot won that year's Tour de France during which Tommy Simpson, also of Peugeot, tragically died. Eddy Merckx had signed for the team soon after turning professional and Bernard Thévenet, his nemesis in the 1975 Tour, winner again in 1977, rode for Peugeot for most of his career. White Peugeot racing frames with the distinctive black and white checker trim soon began to appear in British club races and time trials and the cycling press needed the story.

Liggett walked along the broad, leafy avenue in Winchmore Hill where Bob Chicken lived, gawping at the grand mansions on either side of the road. Could one of them really be the head office of Peugeot UK? He walked up the drive, knocked at the door of the Chicken household and waited in some trepidation. Bob Chicken opened the door. Liggett introduced himself and asked if there was someone living in the house who was importing Peugeot bikes. 'Yes, my son.' Liggett went in, did the interview and wrote his 'the bike that Simpson rode' piece but, more significantly for him and Bob Chicken, his arrival on the doorstep of the big house initiated a long and warm friendship.

Four years later, when Maurice Cumberworth, who had taken over from Chas Messenger as race director of the Milk Race, announced his intention to withdraw and set off on a world trip, Liggett was mentioned as a possible successor. He took over the job in 1971 and set about routing the 1972 race in conjunction with Bill Squance, the organiser since 1969 who had been associated with the race in one capacity or another since 1958. Bob met Squance in 1969 and had been donating prizes for minor competitions in Britain's major stage race since then – 'gentleman's suitcases' for example. The prime motive was to put something into the sport but, perhaps closer to his heart, he was determined to fight back against the creeping invasion of manufactured components from Japan and Taiwan. His belief in the European manufacturing base was paramount and he felt it incumbent on European dealers to back their own industry to the hilt. Shimano had launched its sponsorship campaign already, putting money into the Milk Race, and by 1973 shared sponsorship of a continental pro team with Flandria, a bike manufacturer.

The Milk Marketing Board (MMB) allotted a large enough budget to cover the basic costs of organising and running the race but prize money, cost of competition jerseys and so on had to be funded by the organisers through outside sponsorship. It was difficult to find any large sponsor in the UK because no company would wish to be ' overshadowed by the MMB, as they must surely be. Shimano, accelerating their growth within the European market, were already investing through their concessionaire Tom Vickery, Managing Director of Middlemores in Coventry. Then in 1972, Chickens' added their own contribution and stayed with the event until its demise.

En passant, why *The* Milk Race? In 1964, the Scottish Milk Marketing Board had taken over sponsorship of the five-stage Tour of Scotland and Squance, wishing to keep the English event distinct, insisted on calling it *The* Milk Race. Why not *Tour* on the analogy of the Tour de France? Squance told me that there was a popular aversion to the use of the word *Tour* perhaps for that very reason – it was too French sounding, or else smacked of light-hearted jaunts, touring gallivants. 'We don't have tours' people told him sniffily 'we have *races*'. Races, by implication, are for serious bike riders. The British also disliked trade teams, which smacked too much of professionalism. The Earl of Roseberry, he who told an audience in Adelaide 'The Empire is a Commonwealth of Nations' in 1884, said, with some dismay, in 1900: 'It is beginning to be hinted that we are a nation of amateurs' but his dismay was not generally shared.

The Corinthian spirit – play up, play the game – was rooted deep in the public and authorities alike; mixing sport with commerce simply wasn't on. Monetary reward for the free-spirited engagement in sport corrupted competition. The lust for money is the root of all evil, saith St Paul. (Current levels of remuneration of professional footballers rather proves the point.) Indeed, from 1930 to 1961, teams in the Tour de France rode in national and regional French colours before reverting to the earlier format of trade teams, apart from a brief relapse to national teams in 1967 and 1968.

Yet in spite of any lingering doubts over professionalism, the success of The Milk Race in boosting the image of the sport was phenomenal. A marketing survey showed that 98 per cent of people asked about it knew what The Milk Race was. But in the long run this proved detrimental. The Tour of Britain became so closely associated with The Milk Race, in the absence of any other large sponsor, that, after it had gone, whenever a similar race appeared – the Kellogg's Tour of Britain, The Pru Tour – popular reaction was 'Ah, The Milk Race is back'. The Tour de France resolutely maintains its independence from overall sponsorship for precisely this reason. If a single brand name is indelibly attached to a race, no other backers will be interested, even if the eponymous sponsor withdraws. Thus various corporations give their name only to individual competitions in the Tour de France – Crédit Lyonnais the yellow jersey, Champion supermarkets the polka dots, PMU the totalisator, the green, and so on.

The Chickens' contribution to the Milk Race was the Weinmann-Chicken neutral service vehicle, which became a regular part of the back-up for all the riders in whatever team, handing out lightweight spares with prodigal largesse. The Rover saloon routinely carried 7 front and 10 rear wheels, and two spare bikes –
21½- and 23½-inch frames respectively – to accommodate most riders, with easily adjustable seat pins raised to the maximum height because it's always quicker to lower a saddle than raise it. As Monty Young, founder of Condor Cycles and another stalwart of The Milk Race service team said, Bob Chicken was always first there with help – tyres, wheels, you name it. Young, ('the real gent of the cycling industry' Squance called him), also co-sponsored a racing team during the early 60s for which Hugh Porter rode. In time, Bob sponsored three of the major competitions in the race – Hot Spot Sprints, Points and Combine (a classification for the best all-rounder) – and in 1983 the Chicken

brothers, at Robert's instigation, drove up in a vintage 1937 Foden lorry to precede the riders.

The idea was sparked by a visit to France to see the Tour de France, where he was much taken by the crazy medley of vehicles which make up the publicity caravan driving ahead of the race. Motorised bottles of water, coca cola and engine oil, three-wheeled chocolate éclairs, wedges of cheese and bananas. . . all manner of vehicular whimsy, part of the holiday-time razzamatazz. Robert decided that The Milk Race could do with a bit of that. As for the Foden, it is *the* classic British heavy-duty truck: in use on farms since the end of the nineteenth century, popular with showmen, bought for service on the Western Front by the British army and favoured by hauliers from early days. It was Foden 'steam buses', among them the famous *Puffing Billy,* which plied the passenger routes in the 1920s. Edwin Foden, born in 1841, designed traction engines for farm work, principally ploughing, and produced his first steam-driven wagon in around 1880.[24] In the course of his travels up and down the country, Robert Chicken got used to encountering these distinctive old Fodens from the approximately 50-strong fleet, owned by Stan Robson, a haulier based in Carlisle. Each lorry had its own sobriquet and Robert eventually name-spotted up every one in the fleet and even made a fan visit to see Robson, the first of many. Mrs Robson treated him like a son and, when Stan Robson died, he bequeathed Robert his own personalised number plate. Robert bought first the 1937 vintage vehicle (started with a crank) and then a second Foden, a 1960 eight-wheeler flat-back, to appear at the start of every stage, loaded with wooden packing cases stencilled with the names of the various marques of the Chicken agencies. The older lorry headed the race out and was then ferried on a low loader to near the finish, from where it drove into town and acted as an ad hoc stand for Chicken guests watching the riders come in. Both Fodens, devilishly costly, wonderfully flamboyant, heralded the Chicken presence in the race, a stylish moving billboard for the Chicken name and the

---

[24] In 1887, his compound engine won a gold medal at the Royal Agricultural Society Trials. A compound engine 'is a condensing engine in which the mechanical action of the steam is begun in one cylinder and ended in a larger cylinder,' M. Reynolds, *Engineman's Pocket Companion*, 1886.

brands they imported. Not having Campagnolo limited the impact of the publicity, given that Shimano were getting a lot of coverage. However, the Chicken hospitality tent for their suppliers was a byword for lavish entertainment and the Chicken publicity girls worked hard selling Weinmann t-shirts, replica race jerseys and catalogues.

Such was the infectious enthusiasm of the Chicken involvement in the carnival side of Britain's national cycle tour, the fun side, that Robson himself got involved. When Robert asked him if he had a driver who could help out, Robson not only assigned a driver but sent him down in a brand new DAF truck. Then he took on the onerous but essential labour involved in erecting and dismounting the lines of barriers either side of the route on the approach run to the Finish each day.

Birmingham Outskirts. A pub.

About 2.30pm. Standing idle in the car park, their engines long since cooled, a number of RJ Chicken vehicles, including the 1937 Foden. Inside the pub, Cedric, Robert, the publicity girls, the drivers. A good time is being had by all. Indeed, a very good time has been had by all since they arrived a good while earlier. Suddenly, just audible above the hilarity and jocular persiflage, a wild root-toot-tooting of car klaxons down the road and past the pub. Blimey. It's the fifteen-minute vehicle. Race coming through. Oopsadaisy let's get out of here. Mad scramble into the lorry cabs and car seats. Tally-ho and into the city centre. No time to waste, floor it, matey. Cedric ahead, Robert behind, they are driving the old wagons like a pair of racing cars, swerving round the bends, scorching along the white lines, into the final strait and the barriers. Trouble ahead. A policeman waves them down. Crash gear changes, pull up. The policeman walks up to the 1937 Foden. Robert fumbles with the window – there's no catch, just a leather strap hooked onto a brass button. The leather strap free, the window crashes down and Robert leans out and peers at the copper, unleashing, as he does so, an alcoholic hogo that would have floored a nun. The copper is made of sterner stuff, waves him through, for this is The unalcoholic Milk Race, is it not?

Blackpool. Outskirts. Final stage of the race.

Robert, stone-cold sober, drives into town and is waved down by a policeman. A brief exchange.

'Where you going, sir?'

'Race Finish.'

'Down there.'

'Thanks.'

'Down there' is a narrow, single-track side road leading to a low bridge whose arch is, as Robert gets nearer down the road back up which he will never be able to reverse, not much higher than the height of his Foden cab. Brilliant. Copper must be a comedian. Or a marplot in the pay of the Road Time Trials Council. If the Foden gets stuck under the bridge, the entire Milk Race is (a) going to pile into the back of it at worst or (b)at best, be forced to loll about behind it, waiting to be rescued. The entire Milk Race. Who won overall? Couldn't tell you, they got stuck up the exhaust pipe of a 1937 Foden. Suddenly, a chance. On the far side of the bridge, a vintage car. Driver must be a clairvoyant. He stops the motor, leaps out and sprints over. Inch by inch, the Foden moves forward, the car driver doing the this-way that-way tick-tack and gently, so gently, the lorry is through and on its way to official duty at the Finish on the seafront.

Riding the 1984 Milk Race was a team co-sponsored by Raleigh and, at Bob's instigation as he had announced in December 1983, the company for whom Chicken and Sons acted as sole agent, Weinmann. In fact, after the MMB itself and the National Dairy Council, RJC were the biggest sponsors of The Milk Race. The team included his old muckers, Barras and Lambert, as well as a rising star, Malcolm Elliott, all riding Dawes bikes carrying a lot of equipment supplied by RJC. 'Supersid' and 'Legs' had ridden with Phil Thomas in the four-man Falcon team throughout 1983, the first year of what became a highly popular series of five city-centre races sponsored by Kelloggs.

Thomas won the championship overall, Barras took the fourth race in Manchester and came fifth overall, while Lambert and Ian Greenhalgh gave formidable support. Thomas won the '83 National Championship, Lambert was National Criterium Champion and came second in the national road race, and Barras won the first stage of that year's Milk Race. Their ascendancy marked an era in British road racing which bristled with talent and signalled a general mood of bright optimism in the sport. The first Kelloggs races, each an hour long, held in Bristol, Glasgow, Nottingham, Manchester and Birmingham, attracted 45 pro riders from Britain, France, Holland, Belgium, Ireland, USA and Australia and drew huge crowds. They gave further irrefutable evidence of the potential in road racing: tremendous popular appeal and a punchy sporting drama ideal for television.

The return of Chicken and Sons to direct sponsorship in 1987, in addition to their continued support of and contribution to, The Milk Race, was in part due to a new deal struck in late 1982. At that year's Harrogate Show Dinner, which Bob had inaugurated in 1976, he announced that he had reached a tentative agreement with Simplex to handle their agency in the UK. Whilst Simplex had always commanded huge respect on the continent and was riding high – the great Bernard Hinault (winner of the Tour de France 1979, '80, '81, '82 and '83, three times winner of the Giro d'Italia, etc.) had signed to ride the Simplex marque – as Cedric Chicken put it 'Simplex hasn't exactly been hitting the headlines in this country for a number of years'. Although the Chickens had been supplying chains and chain- and freewheels for a long time, now they would complete the transmission set and deal in gears. Of the teams riding in the Tour de France, 90 per cent used Simplex; in West Germany alone they sold around a fifth of their annual output of 4 million, and one of their biggest growth markets was in Japan. But the Simplex share of the UK market had fallen over 25 years from 70 per cent to a mere 5; this decline was most rapid during the last ten years, due to a massive and unstoppable distribution and take-up of Japanese components. However Dawes, the first bike manufacturer to fit Simplex in the early 50s, had agreed to fit them once more. The

Dawes company was holding its own in the UK market, working as ever on their prime requisites – quality and service – and not price alone. Their and the Chickens' espousal of Simplex was based on a central credo voiced by Bob: 'We have always had confidence in European products because European cycling has a rich tradition and history.'

Sadly, he was bucking a growing trend for recourse to the Far East. The world boom in sales of bicycles at the end of the 70s had put enormous pressure on many European component manufacturers. They simply could not meet the huge increase in demand from manufacturers and dealers; the usual vagaries of boom and bust. When factories could not get supplies from Europe, they went elsewhere and elsewhere was the Far East. But there was a lack of enterprise and even laziness in their disaffection with Europe. When RJC met a shortfall of supplies, they went to Germany, asked for help with components and got them. As so often, the personal touch can make all the difference.

Unhappily, the Simplex hook-up proved thorny. The bad representation before RJC took over had damaged them too radically and the name never caught on. Their own complacency didn't help and, in 1987, they went under.

So in that same year, the Chickens sponsored the Great Britain team for The Milk Race in conjunction with Weinmann and Vredestein, with whom they had forged such close ties. They announced the new arrangement on 2 April 1987. Having represented Vredestein for 33 years, Bob commissioned a Gallup Poll to test how well known the name Vredestein was amongst British cyclists. The results were encouraging: a significant majority said they knew Vredestein second only to Michelin and a great number of dealers replied that Vredestein tyres were undoubtedly the best for quality and reliability. The new company would be called Vredestein-RJC Ltd and reflected a confidence in this already lengthy collaboration. Bob took the opportunity to rebut remarks made by John Moore, director of the importers Moore Large in the *Daily Telegraph* during the Cyclex show, which suggested that the British bicycle was extinct.

'The Far Eastern bike has taken the place of the cheap European bike' said Moore. It's a little more complicated than that but basically that's it.'

Britain, replied Bob, was an intrinsic part of the European Community, not a mere member, and its prosperity would depend on closer associations within the EC. Moreover, Western Europe formed Britain's largest export market. To celebrate the closer Vredestein links, RJC would also be sponsoring Southend and County Wheelers, the biggest racing club in Essex and announced a big meet at Rayleigh at which Tony Doyle, the Worlds 5,000m Pursuit Champion, would make a guest appearance.

In that same month April 1987, three other items of news told a sadder story. The Chater Lea Manufacturing company, which had been set up in Banner Street in London's East End in the 1890s making cycle components and then motorbikes, seemed likely to go under because of cash-flow problems. Secondly, Alan Leng of the CTC expressed concern that the ethos of the club was, willy-nilly, still rooted in the days, particularly the 1930s, when it had been a club serving the needs of 'a small elitist core of dedicated cycle tourists'. He added: 'We've still got this slightly cloth-cap image in the cycling world which we're trying to lose'. Whatever efforts he applied, he didn't succeed and the CTC still has the same problem, of perception, to this day, that it is for eager-beaver diehards in retro clothes with decidedly uncool notions about bikes and cycling, the sort of dippy dilly friends whose championship of cycling make enemies of the bike redundant. It's a pity. The membership of the CTC is roughly the same today – circa 40,000 – as it was in its heyday and the message is, at heart, sound. Perhaps the quasi-mystic, soupy language in which the message is couched puts people off. Here is H.H. England, editor of *Cycling* (precursor of *Cycling Weekly* and popularly known as 'the comic'), writing in 1950:

[A bicycle] is the complete antidote for work strain and the anxieties of the age in which we live. The cinema or dance hall, although both provide pleasure and sometimes relaxation, are little more than a change of scene and action from the workaday round;

cycling provides change, but also acts in a way that rekindles energy and develops tissue . . . Cycling in the pure air gets the blood moving – cleansing – tingling. Cycling is rhythmic, and it is a truism that all "patterned" exercise is pleasant, efficient and beneficial. . . Cycling is the Seven Leagued Boots of modern civilisation.

Allowing for a certain period atmosphere about the writing and social reference, I wouldn't quarrel with any of the substance of that but I do wonder how much time H.H. England had spent in dance halls or even cinemas, come to that. Perhaps he was a rare bobby-dazzler about the London palais, another Bob Chicken, forsooth. Curiously, the big new premises Raleigh built on Lenton Boulevard in 1930 included a concert hall, a dance floor and a 'cinematograph theatre' for the use of all employees. However, the point about England's soft-focus rodomontade is that he sounds altogether *too* strictly ballroom. When he tells us that 'bicycles are the people's transport . . . ' that a bicycle is 'handy' and puts a new meaning on 'freedom' he is merely preaching to the converted. Even to the introverted. Cycling needs more forthright opinion, more practical champions, if it is not to remain forever caught up in the rose-tinted, dappy Olde Englande idyll that John Major wittered about – warm beer served in country pubs beside village greens whereon can be heard the thump of leather on willow and the tinkle of bells as little old ladies pedal by on their way to Evensong along tranquil lanes, fringed with spreading chestnut trees 'neath which a touring cyclist may take a restorative nap in the warm glow of the late afternoon sun.

Thirdly, the editor of *Cycle Trader* lamented the takeover that January of Raleigh Industries by Derby International. 'It finally happened: TI sell Raleigh to relieve itself of a consistent loss-maker' amid the trumpeting of 'restructuring . . . renovation . . . a new beginning'. In the same issue as his editorial, there appeared triumphalist advertisements from Lenton Road, Raleigh puffing their hundredth birthday: '1887–1987. 100 years of winning. A century of leading the Industry. *We've got it right.*' What, asked the editor, would Derby International, whose board included an American former vice-chairman of a leisure group, the advisory director of an investment bank in New York and a London-based American lawyer, sometime director and shareholder of the largest bicycle company in Latin America, what would they do with the Raleigh names and frames? Would they indulge in some asset-stripping on the lines of what Manganese Bronze had done to BSA in 1973? 'There are those' he wrote 'who are pleased to call cycles assembled in Britain entirely from imported parts "British". What, I wonder, do they call the Washington-manufactured Nissan cars? Raleigh, for most people, means the greater part of our cycle industry and nobody wants Derby International to reduce it to a British badge on a 100% foreign product.' The changeover took place on April Fool's Day'.

CHAPTER TEN
MILK RACE...
HOME AND ABROAD...
HOT COMPETITION

The new chief executive of Raleigh, a 45-year-old accountant Alan Finden-Crofts, had, in four years with Dunlop Slazenger, turned an annual loss of £6 million to a profit of £16m. He promised that 'everyone from the top management down will have their minds focussed solely on bikes.' Slazenger had been similar to Raleigh in that 'both were consumer businesses managed by industrialists and factory rather than product-led . . . Good products are absolutely vital for the success of the business and we'll be working towards a core range which can be sold internationally.'

Yvonne Rix, who had worked for Raleigh for some years, took over as Marketing Manager in 1987. One of the first economies in the new order was to fold the continental TI-Raleigh team that was costing around £250,000 per annum. There had always been a gulf between the great success of the team and the image of Raleigh across the Channel. Their bikes were not much liked on the continent: they had the wrong specifications, their frames had the wrong angles, so they didn't sell, even at competitive prices. Most people in France thought they were Dutch, anyway, and Dutch bicycle meant a sit-up-and-beg machine for town use, *not* a racer. Furthermore the widespread UK approach to exporting bikes was to find an agent on the continent or elsewhere and give him sole responsibility; the firms involved didn't send their own people out to do the job – searching out the market, making contacts, speaking the language and selling direct.

The UK team would race on, but the domestic mood turned increasingly sour, the cycling environment ever more hostile and unconducive to racing and the home cycling authorities more and more strident in their dislike of commercialism. Opposed to the whole notion of sponsorship, they didn't want to see the names of sponsors disfiguring bikes or plastered across clothing, feeling that this contaminated the pure integrity of sport, making it tawdry, no more than a circus. True, Henri Desgrange had railed against the pernicious influence of big bicycle manufacturers on riders in the Tour de France – he wanted no truck with anything which detracted from the heroic struggle of man and machine against the road and other riders, especially not businessmen muscling in to weight the odds in favour of their own riders. Indeed, he once voiced the opinion that the ideal Tour de France would be a race which only one rider had the strength and endurance to complete. However, commercial sponsorship had become an integral part of cycle sport; even amateurs won cash prizes in races, and the nature of cycling was such that without injections of money from commercial interests, the sport must wither and die. A bit of advertising was the smallest repayment a sponsor could ask for. But, like the BBC in those days, the BCF hated besmirching its image with any stain of commerce. Excellence in sport should be pursued for love not money. That's what *amateur* meant – gentlemanly. Professionalism smacked of *trade*.

Rix found this attitude incredible. Consider the glittering successes of the Raleigh riders on the continent: 77 stage wins in the Tour de France alone. What a tremendous boost they delivered for the image of the British cycle industry abroad, in the forum of its highest profile, professional road racing. Compare the buzz of excitement triggered by the victories of Raleigh riders in some of the most prestigious races on the calendar with the refusal of the BCF to allow a winner on the podium to wear a cap or jersey sporting his sponsor's name, their disdain for any big coroporate injection of money (and therefore influence) into cycle sport. Harbouring a sulky almost perverse dislike of professionalism and continental ways, they were decidedly amateur in attitude and approach. Heirs, indeed, to the Olympic committee who snorted their disgust that the great sprinter Harold Abrahams *employed* a coach before the Paris Games in 1924, where he won a gold in the 100 yards.

In very quick time, Weinmann, who had been getting a very poor deal for their involvement with cycling in the UK, pulled out of sponsorship and the domestic Raleigh team was in trouble. Rix looked for other sponsors and brought in Banana, a combine of some 3 or 4 banana importers such as Fyffes. Cyclists eat bananas for their sugar and potassium, so this was a natural tie-in and Banana-Raleigh formed a good team riding frames painted plantain black and yellow. But the sponsorship was complicated. Rix had to deal with individual company bosses in the Banana group, each with their own wants and demands vis à vis publicity and input. Raleigh Banana spent, in total, some £250,000 on the team, of which Raleigh's share was £150–175,000.

Each year, Rix had to justify the outlay of this money on the racing team by reference to sales. Without any kind of incidental publicity – magazines, TV, any papers other than the cycling press – this was a hard task. As the capacity of the sport to boost the sale of racing bikes quickly diminished, there was less and less commercial incentive for any company, even within the industry, to pump money into it.

And, as MTBs (mountain bikes – see below) became the new craze, the new cool, sales of racing bikes fell dramatically from around 250,000 per annum to approximately 30,000. The image of MTB grew more and more prominent, puffed in specialist magazines and men's style magazine. By the end of 1987, with sales of mountain bikes rocketing, the company decided that they must have an MTB team, thus compromising finance for the road-racing outfit. Even this new venture wasn't a huge success. There was, for sure, some return on the efforts of the MTB team, but that was almost counter-productive to continued sponsorship of the racing team, who seemed now to exist in a sort of commercial vacuum.

A further blow came in 1987when the organiser of The Milk Race, restricted in the number of British teams he could choose, selected mostly amateur outfits and not Raleigh. Excluded from the major domestic event of the season, Raleigh had even less to persuade them to persist. Paul Sherwen, manager of the UK Raleigh team, was racing in the Vuelta Asturias when he heard the news of Elliott's victory in the '87 Milk Race. He came home and won the National Championships, but shared the general feeling that Raleigh had been fingered for reasons undisclosed.

Yvonne Rix finished as Marketing Director in 1997 and left the company in the summer of 1999. Almost inevitably, Raleigh bowed out of all sponsorship as soon as she went. They had, by then, stopped making their own bikes and something unique was lost. They did try to stick to European components for a while. As Rix told me: 'We did have the best that Europe could offer but the Japanese were switching to alloy and the European manufacturers were slow to follow suit. Then Taiwan entered the market and the Japanese themselves were up against it, to an extent.'

In her time with Raleigh, Yvonne Rix had the idea of combining the best of the MTB with the best of a racing bike. The result was the Pioneer, later called a hybrid. She looked for suitable tyres, with a smaller gauge than standard MTB tyres, and found none, not even as a last resort in the Far East. But Bob stepped in with just the thing, from Vredestein: hybrid tyres with a central rolling tread. The hybrid was more comfortable than the extreme-angled racer because of its less severe, MTB-style positioning; but this combined with nippier movement than on the big squashy MTB with its lengthened frame, extended position of the top tube, saddle to bars, tyres that were too wide, all of which made riding the Pioneer sluggish and hard work on roads.

In March, Cedric announced that RJC would now start an extra and quite separate service, supplying specialist members of the retail trade through a new Retail List of components. Lightweight equipment became simply too expensive when wholesalers had added their percentage; none but the real fanatics would buy and RJC believed that the greater availability of the best components at affordable prices could encourage more interest in bikes and cycling beyond the narrow limits of club racing. A guaranteed despatch within 24 hours, proper back-up and full supply, the right product at the right price. The radical approach had a hidden appeal. It could even be called risqué: Weinmann introduced an upside-down, (legs in the air) alloy ladies' brake which they called the '69'. Not a very obvious witticism for a Swiss, but . . .

In July, after The 1987 Milk Race, won by Malcolm Elliott, Bob addressed the Pedal Club, (which he joined the following year), as guest speaker: 'Sponsorship is not only necessary but imperative. Most other leisures and sports carry sponsorship, cycling must do likewise.' He said that RJC, as a firm believer in goodwill, had decided to put back into cycle sport some of the gains they'd made from the cycle trade. The problem, he acknowledged, was that the British cycling industry had found it hard to make sufficient profits to finance entry into the sport. Nearly all the current UK manufacturers had put money in at one time or another; now they simply could not afford to. Therefore, Bob said, 'sources must be found from outside the industry. The cycle trade should take advantage of the interest from the press and television. Cycle racing is a growing sport . . . The Milk Race should be regarded as one large family outing.' The MMB certainly promoted the race as a spur to healthy living, with slogans like 'Get fresh, get bottle' and 'Gotta lotta bottle'.

The prevailing mood of optimism was corroborated in December when Kelloggs, clearly delighted with the success of the city-centre races, announced a pro Tour of Britain, to be given full coverage by Channel Four.

The MMB finally quit in 1993, when EEC subsidies on the continent rendered the sale of home-produced UK milk less profitable abroad. The three large dairies who subscribed to the MMB, Express, Coop and United (for whom my own grandfather worked as a milkman, delivering by horse and cart), began to feel the pinch badly. Squance had always faced moaning minnies inside the MMB bitching about the cost of sponsorship and the lack of justification for it, and he had to fight them every inch of the way.

Losing his patience on one occasion, he went to the Board of Directors to confront them. 'I hear you're dubious,' he said. 'Well, just come and see for yourselves. Every dairy farmer I have ever invited has loved the show and gone away full of it.'

The Managing Director took him up on the offer, was bowled over by the enthusiasm of the crowd, the excitement of the racing, the holiday atmosphere, the fun, the spectacle. He told Squance: 'This is fantastic. In future, if you need money for this event you come straight to *me,* do you hear?'

It was a sad day for road racing in the UK when the money did stop. The Milk Race had become a high-profile, prestigious event, a win to grace any rider's *palmarès*. When The Milk Race was established on the racing calendar, UCI rules limited any new tour to five stages only – the Tour of Austria, for instance. However, that rule was waived for The Milk Race. Effectively Britain's national tour, (albeit amateur), the fifth oldest in the sport, it was allowed 15 stages.

The Tour de France began in 1903; the Giro d'Italia, 1909; the Tour de Suisse, 1933; and the Vuelta a España, 1935

The triumph of The Milk Race depended on several factors: the full backing by its major sponsor from the start; the strength of the race organisation – Liggett pretty well single-handed took on planning the route, booking accommodation etc; friendly working relationships both with town councils (Squance's brief), particularly those who hosted starts and finishes, and with the various police forces up and down the country in whose hands rested the safety of riders, other road users and spectators alike; and its popularity as a spectacle. Squance even persuaded the Association of Chief Police Officers that it would be a good idea, for all sorts of reasons, to have a number of police motorbike outriders following the race from start to finish, as happens in France, above all because they would get to know the job inside out, instead of there being relays of men covering single days only. The fact that a government White Paper had sanctioned the race was a huge benefit in fostering this close and friendly relationship between police and race organisation. Town councils, too, were generally very eager to help and please. One year, the local council had thoughtfully resurfaced the road into Blackpool, where the race generally finished, and Monty Young ran out of spare tyres for riders who had punctured on the nasty little granite chips of the spanking new approaches.

The demise of The Milk Race – a cruel blow to a healthily burgeoning racing scene in the UK – was partly due to the advent of open racing, where pros and amateurs could race together, in the late 80s. The MMB were not keen on the intervention of the pros; they wanted an all-amateur race. The withdrawal of their support conjured up all the latent resistance to the sport which the undeniable success of The Milk Race had kept suppressed for a long time.

Sadly, objections to road racing in the UK have hardly changed since the beginning. It's too difficult to organise, say the detractors, too difficult and far too dangerous. It inconveniences other road-users – the car lobby, of course, became more and more strident and powerful as ownership of cars increased – and Robert Chicken told me that occasionally he encountered apopleptic motorists shouting and screaming at the cyclists on the race. 'Very sad,' he said, 'to live your life like that.' Alas, even widespread popular support of the events did not persuade big sponsors to get involved. The bike trade, rather defeatist and readier to accept a decline in interest than to fight it, was also slow to appreciate the potential commercial benefits from substantial backing of what they saw as essentially a continental fad. It's all these limp, lame and woebegone flails of negativity that for far too long have militated against the enjoyment and proliferation, in Britain, of one of the very best *free* shows on earth.

Yet as was evident right from the start, when the BLRC organised road and stage races, cycle sport in the continental style – bringing races to a public who could stand by the side of the road or gather in large crowds in city centres to watch – was hugely popular here as across the Channel. Yet it was evident right from the start that when the BLRC organised road and stage races – cycle sport in the continental style – that enabled spectators to stand by the side of the road or gather in large crowds in city centres to watch, it was hugely popular here as across the Channel.

Mistakes were made. When the Tour de France came to England in 1974, sponsored by a local association of Devon asparagus growers, much of the route – a circuit out of Plymouth and back – followed a motorway, a long, wide and soulless stretch of anonymous road. This was not encouraging. However, when it returned in 1994 and took the riders through leafy Sussex and over one of the most famous landmarks in British cycling, Ditchling Beacon, dense crowds lined the side of the road and what cheering there was when Sean Yates, in Tour tradition, went ahead of the peloton into his home town Forest Row to greet his family and fans. A couple of days before this he had been in yellow.

It was calculated that some 3 million people watched the race out on the road, and when the police were asked how many complaints there had been about the race they said they could be counted on one hand. The fact is that the police *can* manage road racing in this country but because of the lack of drive from the cycling authorities and the absence of substantial sponsorship to cope with the additional policing costs involved in closing roads, the prevailing attitude is one of laissez-faire and 'too much of a bother'. Consider the USA, home of the petrol-guzzling motorcar and the drive-everywhere, why-walk-when-you-can-hop-in-a-car? mentality. For the San Francisco Grand Prix, a one-day race in early autumn, the entire city centre gets closed. The police authority commandeers every single parking lot in town, most of them owned by big corporations, and the crowds turn out in their thousands for a good day's entertainment. The city cafés and bars do a roaring trade, it's party time and good fun. The same used to happen in Britain, with a series of city-centre criterium races which were hugely popular with spectators and local tradespeople alike. No more. Too difficult. What's the point? The television companies didn't latch on so enthusiasm waned. To begin with, television companies, both BBC and ITV, did show interest and Squance had a happy relationship with them. However, they began to dictate when live coverage could and could not be shown. In the nature of bike racing this is impractical: tail winds and a lively field or headwinds, rain and collective apathy can make nonsense of a predicted average speed and arrival times. Instead of allowing some flexibility in their scheduling, the television people got stubborn – if times couldn't be guaranteed there'd be no live coverage, so reportage was cut to the minimum and then dropped altogether. But a bike race is always filled with the unpredictable. As for the continued obstinacy of the cycling authorities, they back track racing because it's so much more predictable; also funding is easier because the dividends can be more readily projected. It is no exaggeration to say that The Milk Race helped give road racing in the UK, pro and amateur, a higher profile than it has ever had.

A stage in Yorkshire.

Four Czech riders are in a break. The roads are narrow, the bends sharp, the drystone walls to either side high enough to obscure the way ahead. The fleeing quartet hits a bend too fast, they overshoot straight into a field. Monty Young, in the following car, follows them into the plough, leaps out and gets cracking on the repair work, up to the tops of his shoes in soft mud.

The approach to Harrogate up through the bleak steeps of Coverdale: the race radio crackles and Phil Liggett announces: 'No service to be given on top of the moors.' The motorbike outriders with minimal spares shoot past, one comes too close to the Young vehicle, Monty swerves and nearly whacks into a tree, one of the branches of which, however, hooks a spare red bike off the rack on top of the car. The cars following come upon this grisly trophy dangling in a tree as if its rider has flown off over the edge of the road and down the bank. Wasn't Jerry Taylor of Haverhill riding a red bike? He was. Poor old Jerry. Hope he's okay . . .

English riders won seven of the first ten editions of The Milk Race, Bill Bradley twice (once second), Les West, whom Liggett reckons to be one of the finest racers who never crossed the Channel, twice – 1965 and 1967. But, in the early 60s, teams from Eastern Europe began to turn up regularly and their riders – Czech, Soviet, Polish –imposed an iron grip on the racing throughout the years of the amateur era. They were tough, well-trained and rode like demons, enjoying temporary respite from the tight restrictions of the communist regime back home. While injured American riders complained that the private rooms in English hospitals had no colour televisions, the Soviet Bloc casualties plied the race doctor with bottles of vodka in stunned gratitude at what they took to be special, not simply routine, treatment.

Such was the international prestige of the national tour that droves of foreign riders competed and it certainly proved to be a fine nursery of future professional talent. Bill Nickson, the 1975 winner, then signed for the TI-Raleigh team and rode the 1977 Tour de France. Fedor den Hertog of Holland, winner in 1969 and 1971, went on to a fine professional career. Another Dutchman, Hennie Kuiper, winner in 1972, won Olympic gold that summer. He took the 1975 World pro Road Race title and was twice 2nd overall in the Tour de France, 1977 and 1980. When the great Sean Kelly rode The Milk Race in 1975, he was only 18 years old and lay 3rd overall when the race crossed the Trough of Bowland on the way to Manchester. Kelly had trouble with his brakes and lost so much time he tumbled way down the order into the 20s. But, the disappointment didn't get to him. There were no tears, no outburst of rage, no reaction at all. He seemed utterly impassive to the dreadful bad luck. It was an early showing of the imperturbable strength of mind and will which made him such a formidable champion. He took one stage victory, into Norfolk Park in Sheffield, riding in with the eventual winner, Bernt Johansson of Sweden. He stuck to the Swede's wheel and jumped him for the line. Johansson bitched to Liggett that the man had done no work. 'But he's 18 – what do you expect? Besides, it was a good tactic, wasn't it?'

Kelly certainly became one of the most guileful men in the peloton but it was his no-nonsense, grounded attitude which marked him out as a great rider, impervious to difficulty, utterly composed, never ruffled. Very early in his career, he just missed out on a win in a citerium in the south of France, the Grand Prix de Peymeinade, March 1977. He started the sprint simultaneously with Jos Jacobs. No one else was remotely in the hunt. The Belgian just made it and across the line Kelly remarked, 'No excuses, just a bit fast for me.' A week later in Lugano it was Kelly who was just a bit fast for the rest. Liggett is convinced that several of the British professional road racers of the 70s and 80s were quite the match of their continental rivals. However, very few of them were prepared to move away from home. It was as much a temperamental decision as practical. The wrench of leaving England for an uncertain life in a foreign country added to the demands of racing in the European bunch was simply too daunting for most men. It takes an exceptional indifference to domestic comfort and the familiar to ditch both for a precarious existence where nobody speaks your native tongue. Latterly, Chris Boardman negotiated a special clause in his contract with Crédit Agricole to allow him to remain resident in the Wirral when he was not racing on the continent.

Some riders, like Bill Nickson, did flirt briefly with continental racing. So, too, Dave Lloyd of whom the great Eddie Soens said, after their first encounter on the track, 'He's one of those,' meaning a no-prisoners winner. Lloyd was set to race abroad but a routine medical examination detected an irregular heart rhythm and, unhappily, he was barred. Adrian Timmis, who rode the 1987 Tour de France with the ANC-Halfords-Lycra team, spoke of the experience as the worst in his life. Two of his team mates did persist: Malcolm Elliott and Graham Jones joined others who had already established themselves in the continental peloton. Elliott didn't feel wholly at ease. He found the provision of red wine at the team dinner table bizarre, especially in the absence of his preferred healthy diet of salads etc. Paul Sherwen and Sean Yates had not bothered overmuch with the British racing scene and went straight from the amateur ranks to France. Yates had the ideal temperament, a no-fuss get-on-with-it attitude. He began his pro career as a vegetarian but, summoned to a local restaurant at 4am on the morning of a race to eat a manky steak, blue with age and frilled with yellow fat and gristle, plus a mound of rice, he complied because that was the regime, it always had been and who was he to complain? Phil Bayton, nicknamed 'The Engine', a rider of great aggression, perhaps typifies the influence of time-trialling, the British obsession, on a competitive mentality. Henri Desgrange said that to win the Tour de France a rider must have head *and* legs. In other words, nous, intelligence, guile, a good tactical sense and knowing when to apply full effort and when to hold back. Bayton, an exceptional rider in some ways, simply was not canny enough to succeed on the continent. The discipline of the time trial – flat-out, concentrated effort – will certainly develop a highly aggressive attitude, but at the risk of being blinkered and inflexible; a racing intelligence is quite another matter. Every racer who has left these shores to ride on the continent began as a time trialist – Sean Yates is still turning in remarkable performances against the clock – but each one became an adept in the mind games and hidden stratagems of bunch racing, the *métier*. There is an admirable bluntness in the men who have made it in the pro game, too. After his victory in a Nissan Classic one-day race – typical 100-mile lone break, bunch let him go but couldn't reel him in when they put down the hammer – Yates was pressed to describe how had he managed such a ride. What was the secret? A man of uncluttered mind, he looked back and, bluntly, told it exactly how it is, unlarded with flim-flam: 'You just go as hard as you can for as long as you can.'

Nevertheless, the home riders mounted formidable opposition to any men from continental teams who crossed the Channel to race in the UK. There was, inevitably, a lot of needle, too: the British keen to show they were quite as good as the foreigners, any lone interlopers from abroad vulnerable to the pack of home riders hungry to give them a pasting. Not so if they came as part of a team, in which case the hardened peloton outfits could command a race with some ease. Another bone of contention? Money. In April 1978, Liggett organised a big pro race at Crystal Palace. Eighty-eight riders signed on, including several stars from the continent – Bernard Thévenet, winner of the Tour de France 1975 and '77, Gerrie Knetemann, one of the fastest men in the bunch, winner later that year of the road-race rainbow jersey, and Barry Hoban, then at the end of an illustrious career. Such competitors guaranteed a good crowd, outstanding men in the continental peloton being the great draw, but still the British riders kvetched. Hoban, for instance, was no better than them, they said, so why should *he* get £800 starting money? (As an indication of how seriously they take these things across the Channel, Brian Robinson, the great pioneer, is well-known, recognised and admired in France to this day.)

For a while, bike racing seemed to have arrived in the UK. The image of cycle sport was strong. Home riders showed well in the last years of The Milk Race and won four editions: 1986 Joey McLoughlin, 1987 Malcolm Elliott, 1991 Chris Walker, 1993

Chris Lillywhite. The home-based pros were riding a full season. The future looked rosy, newspapers paid attention to the sport, the Tour de France graced these shores a second time, Jones, Yates and Sherwen and the Scot Robert Millar were highly regarded on the continent – ample encouragement for others to follow their lead. Alas, the promise did not deliver. In America, the promise was barely uttered than its fruits ensued.

Liggett was actually the first international race organiser to bring an American team to Europe in the mid-70s, and in 1983 the American Matt Eaton won the Milk Race, to the surprise of himself and the rest of the team. He had done little before and did not do very much after, but the Americans had patently accepted that top bike racing happened in Europe. The year of Eaton's win, his compatriot Jonathan Boyer rode his second Tour de France and there followed a steady infiltration of Americans in the peloton: Greg Lemond's first victory (of three) in the Tour in 1986, the year the first American sponsored team, *7-11*, competed; there followed another US-sponsored outfit, Motorola, led by Andy Hampsten (4th in the 1986 Tour de France and winner of the Giro d'Italia in 1988), and, latterly, the US Postal team, riding for the six-times winner, Lance Armstrong. In all that time one British trade team rode the Tour – ANC-Halfords in 1987 – only the second to do so, (after Hercules in 1955) and the best British placing ever is Robert Millar's 4th (and Mountains Prize) in 1984. Three Britons have worn the yellow jersey since Tommy Simpson: Chris Boardman, winner of the Prologue on the first day of his first Tour in 1994, Sean Yates later in that same race and, again as a neophyte, David Millar, winner of the Prologue in 2000. Road-racing UK bristles with talent but the talent by and large stays at home. On the subject of cycle sport, Millar is outspoken; as he told me in an interview:

> *If anyone's interested in road racing they should forget Britain. They haven't got a clue. It's a total waste of time. They know nothing about it, the riders and the organisers, and they do everything to discourage you.*

Before I went to France [aged 18] people were saying 'Don't go, you'll only get your head kicked in,' but I wanted to go. I knew it was there or nowhere. The fact is that Britain has nothing to offer pro cycling. If you want to ride as a pro, the best you can do is get out of the UK as soon as possible.

I had lunch with Millar and Bob Chicken just before Christmas, 2004. He had returned to the UK having admitted, earlier in the year, to taking EPO (erythropoietin). He had been understandably reluctant to brave any kind of large social engagement, but came as a guest of Bob's to the Pickwick Garden Party in December. Introduced to the upwards of 650 guests, he stood and was cheered to the ceiling. There were dissenters, notably the President of the Club, but it was, in my view, a welcome acceptance that Millar had come clean, even if, for a while he had not ridden clean, and wanted to get on not only with his life but his racing. Such a marvellous talent should not be allowed to go to waste and if Millar is the only cyclist who has taken dope then I am the legendary king of Atlantis. Millar expressed enormous gratitude to Bob Chicken for his support, and if intelligence, compassion and a certain practical common sense cannot be applied à propos of a young man who succumbed to money, pressure and celebrity but then decided to break out of the nightmare in which he felt himself trapped, then we are all hypocrites and deserve no sympathy, none at all. As ever, the authorities, caught as they are between public obligations and private desires, whatever they be, have shown Millar little regard and less concern. Perhaps they could do nothing else: he let them down and they must abide in silence till he redeems himself through official channels. Until that happens he must be persona non grata. I believe this is harsh and, by his great forbearance, Bob Chicken has made it abundantly clear to David Millar that one mistake does not trash a life and recognition of error is closely bound up with putting it aside. The hostility of the cycling press is harder to stomach. Holier than thou? That and a lot more besides. To use a cycling analogy: when you run out of water you ask the guy riding next to you. Even Coppi and Bartali, bitter rivals, shared water as they shared the rigours of the road.

Official British encouragement of track riders, to the virtual exclusion of any interest in road racers, has had marked success, culminating in Bradley Wiggins's haul of three medals – gold, silver and bronze (individual pursuit, team pursuit and points) – at the Athens Olympic Games in 2004, a brilliant achievement totally and quite disgracefully ignored by the BBC Sports Personality of the Year programme in December of that same year. Wiggins rides on the continent for Crédit Agricole, Boardman's old team, but he is one of less than a handful of extremely talented riders to move from track to road, a progression which ought to be logical. In fact Wiggins rode his last track event for two years – the Points race in the World Track Championships in Manchester, January 2005 – to concentrate on road racing. The Australians have always had this more rugged approach: they move from track to road and succeed in both spheres. Stuart O'Grady, former World team pursuit champion, was the first Australian to wear the green Points jersey in the Tour de France and two others have won it overall – Robbie McEwen (2002 and 2004) and another pursuiter, Baden Cooke in 2003. What of *British* track riders, gold medallists and all? They ride under the auspices of an officialdom calculating results, measuring and monitoring success in a forum where speed and peformance *can* be monitored: the track. Results in exchange for big funding. Road racing? Too chancey. British riders have such a great history in pursuit that the natural step up from track to road ought to be far better established than it has been. Hugh Porter, World 5km pursuit champion 1968, 1970, 1972, 1973, silver in 1967, 1969, bronze 1971; Tony Doyle, World champion in 1980, 1986, silver in 1984, 1985, bronze in 1987; Chris Boardman Olympic pursuit gold 1992, (the first British cycling gold since 1920), World Champion 1994 and 1996, bronze 1993. Britain took Olympic team pursuit bronze, 1972 and 1976 with a team including a Chicken-sponsored rider, Mick Bennett, who then became a noted road racer as did Doyle after and Porter before him. Boardman *did* go on to ride in the continental peloton but, by his own admission, it wasn't a very happy time and his career was, latterly, dogged by a debilitating weakness in his bones which forced his retirement.

The irony is that whereas in athletics it is the short-distance champions who are best remembered – 100 to 1.500 metres – and the long-distance performers who win far less kudos. Cycling, uniquely, honours the endurance riders, the winners of the big tours, the road racers. Track racers, however outstanding they are in the brief blaze of their zenith, soon fade in memory. I do not crow. This is fact. Unjust, perhaps.

In the past, continental riders often rode the pursuit in addition to road racing. Fausto Coppi, gold 1949 (the year of his first victory in the Tour de France); Roger Rivière, gold 1957–59, his Tour career tragically ended in a near-fatal fall into a ravine, 1960; Rudi Altig, gold 1960 and 1961, World road race champion 1966, winner of the Vuelta 1962, wearer of the Tour de France yellow jersey and stalwart lieutenant of Jacques Anquetil; Roy Schuiten, Dutch champion and Raleigh team man, gold in 1974 and '75; Francesco Moser, gold in 1976, to which in 1977 he added the road race rainbow jersey he'd missed out on in '76, Paris–Roubaix 1978–80 and Giro victory, '84; Alain Bondue, gold 1981 and '82 . . . all outstanding road racers. Of course, trends change. However, the natural talent of British track riders deserves a wider nurture as the stimulus to a broader ambition. Demands beyond the wooden boards need to be made, calls to perform on another stage. Perhaps this is happening.

At the age of 14, Mick Bennett had both legs encased in plaster. He was a victim of Osgood-Schlatter diesase, named after the two physicians who identified it in 1903, a year famous in the history of cycling. The disease typically afflicts boys (and latterly more and more girls) between the ages of 10 and 15 who are both physically active and undergoing a growth spurt. Symptoms are extreme soreness and swelling round the upper part of the shinbone to which the kneecap tendon is attached and the complaint is probably caused by the strain of the powerful thigh muscles pulling on that attachment. In the past, treatment was, classically, RICE – rest, ice, compression, elevation.

When Bennett's plaster came off, the physiotherapist in Selly Oak hospital, in south-west Birmingham, recommended a course of rehabilitation on an exercise bike.

Bennett set to. On the wall in front of him hung a board on which had been chalked a number of records set by patients – times and distances. Bennett obliterated them. A passion was born. A neighbour in Sparkhill, nearer the city centre, where he lived, gave him an old BSA bike and he was launched. Two streets away lived Graham Webb, an international rider and Bennett got used to seeing him on the bike in his Great Britain tracksuit as he charged round the tarmac. One day he plucked up courage to go up and ask if he was in a club. He was, the Solihull. Bennett mosied round, parked his embarrassing cranky roadster some way off and walked into the clubhouse *and* the beginning of his life as one of this country's finest racing cyclists.

It was Tommy Goodwin, owner of the local lightweight shop, who introduced him to track racing. Bennett spent hours at the shop, gawping at the bikes, the components – the familiar open sesame – and, when he finally met Goodwin, the guru behind all this technical and aesthetic wizardy, the older man spotted a burgeoning talent and suggested he consider training as a team pursuiter.

The UK, as I have already said, has produced a number of outstanding individual pursuiters, but the discipline is very different from that of the team event. The superlative physical requirements are the same – a high percentage of medium to fast twitch muscles, formidable endurance, cultured speed – but racing in a team of four ups the ante technically. To begin with, there is attuning to riding a fixed wheel. Bennett came a cropper a few times, forgetting that you can't coast on a fixed wheel: the cranks snap your legs on, on, and the momentary loss of poise can be disastrous. In addition to the basics of individual riding, the team pursuit, where each of the four riders takes four turns at the front in the course of the 4km race, demands courage, balance, bike-handling skill, spilt-second timing. There is no margin of error. The lead man has to finish his turn at flat-out speed so that when he pulls off, the man behind him is also riding flat out, just below the aerobic-anaerobic threshold. The rider pulling off goes up the banking and, as the threesome pass, wheel to wheel, he glances left, spots the bottom bracket of the rear man and drops down the banking to take his wheel at a gap of no more than an inch. It is hair-raising even to contemplate; to watch, quite simply thrilling, a balletic grace of movement as the four riders metamorphose briefly into trio and lone satellite in a sudden elliptical curve away from the line and then rejoin to make four again. Each man rides within a very small perspective of vision; the concentration is total; the absorption of the four in their single unit of speed and motion has to be nerveless, the level of mutual trust high indeed; the physical strain of 4km at close to bursting point extreme. As well as the most dedicated attitude to physical conditioning, it takes practice, practice and more practice.

First essays on the track were pretty terrifying. The big 333m velodrome at Leicester, with sharp 42° banking at the bends, was an intimidating arena. Since the start line is halfway down the home straight, a team has to hit top speed very quickly so as to negotiate both the bend and the increased centrifugal force and turbulence at play in the tightest arc of the track. Since the optimum position on the bike, for speed, is upright, there is a danger that if the team doesn't go into the bend quickly enough to get round it in as few pedal strokes as possible, the right pedal may hit the steeply raked boards of the track.

But Bennett and his regular teammates Ian Hallam and Willy Moore gelled and with Ron Keeble making the four they were picked for the Munich Olympics. If cycling is less of a Cinderella sport in the UK nowadays, 40-odd years ago in 1972 it was decidedly on the outside looking in. Bennett bought his bike, tyres, clothing to go to the Games, but what a feeling, aged 21, to graduate from the back streets of Sparkhill to the Olympic velodrome. Through the early stages of the competition, the GB team got faster and faster and suddenly, it was the final. They were riding for Olympic gold on the outdoor wooden track. It seemed unimaginable but there they were. They'd all but lived in each others' pockets for so long, living together, training together, the bonds of reliance and belief were complete and . . . they were on a roll. But, they came away with bronze. Moore punctured – too much pressure in the tyre. They had gone past the point before which a rerun would have been permissible.

Two years later at the Worlds Track Championships in San Sebastian in Spain, they were riding the West German team down in the final. Reduced to three – Rick

Evans had wilted and dropped out – they were heading for gold. The bell rang for the last lap. GB in the lead. A track official, charged with placing the line of sponges on the inside of the track to ensure that no riders clipped a corner, glanced up at the clock, took his eye off his duty, strayed into the path of the approaching Germans, a rider collided with him and the whole team went down. Seconds later, Bennett, Hallam and Moore crossed the line, World Champions. Except that their officials declared they could not take victory under such circumstances. Unfair. Should they claim gold, the Germans would surely appeal. Then we can counter-appeal, said Bennett, but he was overruled.

'They all regret it now,' he told me 'and at the Worlds in 2000, the German team gave us all token gold medals and we were voted Sports Personalities on their television network for outstanding fair play.' He paused. 'I'd rather have had a rainbow jersey.'

The transition to road racing was smooth. Part of the training had always been on the road, anyway, for stamina and strength – The Milk Race, events in Holland and so on. The team crashed at its last event in the 1976 Montreal Olympics, some vital cohesion was lost and the men – Bennett, Hallam with Croker and Ian Banbury – went their separate ways. The problem had always been finding a fourth man, the team necessarily being only as strong as its weakest element. Bennett had spent six years as a team pursuiter and signed as a pro in 1977 for the Carlton-Weinmann team, co-sponsored by Bob Chicken. He won the national sprint championship in his first year. 'When did you learn to sprint?' I asked. 'I didn't' he said, and laughed.

A combination of the pursuit speed and, probably, what had become an instinctive reading of speed was sufficient. He speaks highly of Bob, as do all the riders associated with him: an absolute gentleman and supportive even when the team was not doing so well. He never carped or sulked, care of the riders was uppermost, belief and confidence in them unwavering.

Bennett retired after nine years as a pro road racer, took nine wins one year and still evinces the collected inner strength of mind, spirit and unshakeable self-belief together with the accompanying modesty about their achievements that characterise the men who have raced at the zenith of cycle sport. It's only a bike, after all, they seem to say. Sure, we were good, but no call to live in the past. It's a salutary lesson. I know of an Australian who was nearly picked for the Melbourne Olympics but just missed selection, and that has *almost*? been the compelling raison d'être of his entire life.

Mick Bennett is now Race Director of the professional Tour of Britain. The first edition, in September 2004, having very nearly nose-dived on its opening stage, finished triumphantly on a circuit taking in Whitehall and the Embankment. (Its predecessor, the Prutour, ended in 1999 after but two editions.) As Bradley Wiggins put it to the assembled press the day before the race started: 'I've been World Champion in the pursuit, I've won gold at the Olympics. There's nothing left for me to do on the track.'

The following day: disaster. The organisers had put the race together in very quick order (in three months with a full-time staff of only three) but the problems with traffic on the first stage were appalling and parlous – tailbacks of cars on the left-hand side of the road at traffic lights, car drivers not stopping to keep out of the way at major junctions, poor volunteer marshalling, a general lack of liaison and cooperation. Many riders were on the verge of pulling out. But the costs of official custody are astronomical: a police motorbike marshall must be paid £51 per hour plus mileage and living expenses. Thus the budget for safety on the five-day race was £ ¼ million, the same as for the 8-day Prutour five years earlier.

However mistakes make for overhaul and, by the end of the five days, the race was running very smoothly. Mick Bennett, the race director, acknowledged the need to improve public awareness and to design the route to avoid major areas of congestion. They will also need to secure better understanding from local and highway authorities. So much has been lost, in terms of expertise and experience, in the years since the regular running of road races, stage and one-day, in the UK. However, the will to succeed is there. 'We need the help of cyclists,' Bennett said, 'to help marshall, steward and do voluntary jobs.[As is de rigeur in France, for instance.] It's a call to action.'

Optimism is abroad, but I write this on a day (7 February 2005) when the President of the Bicycle Association, Philip Darnton, speaking to *The Independent*, compares the £21 million earmarked by the Department for Culture, Media and Sport to train forty-four elite cyclists for the Olympics to the lack of any 'overall strategic commitment' to cycling at ministerial level. The UK government spends a mere £1 per person per year on cycling, compared to £5 in Denmark. The Industry Secretary, Alistair Darling, admits he is no cyclist – he described it as 'hard work' – but he inherited a commitment to quadruple the number of cyclists (*active* cyclists?) by 2010. This was ditched in 2004 when figures showed that a miserable 13 per cent of people cycled once a week and 60 per cent never ride at all. As Darnton says, the encouragement of cycling needs an integral policy, pulling in a diverse number of concerns – health, education, sport, transport, local and national authorities – not some vague target for statistical analysis.

BMX . . . MTB . . . NEAR K.O.

By the early 80s, Chicken and Sons were working on around a three months lead-time between placing orders and delivery. By now, their reputation for sound judgement and fair dealing was such that they could sell on their name alone. Knowing all their wholesalers very well, they could phone, say they had a new line – of saddles, maybe, latest design from Sella – and take an order for 500, sight unseen. But, the smooth tarmac under their wheels was about to run out and merge with rough, unsurfaced uphill terrain.

First came the BMX.

Invented as a marketing ploy in California but made entirely, frames and componentry in China and Taiwan with whom the USA maintained trade agreements, the BMX – bicycle motor cross – hit the home market very hard because it was completely incompatible with everything sold in Europe. Different sized wheels and tyres, high cowbars, no freewheel, small frame, the BMX was veritably a cuckoo in the European nest. (A new generation of BMX bikes has tempted older riders as well as young.) Simplex did attempt to join the market, making and supplying plastic BMX wheels, but when an articulated lorry-load of them arrived at Raleigh they were all unusable. Sella Italia swung into action, too, and hurriedly produced a line of knee and elbow pads, but by the time their stuff hit the shelves it was passé, the ephemeral colour fad having already changed. Weinmann started assembling stirrups and other bits which would adapt to the BMX and then tried to sell them at Weinmann prices.

Racing bikes only ever commanded about 10 per cent of the US market but this fun bike was an instant hit, a wholly different concept in bike-riding, and the American bike shops couldn't sell enough. There was hidden as well as manifest damage to the European cycle industry in this. During the boom times, European suppliers had tended to cash in by hiking, even doubling, their prices for the USA, treating it as a soft market. Now the New World found itself in a position of strength and began to flex its muscles: the apparent softie wasn't going to be taken for any more rides.

The appeal of the BMX was as a plaything more than a bike. The frame is strengthened, has a low centre of gravity and the gearing allows for considerable bursts of speed. Kids in helmets rode it round specially constructed dirt tracks or performed a series of gymnastic tricks on the smooth pavements of pedestrian precincts, pirouetting, wheelies, jumps and all manner of swoops and turns. David Millar says that his BMX riding taught him bike handling at an early age, long before he ever mounted a conventional bicycle.

The craze was at a peak for about five years and commanded about 70 per cent of the market but petered out, largely because when kids grew out of their BMXs there was nothing to progress to. The conventional bike looked so *odd*, so *different* from the kickaround machine they'd got used to and the skill and balance required for hopping pavements did not translate directly to the prosaic business of tootling along a flat bit of side street.

Then, close on the BMX's stubby tyres, came the MTB, mountain bike, also from America and, it seems, originally conceived as a handy vehicle for cross-country portage of illegal drugs from remote locations in the hills above San Francisco back down into the city by hippy bike bums who had dropped out and tuned into a more relaxed life style.[25] Alternatively, albeit less colourfully when the California state authority banned downhill racing on motor-cross machines, the downhill fraternity took to utility cycles instead. They cobbled together robust bikes from discarded bits and pieces liberated from garages, skips and back yards. The favoured frame was the sturdy Schwinn, standard for the high school kids who cycled the suburbs delivering papers in the 1950s. These downhill machines were known as 'clunkers', American slang for a dilapidated, worn-out car, bus or other machine, and also applied to early touring cars. They had to be tough to withstand the legendary 'repack run' down the slopes of Mount Tamalpais, in Marin County north across the Golden Gate from San Francisco. This entailed a precipitous drop of 1,300 feet in less than 2½ miles and the overworking of the disc brakes was so fierce that, by the bottom, the grease packing in them had been dried to vapour and needed repacking with fresh. Hence the name of the ride. The bikes had to be carried back up the climb by trailer, so too, for a time, the 'clunkers'. However, as the utility bike became lighter and more refined, riders began to be able to make the steep uphill journeys under their own power. The mountain bike, distant heir to the bikes made by Colnago for the Italian mountaineer infantry in the First World War, had arrived and was sold in the States on the nostalgia kick: here was the machine on which the adult could relive the carefree devilry of youth. The riders who, as kids, had belted round the soft-floored forest trails at breakneck speed incurious of harm on their all-purpose bikes, could do the same in their maturity on a machine custom built for off-road country. A 1992 advertisement for the Specialized Stumpjumper shows a mature man framed in an open doorway, standing on the welcome mat. He, like the bike, slung over his right shoulder, is caked in mud. The caption reads: 'The last time you came

---

[25] Incidentally, 'hippy' is said to derive from the posture adopted by smokers in opium dens, lying on their side, propped up on their hip and elbow.

home like this you got spanked. The Specialized Stumpjumper is not only the world's most popular mountain bike, it's the world's best excuse for acting like a kid again.'

The Stumpjumper first appeared in 1979, resulting from a collaboration between a couple of clunker men and an established frame builder. In 1981, Specialized took over the idea and had it mass-produced in Japan, whence it arrived in the 1982 trade shows.

Once again, the conventional market suffered badly. No manufacturers in Europe had any MTB equipment, no knobbly fat tyres, cantilever brakes, extreme ratio gearing to cope with steep gradients on rough terrain, no chunky tubing to construct a frame which could absorb unwonted shock. As MTB swept the board, demand for conventional components all but dried up too and the dearth hit firms like Weinmann and Campagnolo very hard. Weinmann lasted for a while but closed for business in 1988 and Campagnolo very nearly went under.

Chicken and Sons were taking a bad pummelling from the BMX and MTB too. At one time, every kid would chose a racing bike because that's what the grown-ups rode to work, but the MTB scored over hard saddle, drop handlebars (bad in traffic) head down, bum in air, and the considerably less comfortable ride. Between '87 and '90 the MTB took over as the preferred transport to the place of work.

Before the Cologne Bicycle Show in 1990 Robert prepared a full dossier of their state of business, an analysis of demand related to supply, a brief for discussion of ways and means with Weinmann and arrived with it on the Weinmann stand. Before he had even opened his briefcase, Hans Rahm, the Weinmann finance man, said: 'We know the pound has been taking a battering for some time so we intend to give you a retrospective currency rebate for the last six months – you'll get a credit note tomorrow.' He had summarily pre-empted and boiled down everything that Robert was preparing to ask for. It was the most astonishing display of loyalty, of commercial trust and confidence raised to an essentially personal level. Generally in commerce the first loyalty is to profit, the overriding imperative being what happens tomorrow, no matter with whom you dealt yesterday – the past is dead wood, forget it, you owe it nothing.

Another commercial trend in the 80s hit the bicycle industry hard, the advent of national express carriers like ANC and TNT who offered 24-hour delivery and undercut the old ranks of local wholesalers. One by one these fell away and direct wholesale, of the sort that Bob and then Chicken and Sons had practised all along, became the norm. In the past, a wholesaler had to be bona fide and recognised, this being the only protection afforded to the buyer when the admonition *caveat emptor* had particular potency.

As the competition got even tighter, Cedric and Robert went over to the Ofmega factory in Italy to ask them to adapt their standard cranks to fit a mountain bike. They went off for lunch and, when they came back later, there were samples ready for them to show. Alas, it then took months for delivery on orders and the chance was lost. (Ofmega, a friendly family concern, went under in 2004.) Yvonne Rix, Raleigh's production manager who was also responsible for design and pricing visited the USA and the Far East in 1981 to appraise the new product and foresaw that it would not be long before the bike made for off-road was riding on the road. The Raleigh Board was not impressed and waved her prediction aside. 'England has very few mountains.'

Rix was not one to be fobbed off. 'You don't need a 4x4 to drive round London, either, but there are plenty of Range Rovers in Chelsea.'

While the Europeans were reeling, Shimano embraced the new market with alacrity and invested in what it foresaw as an important and lasting development in the bicycle industry, unlike the ephemeral BMX and Chopper, gimmicks which soon yielded to more sophisticated taste. Campagnolo did, finally, bring out a Bullet groupset to challenge the Shimano MTB components but it didn't work properly and merely worsened their plight. Poor Tullio. Perhaps the traditionalist Campagnolo heart wasn't in this offence to ingrained criteria of purity and style. Compounding the problem: whereas Shimano's supply system was formidably efficient, Campagnolo had always been rather hit and miss on delivery, one of the main reasons why the Chickens did not deal with them for a long time, aside from their connexion with Weinmann. However, other sources soon sprang up. In 1987, the SRAM corporation was established in Chicago and began marketing its Gripshift, a twist shifter on the end of the handlebars.

The genesis of SRAM (an acronym from its founders' names) is an illuminating case study in the way the leading marques of the old world fell to the rising entrepreneurs of the new. The German Ernst Sachs, born in 1867, had to give up racing when he crashed and suffered a multiple fracture in his left leg. On 1 August 1895, he founded a company manufacturing ball bearings and bike hubs in partnership with a friend, Karl Fichtel, and Fichtel-Sachs became one of Germany's leading producers of bicycle components. In 1980, the company bought the French manufacturer of derailleurs and speedometers, Huret, and reemerged in 1985 as Sachs-Huret Incorporated for the sale of components in the USA. After the purchase of Huret, the Fichtel-Sachs end in Germany acquired Maillard, represented in the UK by RJC. Sedis had already been subsumed in the Fichtel-Sachs conglomerate so two of the major RJC agencies had been compromised. Because Huret was the leading brand in the amalgam of companies, it was more or less inevitable that the Huret UK representative, Leonard Newman, the former managing director of Halford's, would be asked to take over the agency for the entire combine, whether he was the right man for the job or not.

The two Huret brothers came to see the Chickens in company with Philippe Maillard, to discuss what was, in fact, a foregone conclusion, viz. that RJC were going to lose both Maillard and Sedis. This stuck in Bob's craw. He remonstrated: RJC had been with Sedis and Maillard for a long time and if either company had a name in the UK it was thanks to RJC. Dumping RJC might seem expedient but that's all it was, an unconsidered folly which offended the basic premise of loyalty to which RJC had always adhered. They deserved better than to be discarded for what was little more pressing than administrative detail . . . or words to that effect. Sachs proposed that RJC come to the company headquarters in Schweinfurt. So all the Sachs top brass on one side of the table faced Bob, Cedric and Robert Chicken on the other. Sachs reversed the decision and RJC took on Sachs as sole agents in the UK. There was an unseemly condition: they were required to take over all Newman's Huret stock, including a huge accumulation of out-of-date items, speedometers and the like, for a sum of £87,000. If that's what it took to land the agency, they decided, they would pay. Newman wanted proforma payment, i.e. the full sum in advance of delivery. Robert told him bluntly that they'd pay in instalments – RJC didn't want the redundant clutter anyway so that's the best they could and would do.

Now Sachs started a fight with Shimano: they introduced no fewer than thirteen different group sets with defiant names – Rival, Success etc – none of which came close to the Shimano quality. Nevertheless, Sachs carted massive consignments to the Bisley works, plagued RJC for targets on sales, and then strangled the entire operation by adding handlebars and stems made by an Italian company whom they had bought out. RJC already supplied handlebars and stems from the 3T company, also in Italy. Sachs told RJC to drop 3T. RJC replied laconically: 'Bollocks'. Not as significant as Marshall Ney's 'Merde' at Waterloo nor yet General McAuliffe's 'Nuts' during the Battle of the Bulge, but adequate for purpose. There had been, alas, no inkling that Sachs would turn out to be trouble but it is apparent that Sachs had taken on the MTB war much too hastily, whereas Shimano had been developing their range for some time with the full weight of their design and engineering expertise. Sachs also relied, insouciantly, on being able to maintain their share of the French market as a bolster for their more precarious undertakings.

In late 1988, Weinmann, for a long time ailing, went under. The company had produced some MTB brakes but tried vainly (unrealistically) to sell them at top-range Weinmann prices. At the same time, Otto senior had been ploughing money into clasps for doing up ski boots to counter the losses on bicycle components and with some success. He adapted the v-shaped straddle wire used in centre-pull brakes. However, when he branched out into the manufacture of the boots themselves, he instantly became a competitor to the boot manufacturers he'd been supplying with fasteners. This had disastrous consequences.

When Weinmann folded, RJC found themselves in even worse trouble. The Sachs connexion was an increasingly onerous liabity. The big conglomerate was still hopelessly disorganised. MTB riders needed helmets: RJC had no helmets. They wanted trip? computers: RJC had some from Sachs but they were inferior. Neither Maillard or Sedis were supplying for MTBs. The German manufacturer of pumps, SKS, for whom RJC acted did not make pumps for MTBs but complained to RJC, their sole agent, that they were not selling enough. Another RJC agency, for ESGE, makers of mudguards and carriers, failed. At around the same time, the Vredestein company was also taking a dive, the quality of their tyres simply not up to snuff, their technology unrefined. And whereas sales of racing and conventional bikes held up in France and the Netherlands for example, between 85 and 90 per cent of the UK market was commandeered by MTBs. The Chicken company needed contingency plans and soon. Robert proposed renting out their commodious warehouse space to third parties and asked his haulier friend Robson for contacts. He and Cedric then bought a number of vehicles – articulated lorries and trailers – to supplement the transport venture. On the point of landing a couple of substantial accounts, they were hit by the recession and had to sell off the recently acquired assets for next to nothing.

On Black Thursday in 1992, Alain Boiret, the export manager, arrived in Bisley from Normandy and dismissed RJC as sole agents for Sachs in the UK. They had decided to work direct with distributors, of which Chicken would be one.

It was a bad day.

The bank was unsympathetic, told them to get into the mass market and ship container loads of merchandise in from the Far East.

This was nonsense. Direct selling via a field sales force was costly and thorny, particularly when they were trying to purvey componentry for an increasingly rare machine, yet somehow they held on and in 1995 matched the '94 turnover. This was a great fillip, but the decision to downsize was unavoidable. Regional wholesalers like the local dealers before them were tumbling one by one, leaving no legacy but bad debts and RJC were swamped with unsaleable stock. As Robert put it they annihilated the rubbish

– sold it at daft prices – and moved back into the original building at Bisley. It was a post-boom recommencement, the reshaping of RJC, the closure of the Penguin and Fishbowl. But, the leaner operation grew steadily and survived and by 1998 the overdraft was cleared.

SRAM of Chicago had taken over as sole owners of Sachs Bicycle Components the year before at what might be called a devouring moment in the cycle industry, quite as climactic as the swallowing up of Raleigh by Derby International. Shortly afterwards, SRAM dismissed RJC as distributors. It was just as well. They had done not much more than mark time for a year or so, entangled with people whom they neither respected nor could deal with. Instead, they returned to their heartland, their European roots and took over the agency for Mavic rim-manufacturers. (Hitherto, dealing with Alesa of Belgium, makers of alloy rims, disqualified them from taking on the French firm.) In Mavic they found a concern entirely compatible with their own ethos: a high quality of manufacture and service, knowledgeable staff and prices commensurate with their own sense of what the high end of the market should demand.

As ever, the secret is the people. Robert spoke with affection of a visit to the small TA company at its works in remote countryside south of the Somme. *Spécialités Transmission Avant* was founded in 1947 by Georges Navet. Fausto Coppi, Louison Bobet and Charly Gaul each won the Tour de France on bikes fitted with the aluminium TA chainwheels and crank sets invented and shaped by Navet. The firm is still very much a family outfit, Navet's spirit pervading them in the harsh modern commercial climate, reminiscent of Portia's comment in *The Merchant of Venice*: 'How far that little candle throws his beams. / So shines a good deed in a naughty world' where 'naughty' has its original more potent sense of 'bad, wicked, blameworthy'. As the Chicken men say of the cycle industry, it is a business where the bad boys stick out like pantomime burglars.

TA is also the last surviving manufacturer of seat pins in Europe and typifies the traditional approach. As the head of the firm told Robert Chicken, 'We've got fine computerised machines, everything of the best that's available, but we're not really commercial, we're artisans.' Such computerised machines will take a solid cube of aluminium and extrude a spider, the cassette block which is the quintessence of the modern freewheel, almost a magical process, a triumph of the sort of wonderment that has always attached to the best engineering: to produce an article of precise usefulness that is also aesthetically pleasing, a thing of beauty. It's still being done for the bicycle in Europe, across the Channel from the UK. In the UK? Ah…

Campagnolo had been the first manufacturer to produce a groupset, an integrated assembly of chainset, gear, freewheel, brakes and headset. Shimano seized on the ploy and marketed their groupsets so aggressively that they all but took over the market. Buying all the bits as a set kept the overall price down; it is also a good branding ploy – bikes could be categorised as such and such a frame with the Shimano Dura-Ace groupset for example, at a time when top riders of the peloton were choosing Shimano Dura Ace. (Shimano had entered sponsorship of professional racing with Flandria in 1973). Makers of individual components simply could not compete with the ruthless Japanese ethos of squeezing and then forcing out competition.

Shimano, still very much controlled by family members, was founded in 1921 as a manufacturer of freewheels. It later expanded to produce other components and, in 1970, began to make fishing equipment for another booming market. The Shimano fishing-reel technology led directly to the introduction of its index gear system for bicycles, which hit the shops in 1987. Hitherto, changing gear by a friction shift was a matter of feel: tightening or slackening the tensioned gear cable pulled the derailleur cage in or out taking the chain up or down the freewheel cogs, but the lever had no inbuilt check. Most experienced riders could judge from long practice how far to pull or push the lever and generally made the shift neatly enough, but the rattle of a badly shifted chain, dancing homeless across the teeth of the freewheel block that signified a fluffed change in the tension of a close race, might well alert rivals to attack on the instant, enabling them to gain a few yards before the recalcitrant chain was properly settled onto the cogs. The Shimano Index System (SIS) worked on a preset spacing in the change mechanism. One click of the gear lever shifted the chain from one sprocket to its neighbour with precision, every time. Undoubtedly, the Shimano application of expertise and its investment in research and development not only advanced bicycle technology to the great benefit of the whole cycling world – from leisure riders to professional racers – it also woke the older establishment, some of it pretty moribund, to the desperate need to compete or die. A similar case, indeed, to that of the impact of New World wines on European *viticulteurs*, especially the French. The sniffy old guard attitude lingers. A French wine grower, pressed by an enthusiastic Aussie to taste a beaut of a wine, mate, reluctantly swirled the buttery white round the bowl of the glass, dipped his proboscis to draw in the bouquet, took a mouthful, slooshed it round his palate, 'chewed' the liquid, that is sluiced it through his teeth, swallowed, raised his eyebrows and, evincing that glum morgue particular to the man who knows when the earth speaks in a vintage and, decidedly, when it does not, pronounced flatly: '*Oui, c'est un chardonnay Australien.*' But, as California, Australia, New Zealand, Chile, and Argentina despatched their wines to an ever more enthusiastic public in the Old World, parts of the French wine industry, so long dominant, finally recognised that it had a real fight on and it has responded with energy, to its credit and our relish of what their growers produce.

The Shimano approach evokes that of Campagnolo in the early days: to refine componentry to the benefit of cyclists, thus building loyalty. The commercial motive is sound. Loyalty improves sales; improved sales keep prices down. However, Shimano have repaid loyalty with what many see as reptilian manipulation. They are accused of not producing samples in advance of a launch; of refusing to supply dealers with individual components, insisting that they take complete groupsets and offering discounts only on large bulk orders. And they fasten on customers through a deliberate policy of making even one item of Shimano incompatible with another. In the mid-90s, they introduced Shimano Total Integration which linked together gear shifting, braking and transmission. Thus, when one part wore out, the whole lot would have to be replaced. Other brand chains would not fit, for example, and you would have no option but to stick with Shimano, with the new and improved Shimano, because the latest gear, even though only minutely different from its predecessor, will not fit on the old cassette – the whole assembly must be changed.

European manufacturers, by and large, have dealt on more firmly settled principles of mutual loyalty. For example, TA of France (whom RJC have represented for a number of years) invented the cotterless alloy crank and have only just withdrawn replacement left and right cranks with matching chain rings as spares after thirty-five years of supplying these necessary bits rather than the whole package, take it or leave it.

Campagnolo gradually woke to the fact that it had to smarten up its marketing and delivery act or else go under. There has never been any quarrel with the Campagnolo ethic which is for superior systems of design and manufacture regardless of time, forget the fast buck, quality above all. A watchman at the main Campagnolo plant in Vicenza said of Il Maestro. 'He's an incredible person. We work not for the company but for that man. Until a component is right for the Commendatore, it won't carry the name of Campagnolo.' It meant that innovation was slow to emerge but, when it did, the quality was assured.[26] Once the works in Vicenza added a solid, dependable service to the quintessential Campagnolo genius, they began, once more, to command a reputable share of the market including, since 2002, via Chicken and Sons.

---

[26] Shimano has even been accused of cynically floating inferior parts onto the market so that when the genuine improvement arrived, they could lay claim to exceptional technological advance.

CHAPTER ELEVEN
DEATH BY A THOUSAND CUTS...
HAND-BUILDER HEROES

Philip Darnton joined Raleigh as Managing Director in January 2000, having been head-hunted from Reckitt and Colman. Raleigh was in serious decline, its business decaying. Some two years earlier, a couple of venture capitalists based in Washington DC had bought the ailing giant from the previous owners, Derby International and its chairman Alan Finden-Crofts, for the whimsical reason that they loved bikes and happened to have a lot of money to throw around. The Raleigh brand still enjoyed that much allure, that much cachet. However, in taking over the company en bloc, namely Raleigh UK, USA, Netherlands, and Raleigh distributors in Scandinavia, Denmark and throughout the old Commonwealth – India, South Africa and Australia – they paid a wildly inflated price. It was more a case of throwing money away than around. That said, Finden-Crofts is a formidable negotiator and he was in possession, at the time, of what appeared to be an attractive outfit to sell: between 1980–95/6, Raleigh, like the whole UK cycling industry had enjoyed a hugely profitable period, thanks to the sudden craze for BMX followed by Mountain Bikes, followed in time by a renewed interest in road bikes. When diversity offered, diversity, as ever, sold. After a long period of slump, bikes were making money again, lots of money. This had always tended to be the pattern: innovation kicking a sluggish market back to vibrant life. What is more, Finden-Crofts' recent track record in stimulating growth persuaded the Americans that, quite against the odds, the Raleigh of old had been revived and was, once again, bursting with vigour. The purchasers called in a chief executive to control the entire organisation from a base in America and, confusingly, called themselves Derby, apparently from the American slang 'darb' for 'any remarkable or excellent thing'.

In August 2000 Gary Matthews, just over 40, a graduate of the Harvard Business School, (BUITW . . . 'Best university in the world' say Harvard men) and had won an egregious reputation in the commercial world of fast-moving consumer goods, that is items which disappear quickly from the shelves into homes and are in constant need of replacement – soap, toothpaste, food, drink and so on. His entire experience was in this field, with, successively, Proctor and Gamble, Coca Cola, Guinness USA and Guinness UK. Full of zip, energy and drive, he arrived at a newly designated HQ in Greenwich Massachussetts as world head of Raleigh. Here he gathered a team of highly paid executives with whom he had worked previously, men who could apply his fast-moving sales methods to the shifting of another commodity: bicycles. A very smart individual who had never yet come unstuck in the very limited field he knew so well, Matthews nonetheless made no adjustments to this new field he knew not at all. He did not revaluate his well-tried business practices in consumer non-durables vis à vis a very different sort of merchandise. Instead, he applied the same methods he had always relied on, namely the Proctor and Gamble model. Herein lay a fundamental anomaly.

For example: when a consumer buys somewhere between ten and twenty packets of Brand X soap powder, say, in a year, as well as other rapidly-used Brand X items, the Brand X company can – indeed must – spend a lot of money on advertising to secure customer loyalty. When the unit price is low, room can be made in the overall budget to allow for hard-sell promotion. 'Brand X customers know they are safe with Brand X whatever they buy.'

This does not apply to the sale of bicycles.

Most individuals, serious cyclists apart, will own perhaps no more than five bikes in their life-time, at least two of them purchased by someone else, probably grandparents or parents as the child grows up. Kiddies trike . . . first grown-up machine at secondary school age. Indeed, one of the bikes may well be second hand, passed on by an elder brother, sister, cousin who has grown out of the machine and moved on. Loyalty to a brand is, therefore, only ever intermittent, certainly not amenable to high-powered, fast-sell, short-lived advertising campaigns.

Matthews and his thoroughbred team working from a de luxe central office already burdened with extremely high overheads, (itself very dangerous in the bicycle industry as the decline of the vastly overweight Raleigh had proved) applied the Proctor and Gamble speed-up methods of selling soap to the sale of bicycles. The rationale was that, just as manufacturers of toothpaste and washing powder could simplify their branding in a drive to command a niche in a global market, focussing the basic appeal of the product by using the same, easily identifiable and distinctive packaging in every retail outlet, worldwide – one brand everywhere – the same could be done for bikes. This was a serious mistake. The same error had hurt Raleigh badly after a number of great world-famous brand names – Hercules, BSA, Rudge-Whitworth and others – were subsumed and lost (jettisoned) in the merger with Tube Investments in 1960. Thus, instead of maintaining the Raleigh sweep of factories with *different* brands – in itself a stimulus to innovation – Matthews decided that there should be: first, one single factory producing bikes for all Europe, a sole source with a pared down range and second, a take-it-or-leave it formula for dealing with customers on the lines of 'You want soap? We've got soap. You want bikes? We've got bikes.' Compounding the misjudgement, he insisted that from now on the entire business should be run as an interlocked team with one overarching style of marketing and image. The various members of the team – in Germany, France, UK, the Netherlands – should each collaborate as key elements in the production and sale of a single homogenised Raleigh product under a single brand name.

However, unlike tubes of toothpaste, bikes do not conform to the principles governing rapid turnover onto and off supermarket shelves. Once bought, a bicycle generally refuses to decay, deplete, wear out, wear down or get squeezed dry. It needs replacement bits to be sure, but the basic entity needs to be sound and durable, or it will not sell in the first place. Expensive advertising, therefore, is not cost-effective. Customers are influenced at a more intimate, personal level, by dealers who know the bikes well, by friends who vouch for this bike or that bike, by the fact that famous riders ride a particular marque. Besides, whereas everyone needs soap, not everyone needs a bicycle and the majority of the populace with money to spend are simply *not* interested in bicycles, despite the fact that a reader poll in *The Times*, December 2004, voted the bicycle 'the nation's favourite invention over the last 250 years' ahead of the computer, electricity (a discovery not an invention) and vaccination. This poll may be a blip, answered mendaciously by people who accede to sentimental fancy and nostalgic whooze, equating a bicycle with lazy hazy days of summer in their youth. The fact is that, many people still regard riding a bike as a proof of indigence and mild eccentricity if not radical stupidity, something you do only if there is no more comfortable alternative.

One simplified, stock-model bicycle for Europe? The world? This was mad. Matthews was attacking the bicycle market, as it were, like WWII strategists in bunkers ordering down blanket B42 bombing on remote targets. At that period, a French *vélo* stood out against an Italian *bicicletta* or a German *Fahrrad*. No one knew what a Spanish *bicicleta* looked like because Franco had shut the borders. And, consider the famous Dutch *fiets*: deep frame, sit-up-and-beg handlebars, ample saddle, wrap-around mudguards, chainguard and oil sump protector to keep skirts out of the back wheel spokes, padlock incorporated in the assembly . . . this is a utility machine, in daily use for essential transport, a highly popular substitute for the car in a country which caters routinely and with sedulous care for cyclists. Cycle paths everywhere. Paradise. As such, the Dutch bike is expensive, designed for a solid, comfortable ride *and* built to last. It sells well enough in Paris and a few other European cities with a cycling culture and undemanding gradients; but in Britain? It would have a curiosity value only. Besides, it would be altogether uncool, too reminiscent of the antiquated Raleigh roadster, evocative of dyed-in-the-wool bike retro. The concept of a unified range of bikes across Europe was laughable, wrong-headed and quite out of touch with the realities of the fluctuating bicycle market.

Moreover, the team culture that thrived in the inner circle of Matthews's highly paid executives at the hub was very difficult to inculcate at the further reaches of the company. Under Finden-Crofts, each manager was expected, indeed required, to be responsible for his own province and had answered to more flexible regulation, taking into account local differences and attendant demands. There had been no culture of interdependence: managers did their job and were answerable to Finden-Crofts not the network of other managers whom they rarely saw and with whom they had nothing to do in business terms and, often, in terms of what they were selling, little in common. But suddenly, these managers and retailers, identifiable, distinguishable individuals upon whom a customer could rely for direct concern with their particular wants, were being made to shrink inside a corporate identity, to become faceless and anonymous – both utterly inimical to the one-to-one exchange which is characteristic of the bike trade, whether serving highly-motivated clubmen or casual pleasure-riders.

There were further woes.

Since the late 70s, a number of European bicycle companies had begun to import low-cost, finished bicycles in boxes, first from Taiwan and then from China, because they simply could not compete on price. The capacity to sell at unrealistic low prices is generally linked to heavy subsidies: special allowances on energy consumption, for instance, bestowed by governments anxious to promote the growth of their home-based industry in competition with rivals overseas. This is unfair trading. Removing essential costs from the price of a finished item places market competitors who have to build those costs into their finished price, at a considerable, often crippling, disadvantage. A tariff barrier will improve matters for a time until the government-backed opposition reorganises. This they did effortlessly. When, in 1999, the EU clapped a tariff on goods from Taiwan, manufacturers in the Far East simply moved from Taiwan on to Thailand . . . the Philippines . . . Malaysia . . . Sri Lanka. The Taiwanese government, ready with its subventions and eager to steal a march, was quick to promote relocation of their home industry to wherever manufacture could continue at low cost.

Once the price slashing had begun, there could be but one outcome: victory to those who could survive on the smallest profit margin. Millions of low-paid people in the Far East rode bikes, cheap machines they could just afford. Many people in Europe were attracted by very cheap bikes. These the Taiwanese manufacturers, subsidised by *sine die* unsecured loans from national banks, could not only produce; more importantly, they could also match western production standards, which the Chinese could not yet do. Other cycle manufacturers needed to follow suit or go under. The result was that factories across the world now generated a huge capacity for the production and, within a very short period, the *over*production of bikes. When demand soars, overcapacity ensues. This means there is always someone around with a sizeable parcel of unsold bikes to get shot of at a knockdown price. Competition to sell gets fiercer, prices plummet and no one can break clear of the trend unless there is a revision of quality.

In seeking to reclaim the market from which they had been partially barred, manufacturers in China switched from production of cheaper bikes to those of higher quality, yet still sold them substantially beneath European prices, mainly because of far lower wage costs. Vietnamese manufacturers, north and south, had been crippled by a 100 per cent tariff on their goods in America at the end of the Vietnam War, but, unlike the Taiwanese, they faced no tariff in the UK. Taiwanese companies therefore began to move to Ho Chi Minh city around 1995 and in progressively greater numbers from then on, to avoid these adverse tariffs, and oriental labour practices aided their success: whole families relocated for three months at a time to ensure the custom-built factories worked at capacity.

Chinese bicycle manufacturers had never faced tariff barriers in the USA and, forced out of Europe in the mid-1990s, they began to flood the American market with a new range of high quality bikes. One by one the American bike makers went under; some tried to restart in Mexico and Canada, but the ferocity of the competition from across the northern Pacific was too hot. Nowadays, of a yearly sale of some 19 millions bikes per annum in America, only about 350,000 are made in the USA, the rest come from China.

The venture capitalist duo who owned Raleigh in tandem with Matthews were compelled to address the new onslaught of competition from imports of extremely high quality bicycles from the Far East. Already forced onto the back foot, they'd intended to streamline by closing down some plants in Europe; they now considered closing them all. The cash crisis deteriorated. In 2000, Matthews sold Sturmey-Archer's land to the University of Nottingham for £3.75m, all of which he withheld from Sturmey who had to pay out a substantial sum of their own money in order to relocate. Thereupon, Matthews sold the company itself to Lenark Investments, an operation headed by a self-styled professional gambler in Las Vegas. For thirty pounds. One wonders if, by some humourless twist of mind, he was thinking of Judas's thirty pieces of silver. Worse: this so-called investment house had been involved in a string of failed business takeovers. Any due diligence in scrutiny ahead of the sale would have highlighted the fact and obviated the deal. *BikeBiz.com* found out that, despite saying he *had* ordered formal investigation of Lenark, Matthews carried out no such inquiry. Documents filed to the US Securities and Exchange Commission before the fall-out showed that Matthews appeared euphoric about having off-loaded Sturmey-Archer and bragged disingenuously that he had sold off the company 'for cash'. A less varnished 'we sold it for thirty quid to a bunch of cowboys' wouldn't have sounded quite pukka.

'This was an exceptional transaction for us,' he crowed, 'as we were able to sell an under performing, non-strategic asset for cash, avoid relocation costs and eliminate negative annual operating cash flows.' Some of Sturmey's machines, and all its intellectual assets, were sold to Sun Race of Taiwan.

The 'executive' of Lenark, a recently discharged bankrupt who had once been jailed for fraud, asked the Sturmey Managing Director, Colin Bateman, now deceased, to be on the lookout for any weak bike companies which Lenark could purchase 'for ten to twelve million pounds, not a problem.'

On the first day of IFMA, the annual cycle trade show in Köln, Germany, in 2000, staff on the Sturmey stand learned that their company was insolvent because Lenark could not pay the £75,000 down payment on the lease for new premises in Calverton.

They were out on their ear.

The proceeds from the Sturmey land sale didn't help Derby one jot. Matthews's objective, to secure a place in the global market, had added huge overheads to Raleigh without the recompense of any increase in sales. Long before the absurd hiving off of Sturmey-Archer, it was quite clear that the cash was running out. In 2001, the Derby investors filed for Chapter 11 bankruptcy in advance of certain collapse. This entailed an appeal to the court judge for a stay of 60 days to allow the company to put together a rescue plan for the discharge of debts. All bank loans were frozen. Raleigh would have to manage, somehow, with existing funds. It must, surely, have been obvious to anyone with any concern for the company that the whizz-kid American strategy had failed. The owners were too far distant from the centre of operations to exercise any close check on what had been happening, and hence to call halt to a strategy that was going badly awry. Although Matthews was extremely plausible, the presence of Finden-Crofts on the board (a stipulation of the sales agreement) had sown deep resentment. He was not only blatantly hostile to everything that Matthews did, but expressed his doubts and reservations with a certain sarcasm and veiled mockery which further riled and antagonised the over-serious po-faced Americans, who in common with their fellow countrymen did *not* do irony.[27] The hard-headed Finden-Crofts both alienated himself from the other board members and undermined his own soberly considered but flippantly expressed counsel and criticism. His acerbic opinionising inclined the rest of the board, Americans all, to side with Matthews.

This partisan support, possibly against the grain, permitted Matthews a far, far longer lease on his wayward determination to pursue a hopelessly flawed plan than he should sensibly have been granted.

---

[27] President Roosevelt, a great fan of Lewis Carroll's *Hunting of the Snark,* once paused during dictation to a secretary to advise him, quoting the Bellman: 'What I tell you three times is true.' The secretary, a highly scrubbed and polished, grimly studious young man, looked up, blinked through his clerkish spectacles, gulped and replied: 'But, Mr President, it would never occur to me to impugn your veracity.'

By the time Darnton joined, Finden-Crofts knew it was all up; the venture capitalists were stumped. They simply did not know what to do. Finden-Crofts suggested they hire him on a six months consultancy. He would arrest the runaway decline.

Matthews was fired along with his entire management team, the Greenwich head office was closed, the fancy marketing ploys were dropped and the company returned to the basics of managers managing their own part of the company in a manner that suited their sales area. Finden-Crofts, a money man whose sole interest was in the profit the saleable article made and not in the article itself, immediately sold the Dutch end of Raleigh, Gazelle, which had remained highly profitable, for some $110 million to another venture capitalist group in the Netherlands in order to pay off debts and liabilities. At the conclusion of his consultancy, Finden-Crofts was in a position to take over from Derby. He offered to buy Raleigh back, at **a** rock-bottom price. The owners had little option but to sell. Finden-Crofts agreed to give his new team small shareholdings while keeping the vast majority for himself. As to whether there was any future for Raleigh in the manufacture of parts in the UK, the answer was simple: it was folly even to imagine they could compete with products *and* prices from Vietnam or Thailand, Sri Lanka and, latterly, Turkey. The great giant Raleigh had once bestrode the world. Now the world was swamping a dwarfed midget. And the world it had dominated now bristled with rivals. Bicycle factories had opened in Lithuania when she became part of an extended Europe following independence; German bicycle manufacturers were advising firms in the Balkan states on the industry; Hungarian manufacturers were busily improving quality on bicycles and seeking ways of getting round the anti-dumping tariffs. Raleigh became a mere receiving warehouse for complete bicycles packed up in boxes. Matthews went on to work for the pharmaceutical company Bristol-Myers Squibb.

When Darnton arrived at Raleigh in Nottingham, 550 people worked there. In 1978, on the 64-acre site, the company had employed some 8,500 producing 2 million bikes. Raleigh and three other big companies in the city, Boots, John Player (now Imperial

Tobacco) and Marconi, employed a total of around 40,000 blue-collar workers. Today in Nottingham, Boots employ some 5,000, Imperial Tobacco owns a warehouse with basic staff, Marconi is gone and at Raleigh there are just 80 men and women. (By 1986, Raleigh employed only 1,800 workers producing 1 million bikes. Numbers dwindled in successive bouts of redundancy.) On the other hand, some 42,000 full-time students study at the university, and, whenever they get into a taxi after a late-night party, the chances are that any of the drivers in the cabs queuing for their fares will have once worked for Raleigh. The original 64 acres of the Lenton site had been trimmed to 14 acres, and, in 2003, Darnton sold them to Nottingham University. (Matthews had agreed to give them first refusal.) Raleigh relocated to a warehouse in Eastwood, 10 miles north-west of the city, formerly a mining village where D.H. Lawrence had been born. Thus a complete shift in social strata: undergraduates replace blue-collar workers; taxis are driven by ex-bicycle factory hands.

Until the early 90s, Raleigh made most of the approximately 120 parts which go into the assemblage of a bicycle on the Lenton Road site: frames, saddles, seat posts, forks, rims, nuts and bolts, even, for a while, spokes – everything bar tyres and ball bearings, as they once boasted. The great benefit of an on-site components manufacturing operation was its inherent flexibility. Product specifications could (given management will and direction) be altered rapidly to suit demand. If there was a sudden run on a particular form, colour and size of bike, the manufacturing process could accommodate it. But as imported components from the Far East undercut the home-based prices, the option of buying in parts rather than making them on the spot had to be faced. For sure, they already bought in tyres and Shimano gears, but a *Raleigh* bike still genuinely earned the name that resonated worldwide.

As each decision to import this item then that item rather than manufacture them was determined by cost imperatives, so the Raleigh bicycle became a mongrel, a pastiche, a meccano joining together of foreign bits, from cable nipples to spokes, frames to handlebars, pedals to lights. Still labelled a Raleigh, it was Raleigh in name only, a motley with an original badge, the true substance gone. Meanwhile, on the far side of the world, the logical conclusion for the newly dominant component exporters came in train. 'If we are making and exporting all these bicycle parts,' said manufacturers in the Far East, 'why not make and export a whole bike?'

This story may be apocryphal but, fact or not, it illustrates a melancholy truth, the need to know your opponent and stay ahead. During the interwar years, the Japanese navy bought warships from Britain and, in advance of purchase, asked for the blueprints of the vessels for approval. These plans they handed over to Japanese shipbuilders. When British naval architects got wind of this, they designed an aircraft carrier with a top-heavy centre of gravity. The Japanese built it, launched it and watched it sink.

In 2000, Darnton walked into a Raleigh plant overcast with a pall of moribund gloom. The game was over, morale at its nadir. The dinosaur had keeled over for chronic lack of nourishment and languished in its terminal decline from maker of bicycles to mere assembler. As it were, the high-grade cabinet-maker had become no better than a spannerman for IKEA. Raleigh's factories had not been able to cope with the extraordinary new diversity in the market. The good old policeman's bike, black or green frame, rod brakes, encased chainguard, dependable, the very image of the celebrated all-steel Raleigh bicycle, the celebrated Modèle Superbe, even if that ever-dependable image told but one part of the story, looked hopelessly quaint and outmoded in the flashy, snappy new scene.

There had, too, been a systemic reluctance to embrace new ideas, even in the early days. Having agreed sole use of a process of safety brazing for frames with Victoria-Werke in Nürnberg in 1927, Raleigh installed the requisite machinery. But, safety brazing didn't really suit the American sheet steel stamping introduced by G.P. Mills in the 1890s to make the 'all-steel bicycle'. *All steel* was the tried and tested selling point, no matter that, according to the Raleigh Works Manager, safety brazing 'was much more satisfactory than the old methods, forks which had been treated with by the new system taking twice the amount of force to deflect compared with forks treated under the old method'. All steel it must be. Safety brazing was out.

In July 1922, following a visit to Henry Ford's factory in USA, Sir Harold Bowden wrote:

The traditions of Great Britain have at once been a help and a handicap. They have sometimes prevented us from taking full advantage of new ideas. They have been to some extent responsible for the reputation we hold of being slow to move. But a craftsman does not readily discard a tried and proven tool for anything that is new. He fears for his reputation. Therefore he will often let the young men experiment . . .

But, though this shows commendable candour, he at once condemned mass production, on the Ford scale, as 'quite unsuited to British methods. As a manufacturing nation we are proud of our craftsmanship . . . We can produce on a big scale, but let it be with the craftsman's work.' Disingenuous.

For sure, when pushed, the Raleigh Board had approved a children's bicycle, but they deemed a kiddy's bike no better than a toy. Such disdain for the diversity that had sounded their death knell was rooted in an undisguised contempt for anything at odds with what was and always had been and, therefore, must always remain the core Raleigh ethos, of which the members of the Board were the venerable guardians. They ignored the overwhelming trend for innovation. Hitherto, their share of the market rested on reliable production of road and around-town bikes. Suddenly, the buying public wanted a whole range of machines: BMX , mountain, racing, road, around-town, children's and teenagers' bikes, in a full palette of colours, a wide range of frame sizes, in chrome, aluminium, titanium and carbon fibre, with rear, front or full suspension, side-pull, centre-pull, cantilever and disc brakes, anything from 10 to 24 gears, *derailleurs* for heaven' sake, not just the same old passé three-speed Sturmey-Archer, but rather anything and everything to make the bike look distinctive, different, cool, saleable. But no one factory, let alone one manufacturer could ever match this variety of demand for a calculated 700 different combinations of bicycle in one form or another. Raleigh's problem was that for historical reasons it simply wasn't structured with the internal flexibility required to meet such a challenge.

The merger of Raleigh and Tube Investments in 1960 had put paid to consumer *choice* via a plethora of *brands*; now when these were needed to satisfy customer demand, they weren't available. David Duffield, who joined Phillips, then part of T.I., in 1952, said the merger was the worst thing that ever happened to the UK bicycle industry. Firstly, the new combine cornered 80 per cent of the home bike market at a time when 99 per cent of bikes bought in the UK were British-made. (Such an overwhelming market-share merger would not be allowed by today's Competition Commission. Moreover, such market domination can lead to complacence and arrogance.) Secondly, the merger translated all the faults and frailties of the Raleigh company, itself going downhill, into confused attempts to shore up an already declining market. Two thriving companies, former rivals, were swallowed up: Hercules (best known for the production of lower cost machines) and Phillips, (trademark lion and motto 'Renowned the World Over'). They were tightly run, efficient businesses producing good quality bikes at competitive prices, including sports bicycles fitted with alloy pedals, brakes, handlebars, hubs and derailleurs. Viking, Dawes and a number of hand builders were the only manufacturers who remained independent of the huge TI-Raleigh conglomerate. Control of the bicycle division having been given to Raleigh, the Nottingham council of elders duly imposed its in-house style and practices with a dead hand. The creative exploratory energies of a substantial company like Phillips had to conform to the original Raleigh credo – if it wasn't invented in Nottingham or made there, we don't use it, and we standardise *our* thread sizes not adapt to those of other people – even if force majeure had softened this approach somewhat. Raleigh did, under sufferance, finally produce a derailleur gear, which club cyclists likened to 'a bloody mangle', but Phillips had been manufacturing good-quality derailleurs under the Resilion brand name as well as handlebars. Raleigh might simply, and profitably, have taken over this operation. Instead, it closed Phillips down.

Importing parts from the Far East further complicated the supply chain: the customer asking the dealer for a specific machine, the dealer placing the order with Raleigh, Raleigh sourcing the necessary bits and pieces from its supplier in the Far East, the delay of transit by ship, more time spent going through Customs . . . perhaps three months between the exchange over the shop counter and delivery of the order. Meantime, as often as not, the customer had got fed up with waiting and gone elsewhere, so the dealer had to put the bike into stock and, at the end of the season, sell it off at a distressed price. For the bike trade had now assimilated certain aspects of the fashion industry which, since the swagger and strut of the Swinging Sixties, had dominated popular culture, along with rock and roll. Teenagers and youth had taken over. Dolly birds in miniskirts, kinky boots, hot pants, The Beatles and The Rolling Stones, and, in the words of the Kinks' song, 'the dedicated follower of fashion' dictated the pace. Fashion called the tune on everything for purchase. The smart money was on *the look.* People wanting to buy two wheels didn't want *last year's bike.* They wanted the up-to-the-minute newest and best, with the latest tweaks, the nerdish detail, the singular visible showy differences. And they wanted it *now.*

Part of the trouble was that the Raleigh Board conducted itself as if it were the committee of a gentleman's club. They were people of good education and background, highly paid, jolly good eggs, but they neither rode nor talked about bicycles in the way that people who love bicycles do.[28] This was intrinsically bad management. Anyone involved in selling a product needs, de rigueur, to know if it works *and* matches popular demand. They need to apply feel, instinct, flair to what might seem, on the face of it, to be an economico-mechanistic process, at the grave risk if they don't of being detached, out of touch. The number-crunching of accountants and actuaries is vital for certain aspects of business but it must be kept in its place.

---

[28] The photograph of Gregory Houston Bowden, great grandson of Frank, the founder, on the back cover of his book about the company shows him astride a Raleigh bike. He looks decidedly uncomfortable.

The non-cycling Raleigh Board preserved the aloof hierarchies of empire and the officer class like a secret priestly order. For example, the Nottingham plant had seven categories of lavatory, from the locked private water closets for the top echelon, each of whom was supplied with his or her own key, down through the middle order loos to the common bogs for the workers on the shop floor. Similarly, there were seven categories of eating-place, from the silver service boardroom via the assistants and the assistants to the assistants' mess to the works canteen. The Commercial Manager in charge of UK North, Midlands and South once asked Duffield, who had just been walking round the factory: 'Walking round the *factory?* Why on earth would you want to do *that?* If you have to find out something from the factory you send your assistant.' Yet Sir Harold Bowden, as his father before him, made frequent visits to the shop floor to walk round and report on the humour of the workers in what he was pleased to call the 'Raleigh family'. Perhaps such a paternalistic approach could not survive the post-war social upheavals.

The distancing of management nobility from drones was rooted in a post-imperial, twilight attitude which pervaded other industries as well – motor and light engineering – and militated grievously against a trait essential to the prevailing circumstances in industry and commerce after the War: adaptability. In 1961, Raleigh ruled the roost and behaved accordingly, with a magisterial arrogance. Presiding over a market in decline, they closed down factories which might have kept abreast of modern development and innovation – the alloy wallahs at Phillips in Birmingham, for instance – in favour of Nottingham.

In a buoyant bike market, Raleigh was indeed a world beater, just as 'Zimmy' Zimmerman, their Yankee world champion, had been in the early 1890s, but when the market changed the Raleigh bosses neither understood what was happening nor sought to comprehend it. Most of the individual expertise they mustered went to waste. The O'Donovan operation was an exception but was of itself too small to make much of an impact on the whole. It was above all the blinkered *attitude* which so squandered resource, the failure to accept that a bike is made of bits and that trying to make the whole gallimaufry of bits for a complete machine had outstretched the capacity of a single manufacturer. The same did not happen in France and Italy, for example, where a number of component manufacturers battled through the vicissitudes and still survive. Willing to adapt and innovate, to utilise new materials and new designs, they stayed ahead. Perhaps symbolic is the purchase, in 2004, by Selle Italia of one of the most famous brand names and marques of British design and manufacture, the last to have endured against foreign competition: Brookes Saddles.[29]

Four cautionary tales:

1.   In early 1962, Roy Day, formerly a draughstman at BSA, was strolling through the grounds of the Hall at Bradford-on-Avon, Wiltshire, and spotted an out-building which housed a drawing office. He peered in through the window and saw a form of bicycle he had never seen before: a frame comprising a single, long transverse member to which was attached a short head tube, front forks with suspension, a short seat tube, suspension on the rear stays, two tiny wheels. This was a prototype of Alex Moulton's unisex F-frame machine for adults. It was radical, the first ever departure from the standard diamond frame which had, from the start, so magnificently defied improvement. Moulton had taken the small wheels as the first and determining feature of his revolutionary new idea. In a 1979 lecture he said that in all other vehicles, evolution of design had been directly linked to the reduction in size of wheels because, in most cases, so many advantages flowed from that. He added suspension to counteract the shock associated with smaller wheels.

---

[29] A historical note: the famous Brookes big rivets come from the days when racing cyclists rode their Brookes in for a while and then had specialist saddle-formers reshape the saddle to the exact profile of their seat. This required the removal of the original smaller rivets, a certain amount of twisting and forming of the by now suppler leather, and rerivetting with the larger brass or copper rivets to disguise the first puncturing. Thus, too, 'on the rivet' meaning with the eyeballs out or, as the French say, 'nose in the handlebars', meant at full effort, bum perched on the big rivet at the front of the Brookes saddle.

Moulton had been working on the design for some time before he took the idea to Raleigh in 1958. For about two years they sat on it – the idea, not the bicycle. Finally, the research and development people in the factory who had been working desultorily with Moulton, approached the Sales Director, Jim Harrison: would the company take on production of the revolutionary new bicycle? Harrison pondered and said they would, so long as his sales managers guaranteed that they could sell 200 per week. His sales managers had a conniption: 200 a *week?* They could never shift that many. Never.

Moulton, in sheer frustration at the endless procrastination capped by the failure of trust, confidence and sheer obtuseness in a combine which had the means to act but not the will, the almost innate lack of *excitement*, decided to go into production on his own account. He launched in November 1962 and, in the first year of manufacture and trading, he sold 40,000, that is 800 per week. He had to double the size of his factory to cater to the huge demand for the handy little shopping and gadabout bike with adjustable saddle and handlebars and front and rear suspension centred on a compressible rubber ball joint. The Moulton's extremely low centre of gravity made it very stable and wonderfully comfortable in town, a smooth glide, even on roads not so oppressed with traffic as they are now, particularly for people who hadn't ridden a bike because they did not feel safe or confident on the larger machine. It suited men and women, young and old. It rolled over bumps and ridges with uninterrupted ease. And, not only did Moulton bikes sell, their great popularity gave bikes in general a cooler, friendlier image and promoted sales of the larger machine, too.

Raleigh had missed out spectacularly.

At last the leviathan ground into what may be described as action. Their chief designer, Alan Oakley, had been working on his own idea for a small-wheel bike. He now produced a Raleigh-style simulacrum of the Moulton, the over-heavy (42 lbs) unsuspended RSW (Raleigh Small Wheels) 16, with 16-inch balloon tyres, (the Moulton had slimmer tyres) a kick-stand which made it easy to park and a capacious shopping carrier affixed to a rear rack. This machine the company backed with a stupendous £100,000 publicity campaign, roughly £1 million today. Quite contrary to what Moulton had said, Oakley claimed that whereas Moulton had made *suspension* his first principle, Raleigh concentrated on the small wheels. An RSW Compact folded in two to fit into a car boot. Oakley was, even so, sceptical. 'If your bicycle has very small wheels,' he said, 'then suspension will not make the ride ideal as the whole wheel will tend to drop into large holes [as if any size of wheel other than the huge Ordinary front wheel can manage a pothole]. With a larger wheel, suspension really does not seem to be necessary.' Doesn't make a lot of sense to me.

2.   The Raleigh old guard had, initially, held off from making sports bikes in any great numbers. But, the market was not to be denied. In 1971, the UK operation was devolved into three areas: North, Midlands, South. A new Sales Director, Archie Hutchinson from Hoover, had swept aside the fuddy-duddy notions which had hampered the company for so long, and Peter Seales, Marketing Director, from Gallagher cigarettes, introduced an altogether racier, glitizier, more dynamic promotion of the Raleigh image. While these two firebrands transformed and (dread word) *modernised* the marketing side of the company, the manufacturing division was cumbrously slow to follow. The vibrant spirit which tingled through one side of the company was amply doused by entrenched and arthritic caution on the other side. Why could they not hear or heed? The British market demanded sports bikes. When Raleigh *did* eventually join the trend, prices were already going down. So it goes with any new idea: once the competition catches on the price falls, and there was little brand loyalty left in the bike-buying public to support a late-starting Raleigh venture. Nevertheless, by around 1973, they were selling some 400,000 10-speed sports bikes to America. To keep the overall price down they fitted poor-quality leather Wright's saddles. Since the sports machine carried no mudguards, these saddles got soaked by spray off the back wheel when it rained and rapidly became sodden, misshapen, useless. The Americans discarded them and fitted all-weather plastic saddles. This was not good for the Raleigh name. However, Raleigh's Toy Division said they could produce a well-shaped plastic saddle onto which a non-racer could fit a foam cover to render it more comfortable. The Concept Designs department agreed production costs and numbers and Duffield, now in the Marketing

department, made a presentation to the Board of Directors. There was already support from the export people who actually had to sell the bikes but, as Duffield walked into the room, the USA Export Manager whispered to him: 'You've lost this one – Mike Smith [the factory director] doesn't believe in plastic saddles'.

Having made his pitch, Duffield sat down whereupon Mike Smith, a man who wielded enormous power and influence in the company, made his response, his defining reply. 'Gentlemen, I wear leather shoes, my Jaguar has leather upholstery, when I go home I sit in a leather armchair. A leather saddle is one of Raleigh's great traditions. I think we do not need *plastic* saddles.'

3.   Gerald O'Donovan, the brilliant frame designer whose family had founded the Carlton works, set up the Raleigh Specialist Bicycle Development Section at Ilkeston in Derbyshire (even the Raleigh nomenclature had something of the old fart about it). He had been experimenting with welded frames, as opposed to fitting tubes with lugs, which are expensive items, and, more significantly, restrict the shape of a frame. Welding allows for a much greater variety of shaping, to suit different heights and physical proportions of a rider. Raleigh were welding some frames, notably on their Chopper and children's bikes where the tubes were thick to withstand a lot of shock, but the welds were hastily cobbled and, by consequence, gobby, angular and uneven, very far from the sort of sleek finish a racer expected on a machine built for speed.

To explain the Chopper: designed by Alan Oakley and launched in 1971, this was a significant departure in the cycle market, and heralded a big explosion of sales. Oakley – who toyed with the design on the back of an envelope on a transatlantic flight home – had been prompted by the shape of the curious Stingray bicycle in America, a low-slung, long-base machine with an elliptical frame, very laid-back, Easy Rider style. Fancy to look at, not much of a ride. All Choppers were fitted with Vredestein tyres which bore a special hand-painted red line, another trim detail in line with the current vogue. Perhaps inspired by the customised Harley Davidson motorbikes ridden by Hell's Angels or the souped-up Vestas and Lambrettas favoured by the Mods, the Chopper gave its rider the authentic insolent cool, slouch style of the two-wheel fast-lick road-strutters, evoking the tough-guy image of the biker, typified by Marlon Brando in *The Wild One*. He strolls into the coffee bar, leather jacket, cap at rakish angle, leans against the counter.

'What are you rebelling against?' the waitress asks.

'What have you got?' he drawls.

The publicity blurb reads:

> *Chopper The Hot One.*
> *Raleigh know what youngsters like. Hot-rod looks, Rakish frames. The power and pounce you see on a dragster circuit. Above all action features. Features like hi-rise 'ape-hanger' bars. Drag-style saddle. Snap-action gear shift. And coil spring suspension. All, giving the hottest ride you'll ever know, all found on the Raleigh Chopper.*
> *Choose this hot one in Golden Yellow, Flamboyant Green or Brilliant Orange.*

The Chopper was sold through Raleigh's Five-Star Dealerships, set up in the 70s, which enjoyed preferential discount rates and treatment for dealing exclusively with the company: premises were upgraded, staff trained in servicing and sales, advertising paid for. However, this was another example of Raleigh's elitist systems: as Five-Star dealers were royally treated, so other dealerships were axed, (sent to Coventry, indeed, former centre of the bike industry) for not coming up to what Raleigh called snuff.

As for the Chopper, Andrew Ritchie says in his *King of the Road: an Illustrated history of Cycling* (Ten Speed Press, 1975) that it was 'not really a bicycle any more [but] a luxury consumer toy'. The point is that the owner of a Chopper wouldn't be likely to go on to ride a *real* bicycle. It was no more than a gimmick, a temporary fun machine which would be discarded without having nourished in its owner any feel for riding a conventional two wheeler. In 1992, Raleigh produced a sort of MTB clone of the Chopper, the Activator, and, in an interview she gave to Paul Rosen, Kath Hamer of York Cycleworks, a cooperative cycle shop with an avowed commitment to promoting cycling, said of the Activator:

> *I think it's the most horrible thing on earth, it represents everything that is bad about the way Raleigh sells bikes. It's unpleasant to ride, very poor quality because they've tried to build something to a price that you can't make for that price. It weighs a ton. I think it would put kids off bikes . . . a bit like the RSW16 with the real fat wheels – basically Moulton invents a bike that's got suspension on, skinny wheels, and they're really titchy and it rides really well. Then Raleigh crush him, buy the name, [when Moulton got into financial difficulties in 1967, Raleigh bought him out and almost at once produced a Raleigh Moulton] produce a bastardised version of it with huge wheels and the whole thing feels like riding through treacle.*

The Activator *looked* cool and, when kids aspired to own all the new superlight mountain bike components on a lightweight frame, they got a lumpen freak of a machine weighing around 40 pounds. Useless. The range lasted three years before being dropped.

Back to lugs.

In the late '70s, O'Donovan was one of the few men associated with Raleigh intimately attuned to bikes because they rode them, a man who had sympathy for the *matter* of the bicycle as well as the *business*. He knew that the days of lugs were numbered. Hence, he had purchased welding equipment, with Mike Smith's approval, to build frames with SIF bronze welding. This demands extreme accuracy in the mitring of the tube ends to be joined. It is a job for a first-rate craftsman. O'Donovan had already broached the possibility of making bikes with welded frames and selling them under the Sun brand, acquired from TI. Duffield made another presentation.

Duffield has always been a passionate rider of as well as talker about the beautiful machine. He held an array of tricycle records between 1955 and 1971 – London to Bath and back, John O'Groats to Land's End, London to York, London to Cardiff, 12 hours, 50 miles, 100 miles, 1,000 miles. Alerted by the dogmatic reception he'd hit last time, he intended to wing the opposition and concluded his pitch by referring to the fact that Mike Smith 'had approved the installation of welding plant in the Ilkeston works.'

Smith, far too comfortably aware of his own eminence and clout in the Raleigh inner circle to be fazed, rejoined: 'We have had disappointments with welded frames in the toy division [one can hear the scoffing emphasis on *toy*] and I now have my doubts about this project. Nevertheless, we have tried it and in my opinion we should not go ahead in view of past failures.'

There would be no welding at Raleigh, toy machines aside, while *he* was in control, nor even testing of the process. The obsession with Raleigh as it had been, continued to be and, all militating contrary factors ignored, would continue to be, proved impossible to shift. The legendary 'all-steel bicycle', though doomed to extinction, must strive in vain to keep up with the alloy machines of the modern era. Raleigh did experiment with titanium when it was first introduced in the early 70s but the frames were glued, not welded, and the joints rarely held for long. Not until MTBs were firmly established in the market did Raleigh adopt welding. Entirely in line with their reaction to the BMX when it arrived: 'It'll never take off in the UK'.' And when it did, and the market was awash with BMX, Raleigh belatedly produced their own version, the Burner, but still could not bring themselves actually to call it a BMX. Once again they had missed out.[30]

---

[30] In an interview with *Cycle Trader* (September 1982) Duffield said: 'BMX was . . . going to happen because kids have been riding bikes over rough ground for years now and, when one went and saw what they'd done in America, the kids were just harnessing that natural desire.' He admitted there had been a risk but risk can be reduced, if not eliminated, by research.

4.   In 1985, the Bluemel company, a third-generation firm and principal makers of bicycle pumps and mudguards, for long a fixture in the home trade, succumbed to bank calls to end trading.[31] The overdraft stood at over £1½ million even as the Board sat in a plush, wood-panelled boardroom graced with fine furnishings, drinks cabinets and the glossy patina of wealth and success. The Chairman, Sir Ronnie Atkins, described by the late Ron Kitching as 'an insufferable prig', arrived for a Board meeting at 3pm, shook everyone (including Kitching) unctuously by the hand, sat down and called for the agenda. Instead of the agenda he was given a letter requesting his resignation. He got up and went back to his Rolls Royce. It was 3 minutes past three.

Bluemels went into receivership. The receiver contacted Bob, because he had known three of the company's Sales Directors well, and sought his help in assessing the worth of the operation. He insisted that he was going to sell the entirety, not parcel it up. Bob called Willie Blome of the SKS company in Germany and told him that Bluemels was going to be sold and that if he made a reasonable offer it would almost certainly be accepted. He added the caveat that 60 per cent of the lot was junk and worthless. Blome bought the entirety, dumped the junk but, crucially, bought the expertise and plant for the manufacture of mudguards, which always had been the mainstay of the Bluemels output. SKS is now a world leader in the manufacture of mudguards.

Robert Chicken organised the dumping of the junk – all the plant and the work in progress as well as the racking, some of which RJC is still using at the Bisley site.

In the view of many, Raleigh, faced by a radically changing market, should have faced uncomfortable facts as soon as they presented themselves and slimmed down in order to concentrate on the manufacture of components rather than teetering between the manufacture of whole bikes and the assembly of imported bits. Instead, they shed their expertise, perhaps their greatest asset, and ditched the true base of their and the UK's

---

[31] They also made car number plates, foot pumps and steering wheels, extruded plastic for gutters, brass and pewter giftware.

economy and erstwhile pre-eminence, manufacturing. This affected other concerns badly. Individual UK component manufacturers went under as the creaking megalith foundered. Coventry/Reynolds chains . . . Bayliss-Wiley freewheels. . . Williams chainwheels and cranks . . . Phillips handlebars and brakes . . . all disappeared to the great detriment of the home industry and the profit of foreign rivals.[32]

A notable clutch of European component and frame manufacturers survived the slumps and continues to prosper. SRAM made its gears in direct response to market needs. The de Rosa family business manufacturing bike frames continues to thrive. Campagnolo is still Campagnolo. Colnago and Bianchi are still making de luxe frames, Bianchi promoted by the great champion Felice Gimondi, winner of the Tour de France in 1965, Giro d'Italia 1967 and '69, World Road Champion 1973 (2nd in 1971).[33] Trek and Specialised in the USA produce top-end frames for world-class bicycles, albeit the rest of the parts are brought in from abroad. When competitors were using names which might appeal to a continental buyer, Raleigh, good old stiff upper-lipped Raleigh, remained obdurately averse to any modification of the upright (uptight) British signature.

So long as the bikes arriving from the Far East were of lower quality than those produced in the UK – poor welding, sloppily applied decals, low-grade painting – Raleigh could match the competition. But once the purpose-built factories in Vietnam began to produce high-quality machines, the foreign competition inevitably, and rapidly, outstripped them. By 2003, an exact replica of a Raleigh bike made by the Taiwanese in Vietnam sold at 22 per cent cheaper than its home-built counterpart and bikes from Vietnam were supplying not only the UK but other markets as well.

---

[32] James Dyson was much criticised for relocating his manufacturing to Malaysia, though he pleaded impossible difficulties from government legislation, planning restrictions, banks wanting a quick return. In Malaysia, everything is made and supplied to the assembly plant from within a ten-mile radius and Dysons now employs *more* people at the HQ in Wiltshire than they did before the move. The profits generated in the Far East help promote schemes for education of the work force as well as funding research and development.
[33] Duffield once remarked: 'Raleigh wouldn't use Gimondi – they wouldn't know who he was.'

Before Darnton joined, a number of people advised him that Raleigh was beyond help, that it was far too late; they even said he was bold to try but naïve to take on the job. A colleague looked at the company's balance sheets and said, 'Philip, don't touch it.' But Darnton decided the challenge was there, to settle the affairs of what remained of Raleigh Industries. Even if the attempt ended in tears, it must be possible to manage the demise humanely, decently, at least to defend the redundancy and pension rights of the 500 people still working in the once-proud firm, as it were a forgotten rump of disillusioned, depressed labourers in an abandoned collective.

The seeds of the decline, Darnton believes, were sown in the late 1970s when a lack of investment and failure to innovate, overlaid with a stiff-necked, old-school arrogance blighted the future irreparably. The increasingly preposterous belief within Raleigh that, commanding a 60–70 per cent share of the market, it need heed no other dissenting voice or opinion, proved fatal. It also bred poisonous resentment among those on whom it relied, the dealers, some of whom were classified as 5-star and marked out from the rest, the hoi polloi, for special treatment and terms. Such pulling of rank was positively feudal. The Raleigh policy men also bullied dealers, squeezing on prices and deliveries, incessantly hectoring on the phone.

In common with many other manufacturing businesses of the time, Raleigh missed a new commercial trend that became established in the mid-60s. When Darnton joined Unilever in 1966, the company was putting many of its brightest new recruits into the marketing department. Their brief? To analyse and make profiles of the target audience, to push the precise benefit of Unilever products, to investigate and identify consumer interests vis à vis those products and to work on means of distinguishing the Unilever brand as against those of its competitors. This required a new concentration on advertising, packaging and the locales in which advertisements were seen. (Pointless, for instance, to advertise Ferrari cars on television.) Above all, this meant linking the life style of the consumer to the appeal of the product. Indeed, company managers with sharp acumen were beginning to ask that very question, obvious to us now, maybe, but not at the time: what is a consumer? What does she or he do for a living, for leisure?

How do the consumers we are seeking to attract spend their money? Where do they spend it?

For the first time since the War, ten years after the end of rationing, goods were in plentiful supply. MacMillan had told the nation, 'You have never had it so good,' in 1963 and now the market was awash, supply handsomely exceeding demand. While goods were scarce, there had been little need to encourage purchase. Retailers could stock their shelves in the placid expectation that the shelves would be emptied. Once supply boomed, manufacturers had suddenly to be alive to the need to promote, to carve out a niche in the newly bustling marketplace. Neglect that and sales would tumble. Unadventurous shoppers for essentials had become eager consumers exercising choice, on the hunt for variety, innovation, competitive prices.

Raleigh simply did not accommodate this radical new trend. Their operation was driven, from start to finish, by production men. 'We make the stuff,' they said breezily, 'and to a high standard which people want, so people are just going to have to pay commensurate prices, and that is that. End of story.'

They lacked consistent marketing strategies, and no powerful intervening voice of the consumer would be allowed to affect how they ran their business. The consumer, as far as they were concerned, would bloody well accept what he or she was given. It was bloody good quality and they should be bloody grateful for it and bloody well shut up. Nothing was better guaranteed to make the consumer bloody well go elsewhere and go elsewhere the consumer bloody well did.

Raleigh continues to exist, continues to trade, but there is no soul in the business. It peddles an anonymous commodity toting a once-famous badge. Earnings in the company all but trebled in the years 2003, 2004. Why? Because Raleigh relaunched the Chopper, not a bicycle so much as 'a luxury consumer toy'. A newspaper article touting the success story shows three Raleigh executives astride their Choppers, grinning glassily, feet firmly *off* the pedals and *on* the ground.

There is one sector of the UK bicycle industry which has, somehow, survived all the vicissitudes of a fluctuating market, variable trends, vogues, fads and caprice, and is still going strong, albeit in miniature, entirely dependent on native expertise, flair and sheer bloodymindedness: hand building. Napoleon described Britain contemptuously as 'a nation of shopkeepers' yet the hand-builders of frames turn the contempt back on itself. The men who worked on a kitchen table at the back of their shop or even the back of their house – an authentic cottage industry – deserve particular recognition as upholders of a very British tradition in native craft and independence of mind. They put their names to the frames they built, to the racing men they sponsored, to the rich history of cycling, names revered by the cognoscenti as purists, enthusiasts, men who made a mark on cycling and cycle lore. When lightweight frames were not available in the UK from any other source, the one-man bands supplied the racing men with frames to rival any built on the continent far away over the Channel, the slim-tubed elegant steel-framed bikes ridden by the star racers. In no particular order, and by no means a comprehensive list, up and down the country, from Stockton to Kent, from Accrington to Plymouth, all producing 'a frame with a name': Harry Quinn, Ellis Briggs, Rattrays of Glasgow, Ken Bird, Alec Bird, E.G. Bates, Reg Barnett, Tom Crowther, E.F. Russ, Alan Shorter, Freddie Grubb, Norman Shrubb, Ron Cooper, Norman Fay, Jack Taylor, Dave Russell, Bob Jackson, Henry Gregson, Higgins, Hetchins, Walvale, Woodrup, Don Farrell, Fred Baker, Claud Butler, 'the road to fame is a Roy Thame frame', Charlie Roberts . . . and Chas, his son, carrying on the family tradition, in Croydon.

The first time I cycled to Croydon from my home in Sevenoaks (to gather up a few bits of furniture from IKEA and load them onto the uncomplaining vélo), I went over Titsey Hill and downhill, very downhill, into New Addington, past a large signboard by the roadside, like a 'No Casualty Department' placard outside a hospital. It reads: *Welcome to Croydon, the natural choice . . . Twinned with Arnhem.* The natural choice. Choice of what, you wonder.

This time, en route to visit Chas Roberts at his workshop in the town described by one noted urban planner as 'Where?', I chose the hill whose name best fits the brief but profound misery of getting self and bike over the North Downs escarpment: Hog Trough. After a murky, rain-drenched start, the day had blossomed into a beautiful autumn morning. On the high steep of the hill, just as I was thinking my legs had taken all the lactic acid they could hold, the road suddenly eased a fraction through a spinney of ancient beech trees. A fine, sunlit view back down over the valley, the low murmur of the M25 traffic almost inaudible now. My heart lifted. On over the Bump – Biggin Hill – and away from the main road curse of school runs and white vans, into the winding rural back lanes past Keston church and the remains of a Roman Mausoleum (probably twinned with Titsey Hill), finally, into the latticework of the Croydon tram lines. If the road hogs don't get you the sunken rails will. You have to be intrepid to research books these days, I tell you.

Chas' workshop is at 89 Gloucester Road, just past The Drum and Monkey. Andrew, the technical assistant who fronts the shop, a former Ironman triathlete and very well spoken, opened the door and, without blinking, ushered my old workhorse Claud Butler past the lustrous, sleek machines on display into the workshop. It was like tugging a flea-bitten mongrel onto the podium at Crufts. He came back with a cup of black coffee and said with no more than a twinkle of a smile: 'How long have you had that Brookes saddle?' I'm surprised he recognised it as such, so misshapen has it become. Then he told me about a guy who had bought a Roberts frame plus all the trimmings and plonked onto it, in its fine, pristine state, the favourite comfortable battered old Brookes which no bit of unworn sit-upon wizardry could match. That encapsulates the Roberts design philosophy: fit the customer exactly. Chas asks every customer exactly what he or she wants from the bike, what they want it for and then takes the basic measurements which enable him to make the frame fit, bespoke: inside leg, height, weight, length of arms and forearms, shoulder width, shoe size (for mudguard clearance). Weight is important because a beanpole and a bruiser might well have the same skeleton. A lot of women buy Roberts' bikes because the standard, mass-manufactured machines do not accommodate their generally shorter height: small frames with small everything else simply don't work. As for preternaturally tall men: two recent customers check in at around 6ft 9 inches but they don't want the cumbersome huge frame that would ordinarily be prescribed; they need a more thoughtful mix of standard-size frame plus taller head tube and so on. Andrew, for example, had always found it impossible to buy a bike on which he felt at ease. Then he met Chas, who took some basic measurements and told him that his legs were proportionate to his height but that his upper body (torso) was disproportionately long. 'If I'd bought a suit,' Andrew said, 'I'd have discovered that my arms were a bit long for the rest of me.' Frankly, I don't think a suit would be quite strawberry leaf in the context of the front shop just along from the Drum and Monkey, but I take his point.

While I waited, I took in the cork notice board, plastered with newspaper and magazine articles, letters and postcards from happy customers – Josie Drew the long-distance lass, a guy clad in sunglasses wearing a large tattoo on his right thigh and nothing else astride a bike loaded like a pack-mule. A cross-undressed Lady Godiva for our time.

Chas came in at the agreed time – I'd been 20 minutes ahead of schedule. No call to boast. New tyres. Vredestein Fortezza – and we went up the narrow stairs, steep as Hog Trough, to his office in what used to be a cottage. He moved what truly is his cottage industry to these premises some years back when Croydon Council decided to make the estate where they worked wholly residential. They didn't want pedestrians who passed the Roberts establishment emerging with a blue rinse from the paint sprayers. Chas now has only four guys working for him: Andrew and the three in the workshop, each of whom learnt his skill in a larger manufacturing workshop and, over the past 17 years, have refined it in the more exacting work of hand-built frames. Some five years ago, their in-house painter, a brilliant guy who'd worked for Claude Butler and J. Holland, retired and Chas realised that it was going to be impossible to finance a replacement for him. The trade is now so highly specialised, health and safety regulations are punitive, insurance companies so jittery, that small firms simply cannot handle the excessive added financial risks and demands. Now their painting is done by a freelance in Crayford, to whom they sold the plant. (Even Colnago doesn't have its own paint shop.)

The trimmed-down Roberts workshop produces anywhere between 250 and 350 frames per year – some sold as frames, others built into bikes to suit a wide range of needs: a lot of Audax riders want a Roberts for the lunacy which is the driving force of their strange masochistic addiction – e.g. Paris–Brest–Paris.[34] People taking time out from work – six months, a year – to ride round the world or make the big continental expedition, ask Roberts for the exact machine snug for the job. And, all things considered, up to £2,000 or £3,000 for such a specialised bike is not high. Others come in for their own tailor-made version of the racing machines I drooled at in the shop, examples of the bikes ridden by Olympic track-riders and world champions like Tony Doyle, even the prototype Roberts MTB. 'We made that,' Chas explained 'when the mountain bike fraternity were just getting going [c. 1982] and we didn't know what to call it. There was a graduate working for us who read that magazine VIZ. Every other sentence seemed to have "the dog's bollocks" in it. So, that's what we called the MTB.' And there it is, painted on the down tube of the opaline blue frame: D.O.G.S. B.L.X. Cool. Professional MTB riders have homed in on the Roberts off-road machine, too.

Chas is agreeably unselfconscious when he talks about the superb quality of design and finish in his frames. But the casual way he speaks of abstractions cannot mask the passion, the thought, the constant substratum of inventive energy behind the sketch he pulls out of a drawer – a scrap of paper cut to shape, a new thought on disc brakes. He'll go two, three weeks sick to the back teeth of bikes – an extended version of that passage of atrabilious disgust midway up Hog Trough – but then, almost unbidden, comes the fidget of an idea, the need to rethink. This is what he calls 'playing around the edges', where the advances in design come, the edge, the special touch, keeping the Roberts machine ahead. Maybe nothing that'll shake the bike fraternity to its roots, but

---

[34] Just saying this last makes me feel queasy. Every time I see Richard Hallett he fixes me with a gimlet eye and asks me when I'm going to do P–B–P. Either that or, he says, I'm ready for a makeover. Well, I know *that*.

it's part of the responsibility he feels, the pride in producing something with his name on it. You promise excellence and precision, you have to deliver.

Sure, he gets upset when he's knocked by snide individuals wittering on: 'Oh, Roberts – they charge so much bloody extra for this, so much bloody extra for that. Overpriced and overblown.' But I say there's no accounting for ignorance. It's a sour British thing, attuned to the snivelling cloth-cap image of the bike, taking pops at what seems pretentious but is, in fact, top drawer. Ah, how we cleave to *failure*. 'Yes – if you're close to the top of the tree people like to shake it to see who comes down.'

Charlie Roberts, Chas's dad, who died some 20 years ago, started out just after the War making frames for Butler, Holdsworth, Freddie Grubb. He branched out on his own in the 1960s. 'Did he push you to join him?' I asked. 'No, not really. I was always stripping bikes down – get a Phillips, rebuild it as a dirt track iron with cowhorn bars and knobbly tyres. And when most kids my age were doing a paper round, I was earning extra helping my Dad in the cellar of our house in Sydenham every night, brazing up carriers for Butler.' I asked if they'd got on together, when he followed what seemed a natural path to join his father in the workshop. He smiled. Well, there's always going to be some niggle between father and son, but, no, they got on well and it's apparent to me that there is a real family tradition at work here. The fact that Chas designs every single Roberts himself, even if he can't get into the workshop as often as he likes because of ringing phones (importunate individuals like me and the proverbial person from Porlock) and having to keep a bank manager, even an understanding bank manager, happy means that every one of the hand-built frames presents what he calls 'a human face'. Mass-produced models speak 'machine-made' at you. Even the super-duper, top-range, pro-style classy items *as ridden by* . . . are, as he put it, 'very aerospace but they have little character. We were always *drawn* by a bike, a frame and that's the feeling that lasts.'

Chas gave me an hour and a half of his time, happy to indulge the real pleasure he takes in the bike and the idea of the bike. The five-man team works as a cooperative of equals – certainly his workshop men, Winston and Adrian the frame-builders and the mechanic Brian can give him a run for his money. They make superb frames and, yes, 'dog's bollocks' is right. I didn't show him my saddle: I'm sure I was already outstaying my welcome.

We said goodbye and a few moments later, Chas came back with a frame that's ready for painting, just to show me the fillet brazing he'd talked about. A brass and silver solder sealing perfectly mitred tube ends, filed to a satin smoothness: we're talking goldsmith standards here.

I rode home some time later in pelting, foully inhospitable rain, roads awash, down Hog Trough gingerly, at an even slower speed than up it in sunshine. Wet through, for sure, but I haven't started to leak yet. Besides, this day had given me something very special: I'm not speaking of insights, not an acquaintance with the technology of lugs (I'm very attached to lugs) nor even an insane envy of those Roberts frames, though I did bring away all three. No, it was the delight, the sheer delight, of seeing excellence at close quarters, and discovering that, whether Croydon appreciates it or not, Croydon *does* offer a natural choice after all: at 89 Gloucester Road, on the left, past The Drum and Monkey.

According to Richard Hallett there are, today, probably around fifty independent frame builders, by no means all working full-time. Difficult to say. Maybe even up to a hundred including the retired men still ready to oblige and those working at other jobs who will make a frame in their spare time as a favour. During a research trip to Newcastle, I loaded a fold-up Brompton, loaned to me by Carlton Reid, editor of *Bikebiz.com*, onto the Metro at Jesmond and from the station near Wallsend cycled down to the trading estate where Dave Yates makes (and repairs) frames for the shop run by his compadre, Joe Waugh, in Gosforth. He had a stinking cold which he was trying to weld into submission, crouched over the TIG (Tungsten Inert Gas) welding apparatus in a glow of electric blue. He'd told me on the phone he was badly pressed for time, but I went anyway – you never know what you're going to pick up.[35]

---

[35] I once went, unannounced, to see Laurent Fignon. He'd ignored phone calls, letters, faxes, but I went anyway, told his secretary I would like to see M. Fignon, at the time working on the next year's Paris–

Dave Yates told me I had thirty seconds. We talked for about ten minutes (is this, by some arcane ruling, the agreed span of time allotted for impromptu discussion between chance caller and men who have no time to talk, I wonder?) until the delivery man arrived to carry him off, possibly to a rehab centre for irrecoverable TIG addicts, and there really could be no prolonging the conversation with the guy who can't resist talking about bikes and frame-building. Enthusiasm? No, obsession. To do such a job for the derisory monetary reward, it has to be an obsession. A made-up steel frame can be imported from the Czech Republic and sell at £20; Yates cannot buy even the tubes alone for under £40. No contest, except . . . except, there are little pockets of Yates frame/bike owners (the bikes are assembled in Gosforth) all round the country. One guy walks into the workshop, Yates looks at him, scans his existing bike (very rarely does he indulge in Roberts-style measurements) and delivers a bespoke frame with the Reynolds 831 steel tubing he sticks by. The guy's friends see the finished article, ask him for the phone number and

Yates has another customer. It's all pretty seat of the pants, though, and the big market is, and will always be, beyond the reach of him and his ilk. But, they display a similar attitude to the huge Taiwan operations – utterly positive, always *can do*, the very antithesis of the stubborn inflexibility which first dogged native bike manufacturers and then hounded them out of business or, rather, left them stranded, high and dry. Yates says, with admiration, that you can go to a Taiwanese factory, ask for something they aren't yet producing, they'll go away and in a very short time promise swift delivery. 'Do they have big design departments?' I asked.

'Nah, don't need them. There's nothing new under the sun in frame building – we all know the angles and there's nothing that hasn't already been done. They've got the software and all the angles, it's just a case of re-jigging.' After the almost sacerdotal approach in the Roberts works in Croydon, this was surprising and it may simply be a

---

Nice. She went into his office, emerged and said I could go in. He told me he couldn't see me and then spent ten minutes explaining why he couldn't see me . . . a precious chance to get even a small measure of the man.

bluff disclaimer of any special skill or mastery. Take it how you will, but my friend Luke Evans told me that when he went, as a teenager, to Ron Cooper at Honor Oak Park, near Lewisham, for his first custom-built bike, Cooper made no measurements: he just looked Luke up and down and knew.

One company which for a long time straddled the divide between the small workshop and the big manufacturers, was Dawes of Birmingham, founded in 1926, which produced around 30 – 50, 000 bikes per year but retained its credo of ultimate flexibility – mirrored in the later Taiwan approach – yet avoiding the practices of mass production. An article in *International Cycle Sport* (now defunct) of March 1976, when Dawes Cycles were sponsoring two professional riders, Phil Bayton (road) and Trevor Bull (track) records that the company was producing around 1,000 bikes per week ranging from a childrens' model to a wide assortment of sports models and light roadsters. The machines were made in batches of one hundred at a time, deploying a number of techniques more usually associated with hand building. But it was in the final assembly where the flexibility showed itself: each builder was responsible for the entire machine. Whereas in other factories one man fitted the wheels, another the bars and brakes, and so on, the Dawes people built the whole thing. The Works Manager of the day, Reg Ball, was proud to claim that his work force was probably the most versatile in the cycle industry. Some of the wheels, for instance, were 'eye trued' instead of by machine.

Until financial problems and distribution difficulties forced them to sell and surrender their independence to the Dutch cycle firm Batavus in 1993, they remained one of the few family businesses still trading – the then owner's grandfather and a partner produced the Humphries and Dawes OK Supreme motorcycle in 1904. Even today, the Dawes name is synonymous with lightweight high-quality frame building. After various changes – two more sell-outs and, finally, a merger with the group which owned Falcon cycles – Dawes has the frames, for which it was always best known, made in Vietnam (until recently they were being made in the Czech Republic) but still with

Reynolds 631 and 853 tubing and still to the company's criteria of design and manufacture.

Dave Yates made a mountain bike sometime around 1983 and lined up with the rest of the field in Carlisle for the annual Hadrian Wall ride, which ends not far from the works in Wallsend. The rest of the field were bemused. Had the boy Yates been snorting oxy-acetylene? Call that a *bike?* But, like his namesake way to the south, Yates is a-water-off-a-duck's-back sort of man. So. The idea was for him to go like the clappers to keep up with the racing bikes for a few miles and then swap to his own sleeker road machine which Joe Waugh would bring down. Waugh wasn't there. Yates, unabashed, had to slog on aboard the heavy, thick-tyred prototype.

Later, I phoned him from home to ask him about the technology of TIG welding and, still labouring with the beastly rheum, he gave me the lowdown: argon, fusion, oxidisation, the virtues of welding over brazing, the usefulness of brazing over welding, weight proportions – all steel weighs the same on a volume-for-volume basis, so the weight of a frame is reduced by using less metal, but the thinner the metal the weaker it becomes and the more accurate the skill needed to work it. Thus, in a dwindling number of small workshops in outposts of the country, it remains a fact, a happy fact, which outfaces sentimentality, that high quality steel and high quality craftsmanship go together into the making of each and every particular handcrafted frame with a name.

From the Yates workshop, that grey, chill, misty-moisty January afternoon, I cycled along to the pedestrian tunnel under the river they called the Coalie Tyne, an underpass once used daily by around 30,000 workers at the shipyards for which Tyneside was, until the mid-60s, best known. Every day they walked to the gatehouse and rode the wooden elevators, once the longest in the world, down, down, creakily and slowly to the twin tunnel shafts, then walked along one way *to* work and back the other *from* work. Nowadays, one of the tunnels is designated for cyclists and I, a veteran of the Blackwall Tunnel on two wheels, there and back (bloody stupid, bad mistake, terrifying) I rode in tranquillity and alone in the empty place, south and up the far side elevator, each of its timber treads marked with a stencilled number in series, and cycled on to the station at Jarrow. From Jarrow on 5 October 1936, 200 men, mostly shipworkers and miners, set out to march to London on what came to be called the Jarrow Crusade or the Jarrow March. They walked the 280.5 miles to London in twenty-two stages, with overnight stops, sheltered, fed and watered by sympathisers along the way, in protest at the miseries of chronic poverty and unemployment, the desperate straits in which they, their wives and their bairns were irredeemably sunk. Calm, defiant, dignified, like the Tolpuddle Martyrs coming out of the Dorchester courthouse under sentence of transportation, they would cry: 'We shall, we shall, we shall be free.' They spoke for all their kind and theirs was not a new grievance. For nearly two decades, the whole north-east region had been subjected to ruinous industrial rundown and serial, even casual neglect. Like the men of Dorset neither did they 'shame their kind'.

When they'd completed the final leg of their march, the 8½ miles from Edmonton to Marble Arch, Ellen Wilkinson, Labour MP for Jarrow, handed a petition bearing 12,000 signatures to Parliament, but the Prime Minister, Stanley Baldwin, refused to see or speak to any of the marchers.

Their descendants, the shipyards long gone, the mines more recently shut down, find work elsewhere and do not cross the river by way of the pedestrian tunnel. Instead, they get into their cars and drive into the dense and constant traffic which clogs all the roads in and around Newcastle-upon-Tyne and Gateshead, content, it seems, to sit idle and trapped, in their private transport, engines idling too, for however long, no matter how long, it takes the jams to clear, rather than cycling to a Metro station, there to fold up a Brompton and board one of the most efficient metropolitan railways lines in use today, thence to travel at unhindered speed to as close to their destination as they choose.

Carlton Reid's three children, Josh, aged 7, and Ellie and Hanna the twins, 5, cycle to school every day, up the steep, steep bank out of Jesmond Dene (it ain't much fun on a Brompton I can tell you) at remarkable speed. They have the love of the bike and it's a joy to behold. A poll of their fellow pupils showed that fully 70 per cent would prefer to cycle to school, rather than be ferried to and fro in the cars, people carriers and whatnot which are the diurnal cages of their morning and afternoon routine. But the parents vetoed cycling on the grounds that it is perilous, ignoring the fact that the roads are made more dangerous by virtue of their having to cope with the diurnal choking of cars, people carriers and whatnot ferrying children to and from school.

AFTERWORD

In August 1965, I saw a performance of Aeschylus' *The Persians* in the Herodos Atticus theatre below the Acropolis in Athens. The play celebrates the great victory of the entire fleet of 200 Athenian triremes over the 1,000 ships of the invading Persian armada in Salamis Bay in 480 BC. Aechylus had fought at the battle of Marathon ten years earlier against Darius' invasion, and he describes the savagery of the sea action from sharp, firsthand experience of the violence of war. The Persian Messenger reports to Queen Atossa in the royal palace in Susa, giving a graphic account of the battle, the loss of the fleet, her son Xerxes' crushing defeat. Suddenly, the entire audience, it seemed, leapt to its feet round and below me and cheered and bellowed and stamped and clapped. What was going on ? Luckily, an American sitting just in front of me understood Modern Greek and told his neighbour that Queen Atossa, puzzled about these far-off people, the Athenians, who had just annihilated the might of the Persian navy, asks the Messenger:

> *Atossa: Who herds them into battle? What absolute master do they obey?*
> *[The Great King of Persia ruled as an absolute despot and the foot soldiers of the Persian horde were often whipped and cudgelled into the fighting line.]*
> *The Messenger: They are slaves to no man, they acknowledge no master.*
> *Atossa (in disbelief): And can they resist invasion without any master?*
> *Messenger: Just as they destroyed Darius' vast and noble army.*

It was hearing these lines that brought the Greeks to their feet in jubilant acclamation of their glorious past, their sense of history, their stubborn belief that being Greek still marked them out as something special. Indeed, they were the first of the non-aligned states in Europe to ally with the British against the Axis forces. Metaxas' famous

Ochi, No, is typical of that blunt defiance, that *Greekness*, and it is always celebrated on Ochi Day. [36]

However, on that evening in 1965 when the Athenians hollered and roared, Greece had no government, the country was in chaos, the air in Constitution Square had made my eyes water with the residue of tear gas from the suppression of recent rioting and a taxi driver had told me everything was going to hell and then laughed. In less than two years, Greece would be enslaved in the grip of a junta of army colonels, despots for sure. Against this background, the blustering acclaim of Aeschylus' line seems to me not far off a similar nostalgic absurdity in the British pretence of being a world power which festered for so long after the War. It was isolationism imbued with arrogance, together with a myopic clinging onto what had gone for ever. Despite the bankruptcy caused by the War and aggravated by the continued heavy expenditure on armaments, on overseas military postings and the disintegration of her colonial Empire, Britain, like the bombed-out shops in London, kept insisting that she was still 'Open for Business'. Instead, 'Ichabod, Ichabod,' the peacetime politicians should have been saying, 'the glory is departed, *but*, a new role beckons: Europe.' They did not; their assessment leaned more on Britannia still ruling the waves and an attitude of superiority engendered by the past and blinkered to the present reality. Shades of that famous jingoistic headline in *The Times*: 'Fog in Channel. Europe cut off,' or the occasion when an overnight train travelling across Europe halted at a station; after a certain amount of nocturnal banging and shouting a window in one of the sleeping compartments shot up to reveal a bilious, florid-faced individual who barked to the offending nuisance: 'I say, do you mind being quiet out there? There are English people inside trying to get some sleep.'

---

[36] When I rowed in the first sea trials of the reconstructed Athenian trireme in 1987, I thought much about Salamis and told a particular friend, Iannis Manuelides, a highly sophisticated Athenian, educated at Cambridge and Harvard, that I simply didn't know how those men did what they had done. 'Simple,' he said, with a smile, 'they were Greek,' an answer both irrational and succinctly true. He and I celebrated that year's Ochi Day in a *Turkish* restaurant in Bayswater. Iannis explained that his family, originally Byzantine Greeks, had been going there for years and were favoured customers.

Peter Ustinov recounts how, as a young schoolboy, he was shown a poster of Jesus showing a Boy Scout a map of the World and smiling benignly at the areas coloured pink, the British Empire. That summed it up: 'Most of it is ours and God wanted us to have it and to keep it.' Ustinov was not fooled. So many were.

Resentment at the continued existence of the British Empire was not confined to its subject peoples. During the war, German occupying forces in France posted propaganda notices denouncing Britain's continued domination of the world map precisely to alienate the French. Germany had been stripped of her own empire after the First World War and Hitler's call for *lebensraum* was a calculated gibe at Britain's vast colonial holdings. This was sharpened by his personal bitterness at the humiliation meted out to Austria, the country of his birth: the huge Austro-Hungarian Empire had been broken up by the terms of the Treaty of Versailles. When, on 12 March 1938, troops of Hitler's Wehrmacht and the Waffen SS marched across the German-Austrian border and on into the old imperial capital Vienna to annexe the country once more into the Germanic bloc in central Europe – the *Anschluss* – they were heartily cheered by many who saw the glory returned in blessed triumph.

Germany's imperial high-seas fleet – sixty-nine ships, from battleships to destroyers - had surrendered to the Royal Navy in Scapa Flow in November, 1918 and, the following June, their crews, bored and mutinous, scuttled what had been the pride of the German navy. The widely perceived continuing role of Britain's Royal Navy as a universal maritime police force without rival and answerable only to London stuck in the craw of many who believed that the pink patches on the world map were a continuing anachronistic affront.

Most of Britain's colonial possessions had been given independence within some 15 years of the end of the War, and by 1971 all her bases East of Suez had been evacuated. This emphatically spelled the finish of this island nation's role as a world power, even if not as a world leader. And yet, despite a huge shift in the base of what power Britain did retain, the hauteur of the imperial past lingered on. Having given India its independence, the belief was that the new Commonwealth of former colonies, now free states, would seamlessly replace the vanished Empire. Churchill had spoken of Britain's three-fold role as a global leader: as head of the Commonwealth, that special compact of allegiance to the British sovereign; as the country which alone had stood against Hitler's Germany throughout and must, therefore, claim respect as Europe's saviour; and as one of the principal members of NATO, particularly in the context of her special relationship with the USA. Each had significance separately, but the conflicts of interest inherent in juggling all three at once were very damaging.

 In 1963, General de Gaulle, formerly leader of the Free French Army, now the French President, declared that he would veto Britain's first tentative application in 1961 to join what was then called the European Economic Community. Harold Macmillan, as Prime Minister, was convinced that Britain's deepest loyalties were to America, whose influence and intrusive presence in Europe De Gaulle loathed. Whereas Britain *had* played a central, crucial role in the defeat of Hitler, she seemed, nevertheless, compromised afterwards. A story about the two men and their wives meeting privately nicely illustrates the kind of cross-Channel misunderstandings which bedevilled relations at the time – as when the otherwise punctilious Hugh Gaitskell, leader of the Labour Party, introduced the mayor of Berlin, Willy Brandt, future socialist Chancellor of Germany, in 1962 as 'our friend from overseas'.

Away from the antagonisms of international politics, De Gaulle and Macmillan met and were talking about what each would do when they retired from politics. Write their memoirs, probably. Following suit, Mrs Macmillan asked Mme de Gaulle what *she* hoped for after leaving the Elysée Palace. 'A penis' she replied. There was a yawning pause, blushes. The General, not one whit fussed by the somewhat risqué gaucherie, intervened and explained, in an accent marginally closer to the original English, that his wife was actually hankering after *'appinness*.

Given that several countries of Europe had been consistently tearing lumps out of other weaker European states for centuries and that twice, within the space of 20 years, the continental war had spilled over to embroil much of the rest of the planet, the initial impulse to European union – really to obviate any possible recurrence of such monstrous calamity – was not merely sound, but imperative, urgent. The failure of the League of Nations after the First World War and the punitive, humiliating terms of the Treaty of Versailles imposed on the aggressor, Germany (at France's insistence), had made the Second World War if not inevitable, certainly probable. Therefore, a political union reinforced by economic ties was a not merely a desirable, but a necessary investment in the defence of European integrity. However, this alarmed British instincts which were to preserve its trade commitments with America, its continuing tariff agreements with the countries of the Commonwealth and, most injuriously, a radical dread of surrendering its sovereignty and constitution, its unwritten constitution to – heaven forbid – France and Germany.

The satirists were sceptical, too. As Tom Lehrer wrote:

Once all the Germans were warlike and mean
But that couldn't happen again.
We taught them a lesson in 1919
And they've hardly bothered us since then . . .
We've got the missiles, peace to determine
And one of the fingers on the button will be German.

MLF – 'Multi-lateral Force' – 1963.

De Gaulle's opposition apart, the opportunity was lost and the repercussions still impede Britain's fully committed membership of the European Union, on spurious grounds of hoity-toity individuality and sovereign independence against the mush of federalism. Moreover, whilst the beaten nations – Germany, Italy, Japan – were compelled, willy-nilly, to start their economic recovery from scratch, to rebuild their industrial base anew, to apply fresh thinking, new practices, and thus began steadily to thrive, unburdened with the need to maintain a large army, air force and navy, a massive arsenal as well as the cost of foreign policing, Britain continued to fund all the trappings and onus of her former role as world power on the budget of an impoverished nation.

The Suez débacle in 1956 amply demonstrates the delusion at the core of British governmental thinking then as the wicked, the illegal folly of the war in Iraq does today.

Soaring inflation and endless industrial disputes – recrudescence of the class struggle – further hit post-war British manufacturing and, despite a ministerial call for harmony, *In Place of Strife* (the title of the 1967 White Paper from the Secretary of State for Employment and Productivity, Barbara Castle), bosses and workers by and large remained at loggerheads. Entrepreneurial skills there were in abundance, but management frequently failed to address the new flux in society, the need for cooperation rather than rigid hierarchy. Raleigh, for instance, insisted that all its trainee managers should be university graduates, no matter that they didn't know a pump from a down tube. The vision of equality held out by the Labour party in the 1945 election did not materialise. The age-old suspicions about London and government tainted attitudes across the country, especially in the industrial midlands and north. What did London care about them? All they had got from London were hiked taxes and the call-up to war.

The optimism of this young officer speaking about the wonderful spirit that obtained in the Eighth Army, with which he had served, was to be cruelly dashed:

> *They [the Labour party] stand for a square deal for you and me, with food, a house and a job for all who will do it. They stand for everybody having an equal chance and for more even distribution of the wealth of the world – not cigars at the Ritz and starvation at the Rhondda, not duck at the Berkeley and the dole at Barrow.*

Paying such dreams an apathetic lip service, the sclerotic old order, the vested interests of the establishment, made sure that nothing so egalitarian as this could happen and viewed the dread European Community much in the way that toffs always regarded 'trade': grubby and irredeemably proletarian.

Bob Chicken, staunch European, has stuck to his loyalty to the United Kingdom and Europe against the onslaught from the Far East, the economic blitzkrieg from Shimano and the rest. His connexion with the principle continental suppliers, as detailed in this book, simply reinforced a compelling belief that Britain was always and should still be central to the fortunes of Europe as a whole. His espousal of the values for which the many men and women of the British forces fought in the Second World War is an abiding motive. His belief in the unity of Europe, for political as well as economic reasons, underpins his commercial ethic and vision and, when the EEC became the EU, he adopted the twelve stars of united Europe for the Chicken company. It was more than mere symbolism. What failed faith lay behind the refusal of the UK government to join the single currency. In the mid-90s, the £ stood at 1.75 against the Euro; at the time of writing it is 1.42, a figure not much bandied about.

He has been a supporter of the Liberal Party for most of his life and is increasingly committed to and involved with the party's agenda, both domestic and international, not least because of the Liberal Democrat's full-hearted espousal of Europe and their forthright belief that Britain should take a fully integrated role in the EU, not hover about the fringes. The two other main parties have all along been tentative, indecisive, timid, in their resistance to full partnership. They have shilly-shallied. They have preached engagement while practising disaffection. As a result, in the perception of the British public, Europe, the very idea of Europe, is hedged round with suspicion, with distaste, even xenophobia. The negative spirit of isolationism lives on and we teeter between a hesitant 'maybe' to Europe and an incautious, a thoughtless, an injurious 'yes, oh yes,' to America, most recently and regrettably demonstrated in the invasion of Iraq for which there was, plainly, no legal justification, moral need, or practical purpose. A decision made in camera and against public opinion and national interest. A recruiting campaign for international terrorism. An unmitigated and shameful disaster. The Liberals alone stood out against it from the start.

I am one of a generation which, for the first time in recorded history, has had the good fortune never to have been required to go to war or even to have come close to being called into the armed forces. We are the generation who inherited peace, a peace for which our parents fought hard, and I, at any rate, believed from my young manhood that it was incumbent upon us, our deepest responsibility, to manage that peace. It is utterly beyond my comprehension that British politics is bedevilled still by men – and women – who will go to war on on the flimsiest and most tainted of pretexts. Bob, like many others whose own young manhood was lost to the grisly experience of war, had no option of avoiding combat. His passion for peace is, therefore, grounded in bitter memory of friends lost and the harrowing traumas of violent conflict. On the question of the war in Iraq, the Liberal-Democrats have stood fast, in their doughty exception to the vote *in* the House and their clear reflexion of the vast majority of opinion *outside* the House. This stance is intelligent, humane, rational. It has also proved, in the light of the government's flagrant mendacity, to be honourable. It is part and parcel of their general willingness to step forward into a better understanding of this country's place in the world as it is.

For, on the central issue which confronts Britain today, the Liberal Democrats are unequivocal: our future lies with and in Europe; failure to accept and embrace this is, and always has been, ruinous; the little island mentality does no service to Britain's honourable past as steadfast opponent to tyranny and fascism. The world has changed. Britain must change too, instead of either harking back to the past glory (long gone) or else slavishly battening onto the once-steady special relationship with America (compromised). Bob is staunch in his support of the Liberal-Democrat will and desire for joining common cause with Britain's natural partners, both commercial and geopolitical, in Europe.

It is also the fact that the Liberal Democrats are, pro rata, the liveliest supporters of the All-party Parliamentary Cycling Group with 23 members; Labour, with vastly more MPs, has 39 and the Tories, 16.

Receiving a commemorative gift to mark his half century of membership of the oldest cycle club in the world, The Pickwick Bicycle Club, on 2 December 2004, and in recognition of his peerless contribution to the cycle industry and sport in this country, Bob said: 'I don't think it's necessary. It's unwarranted, but that's life.'

His membership of the Pickwick, of which he was President in 1983, emphasises an unmoving principle in Bob's approach to business, that of trust built on good relationships and, in many cases, deep friendship. And, as the saying goes, 'The table wins us more friends than does kindly feeling'.

Ah, the lunches and dinners.

Whether as a member (or President, 1981-2) of the Centenary Club, founded in 1939, or the Pedal Club (President 2000) founded in 1941 by cycling officials and journalists, Bob has waxed strong in the company of friends and associates. Conviviality is the key and dinner lubricates business.

The Pickwick meets twice yearly for lunch and a round of very English eccentric ritual, nicely reminiscent of the great Samuel Pickwick, him of *The Pickwick Papers*.

In 1694, a baby, abandoned by the side of the Oxford-Bath coaching road near Pickwick in Wiltshire, was taken to a house in Corsham. The foundling's benefactors christened him Moses, after the baby in the bulrushes, and Pickwick for the place of his rescue. One of his descendants, another Moses Pickwick, born in 1782, became owner of a famous line of coaches and proprietor of The White Hart (a coaching inn) in the centre of Bath, home, remember, of Bob's Pickwick sobriquet, Angelo Cyrus Bantam. Dickens visited Bath frequently to see his friend Walter Savage Landor, the poet:

> *I strove with none; for none was worth my strife;*
> *Nature I loved and next to Nature, Art;*
> *I warmed both hands before the fire of life;*
> *It sinks, and I am ready to depart.*
>
> *(I Strove with None)*

Business was brisk. Pickwick's coaches plied routes as far north as Liverpool and Holyhead and points in between; south to Porstmouth and Southampton in direct communication with the mail packets to Le Havre and Caen in Normandy; to Weymouth for the packets to the Channel Isles; in all some twenty-four coaches every day, forwarding 'Passengers and Parcels . . . with the greatest despatch . . . to all parts of the Kingdom' as well as an additional service of 'Black Carriages and Horses for Funerals'.

After the publication of Dickens' novel, the real Pickwick's business went into decline and, bridling at the faintly mocking portrait of the fictional character, an unworldly screwball with a decidedly epicurean approach to life, the bustling, hard-nosed coach-owner blamed his failing commerce on the adverse publicity in tuppenny fiction which painted him as a poltroon. Vanity acceded to a lack of commercial realism. The world was changing and Pickwick was not changing with it. A familiar story. For, in truth, the advent of the railways heralded and then hastened on the demise of the coaching runs and the inns en route which catered to the coach passengers, many of them bypassed by the iron roads which began to lattice the country.

The Pickwick Bicycle Club was formed on 22 June 1870 by six cycling enthusiasts who met at the Downs Hotel, Hackney Downs (when they were still open meadows) in East London. The coincidental death of Charles Dickens a week earlier led to the choice of name, in celebration of the genial Mr Pickwick's fondness for fostering good fellowship good food and drink, revelry and sociability. The stated aims of the club are: 'a. The encouragement of cycling, Dickensian fellowship and the Pickwickian art of being happy by communicating happiness,' and 'b. To visit, as a Club, places of interest under the command of the Captain or an appointed substitute.'

In the early days, that entailed an energetic programme of weekend runs into Kent, Cambridgeshire, Buckinghamshire, Sussex, Oxford, Hertfordshire. Sadly, none of the pubs and hotels the club visited features among the many which do crop up in Dickens' fiction but, I wonder if they at least stopped at the Upware Inn near Wicken Fen in Lincolnshire, whose outer wall (according to the February 1912 issue of *Cycling*) sported a large notice outside reading, in black letters: 'Five miles from anywhere. No hurry' which seems to strike exactly the right note.

The Centenary Club and the Pedal Club also organise annual cycling forays in accord with the Centenary Club's object of 'active participation in cycling and social intercourse'. The early bicycles were seen above all as a means to companionship, 'companionable all the way' as Dickens puts it in *The Pickwick Papers*. The short-lived Sociable tricycle even allowed partners to ride side by side.

The municipal borough of Harrogate stands in what was called the West Riding of Yorkshire before the idiotic appellations introduced by the Heath government in the early 70s threw up the bastard nonentity of Richmondshire, Malvernshire and their ilk. Harrogate lies at about 400 feet above sea level on the Pennine foothills, Blubberhouses Moor to the west and the Vale of York to the east. Harrogate became known as 'the English Spa' following the discovery first of chalybeate (iron-rich) springs in the Tewit well towards the end of the sixteenth century and, subsequently, sulphur and saline springs in and around the centre – some eighty in all for bathing and drinking. A common, called the Stray, secured by act of parliament from ever being built upon, stretches for 200 acres in front of the town's main line of houses and it was on the Stray, during the 1870s that cyclists began to hold Meets. (Stray in northern usage refers to the right of allowing cattle to stray and feed on common land.) These Meets on the Stray led to the formation of the Bicycle Touring Club (forerunner of the CTC) in Harrogate in 1878. Nearly 100 years later, the Harrogate Show and Festival of races came into being.

In the 1930s there were two cycle shows in London: the Lightweight Cycle Show held at the Horticultural Hall in Westminster and, a month later, the British Manufacturers' Union show in Olympia. In 1938, having seen off the Lightweight, the Olympia show upped and moved to the enormous hangar of Earls Court for a combined exhibition with motor cycles, the single trade show for bicycles in the UK.

Outside the trade, the York Rally, founded by a group of Yorkshire CTC enthusiasts in 1945, has become a steadfast annual fixture in the calendar, a bumper weekend of fun and serious cyclism. Yorkshire has been one of the great heartlands of cycling in Britain, and Harrogate's role in fostering cycling, for recreation and sport, has been distinguished. In 1956, it launched its French Week to celebrate the twinning of the town with Luchon, still perhaps the most fashionable of the French Pyrenean resorts, home to sulphurous and radioactive springs, popular since Roman times and a frequent port of call for the Tour de France. Of course there had to be a cycle race (promoted by the Yorkshire Road Club) and the organisers decided to make it a woman's event, including a French team led by the French champion, Lily Herse. The circuit included six ascents of the notorious steep incline of Pot Bank – 500 yards on Pennypot Lane between Harrogate and Pateley Bridge to winnow out anyone faltering – and the winner was Millie Robinson of the Isle of Man.

The inaugural 8-day Harrogate Festival of Cycling with accompanying trade show was heralded in the *Cycling Weekly* issue of 21 June 1975: 'Welcome to Harrogate. Sport and Industry combine under our banner.' As well as the commercial display of components and bikes in the town's Exhibition Hall there were time trials, road races, touring rides. By 1980, 132 exhibitors – dealers and companies – attended the show and the Great Yorkshire Classic, a three-stage road race, was established.

RJC were firm supporters of the Harrogate Show but became increasingly vexed that the trade turned up, did their business and then simply melted away. This was crazy. No social? As Peter Crabtree, formerly a prominent bicycle wholesaler, put it to me: 'The Chickens brought a much-needed touch of class to the industry. There were one or two others of a more enlightened attitude than the general run of drab, stuffy, old-school individuals who were too busy puffing their own importance to indulge in a bit of levity, but the Chickens – and Bob was the prime mover – had personality, intelligence and style. They were a breath of fresh air; they got things done. What a contrast to some of the old lags. I had a go at Miller, boss of Miller's Dynamos between Glasgow and Edinburgh when we were short of dynamos. Miller was on the council of the Bicycle Association, typical committee man, full of himself sitting up there. I buttonholed him after a meeting and told him we needed dynamos and had needed them for ages, what was he going to do about it? He just shrugged his shoulders and said they were short of a few components as if having to scrabble around for bits and pieces was beneath him now he was a *councillor*. No oomph. Complacent and dead on their feet, most of them.

'The Chickens were always ready to invest, they brought light into a dim moribund world. One time, a bunch of us wholesalers turned up at the famous Penguin and Fishbowl for an open day and Cedric and Robert put on a presentation. But they didn't do the usual dull old rigmarole with graphs and spreadsheets and statistics and figures, they put on a double act, pretty well unrehearsed, apparently, but it was hilarious. This was before TV chat shows got going and it was brilliant, original and, somehow, typical of the Chickens' way of doing things. Never frightened to go for something new, a bit out of the way, even risky. What a hoot. Their enthusiasm is infectious and they were always great party people, sparkling company. They worked hard but they knew how to entertain, too. That was all part of what made Bob one of the most respected people in the industry.'

One can almost hear Bob's thought processes. What's the trouble with the Harrogate Show? The trouble with the Harrogate Show is that there's no *dinner*. *Quod, my boys, erat demonstrandum*. Ergo, there will *be* a dinner. And so it came to pass, highlight of the Harrogate Show, the Chicken (sponsor not menu) Dinner, by invitation to around a hundred in the trade, the cream of the cream, all paid for by RJC, in the Ballroom of the Crown Hotel, Harrogate. For sure it was a grand – and useful – PR opportunity for the Chicken enterprise, but a mark, too, of their great generosity and the importance they placed on the fraternal feelings that bound them all, the sense that they were friends as well as being in commerce.

The question of cycle shows in Britain has been vexed. Earls Court, too cavernous? Harrogate, too localised? UK too marginal in the world of the cycle industry? Harrogate went into a decline as support for professional cycle racing waned. The local authority no longer wanted the show in the town itself and in the early '80s it moved into what proved to be its graveyard, the Great Yorkshire Showground. The public still came but the trade lost interest and the show finished in 1988. And it was precisely because the public came that Raleigh pulled out; they wanted no truck with the people who rode the bikes, only with those who sold them. Their withdrawal disheartened most of the others in the trade.

The disappearance of the Harrogate National Cycle Show left Britain without an annual bicycle exhibition. This had to be remedied and Bob began to work on the possibility of staging a truly international bicycle exhibition as close as possible to the heart of London. Harrogate may have been good for the trade and people in the north, but London offered a much larger catchment. Over 40 per cent of CTC and BCF members lived in the south-east. London was the best place to attract both national and international media coverage together with overseas as well as UK visitors.

The Bolshoi Ballet visited London in 1988 and performed at the Business Design Centre, formerly the Royal Agricultural Hall in Islington (see page 35). Christina loved the ballet, Bob bought tickets and, during the performance, Bob was captivated not only by the Russian dance company but by the magnificence of the venue, the splendour of its open wrought-iron framed construction, the ambiance. An idea sparked in the back of his mind: this was the perfect place in which to house an impressive cycle show. He went back to the building once, twice and was convinced: he had found his venue, a building acknowledged as 'London's Jewel in the Crown' by *The Times* Exhibition report in the late 1980s, a stunning example of Victorian commercial architecture with superb facilities, on-site parking for 270 cars, NCP car parks adjacent, and easy access by tube and bus.

Unfortunately, the majority of the Bicycle Association, and specifically Raleigh Industries, spurned the notion of a show to which the public would have access and, with most constituent members of the body against him, Bob accepted defeat. Later, in 1991, he put the idea again to the B.A but once more it was voted out.

In 1992, Bob decided that Raleigh was the principle stumbling block and that if he was to get a show on he would have to discount them, if necessary, and take the financial risk himself. However, he did finally get the support of Raleigh's Marketing Director, Yvonne Rix and the MD Howard Knight. He shook hands on the agreement with Knight and the wheels began to turn. He laid out the money to secure the show, the hall, the publicity campaign. As the brochures for IBEX, the International Bicycle Exhibition, put it: 'The time is right . . . The place is right . . . The mix is right . . . The visitors are right . . . The price is right.' There would be free seminars and workshop programmes as part of the 'unique opportunity to convert thousands of visitors to cycling'. Sport for Television had been invited to promote up to three events around the dates of the show whose purpose was to promote the joys of cycling and its great benefits.

Four days after he had shaken hands with Knight, the phone rang. It was Knight. Terribly apologetic, what could he say, had a meeting with his Sales Director, Roger Dear, tried to persuade him this show was to everyone's advantage – great for the industry, retailers, customers – but Dear was adamant: no non-trade involvement, Raleigh was not in the business of exhibiting their products to the general public. That was what dealers were for. Raleigh's job was to make the stuff not flaunt it like clothes on a catwalk. Bob listened in amazement that gave way to anger which erupted in fury and a salvo of expletives. The handset might well have caught fire so incandescent was he at this unconscionable breach of faith. The man was Managing Director, he'd given his word. It didn't even have to be his solemn word and certainly not corroborated by hands on the Bible. Word was word and handshake was deal done. This was barefaced unmitigated perfidy, a disgrace to friendship.

Several other manufacturers, but not all, deserted with Raleigh. The backbone of the trade commitment had gone, the main players abandoned, and Bob refused to put on a second-rate show and deprive the public of what would have been the full spectrum of all the bicycle industry had to offer. With heavy heart and deep reluctance, Bob cancelled the show. The contract agreement with the Business Design Centre, which he had signed on earnest of Knight's agreement that Raleigh would show, left him dangling and substantially – several tens of thousands of pounds – in debt.

On occasions the credo by which we live seems to mock us. For a brief while it seemed to Bob that all he was holding firm to was the huge financial indebtedness with which someone else's dishonour had saddled him. However, his naturally buoyant spirit would not be submerged by disappointment or someone else's faithlessness. He never gave up the vision and was soon beavering away, seeking support for a show despite the financial losses he had already sustained. He was determined, too, that should he get the show on with the backing of the Bicycle Association , and that all profits accruing would be donated to that organisation whose brief is to stimulate interest in and encouragement– practical encouragement by way of official action – of cycling in the UK.

With the active help of Carlton Reid, editor of *Bikebiz.com*, Bob circulated a questionnaire to every cycle dealer throughout the UK. The response was cheery – the great majority were in enthusiastic favour of a Trade/Public Bicycle Exhibition to be staged at the Business Design Centre. Bob didn't stop there: he lobbied everywhere, in every possible area of interest, drumming up *yeas* in what had been for too long a climate of *nays*. He went the rounds of dealers, manufacturers, trade associations, journalists; he badgered and cajoled; he persuaded and pushed. At last, in a meeting in 1993, he persuaded the Chairman of the Business Design Centre, Jack Morris, and his Brother Andrew that now was the moment, and they must seize it. Convinced that it must succeed, Bob sought to take out a 25-percent equity share in the venture, only to be told that this was not permissible. On the other hand, sensible of Bob's losses and the betrayal which occasioned them, they undertook to repay Bob a handsome percentage of his original stake on the first, aborted attempt and they honoured the pledge.

Morris recalls: 'Bob had this harebrained idea of running an international bicycle exhibition, or IBEX as he called it. Being great visionaries, we listened politely, thought "it'll never get off the ground" and got back to our business. But we didn't bargain for Bob. His tenacity and love for the industry is legendary. He spent years convincing us and the industry that his vision should become a reality.'

The decision to hold the exhibition was made in May 2001. Morris asked Bob if he could recommend a knowledgeable and experienced individual from within the industry to organise the event. By coincidence, the former Olympic pursuit bronze medallist Mick Bennett, who had ridden for Bob's Weinmann-Raleigh pro team, had recently severed his association with Alan Rushton, organiser of the Tour of Britain. He contacted him, Bennett agreed and the die was cast.

Cycle 2002 ran from 26-29 September. On the evening of the show's opening day, Bob arrived at Frederick's restaurant in Islington, expecting to enjoy a quiet supper with Dominic Jones, the new Managing Director of the B.D.C. and Mick Bennett. As he walked into the upstairs private dining room, the assembled company of thirty of his friends, prominent in the world of cycling – industry, journalism, luminaries of the clubs of which he is a member, let rip with 'For he's a jolly good fellow . . . ' As Bob wiped away his own tears, his dear friend Monty Young was similarly moved. Their association goes back to the early days of Condor Cycles: one of the first business cheques Monty had was from Bob. A month or so went by and the cheque still hadn't been cleared. Bob rang to find out what was going on. Monty said: 'I'm not going to bank it. I've framed it. It's hanging on the wall. For luck.' It's there to this day – same cheque, new premises.

Speaking at that dinner, Morris said of Bob's tenacity: 'I think it's fair to say that Cycle 2002 wouldn't have happened without him . . . He never gave up until, as all his friends in this room will understand, his infectious enthusiasm caught on and we all got on board with him.' Then, turning to Bob he concluded: 'You are a very special man, a one-off, and tonight we honour and thank you for the contribution you have made to the industry and to us as your friends and colleagues. Everybody in this room has been enriched by knowing you. You have a lot to be proud of and I hope your vim and vigour will continue to inspire us for many years to come.'

A saying current in the navy in Nelson's time, a demotic form of 'England expects' perhaps, Hold Fast, chimes nicely with the motto of Bob's school, *Tenez Ferme*. Not a bad note to end on.

R.J.CHICKEN TODAY

In the late 1990s, Cedric and Robert drew three conclusions they deemed vital to the continuation of RJC: bulk storage being no longer necessary, their Kensworth facility was too big for future needs; the failure to utilise the available space for third party storage during the transporting days had cost much for little return; all available cheap products were being imported from the Far East, moreover, their lead times were far quicker than those of the European companies who had contrived to stay afloat. The Chicken company had endeavoured, unsuccessfully, to compete at the lower end of the market both with cheaper European products and a certain amount from the Far East purchased through a friendly contact. However, the vast majority of UK dealers did not associate Chicken with low-end components and stayed loyal to their long-established wholesalers for such material. However, they still bought high quality items from Chicken, such as SELCOF seat pins and TA rings, because Chicken provided an unbeatable service as well as a comprehensive range of sizes and patterns.

The Bisley works was sold on 8 December 1997.

In the months leading up to the sale, Cedric and Robert had cleared thousands of pounds' worth of cheap goods – notably 12" green pumps and tyres from the Czech Republic – for which there was no space in the original warehouse (now held on a lease back) which they had first used in 1981. The first year's trading under the slimmed-down operation was healthy: RJC consolidated and began to analyse the many changes which the market had undergone vis à vis where their own best interests lay. Alesa of Belgium had gone but Mavic was still riding high and they knew that their attachment to so prestigious a marque would not only be good financially but would continue to confirm their status as dependable dealers in the very best quality of European and American componentry, such as Selle Italia (saddles) and Time (frames, pedals etc). They offered superior levels of service and the trade responded positively. Dealers came to Chicken and Sons because they not only had a ready supply of stock but their prices were fair. On the back of this newly instilled confidence in the Chicken name, the company acquired a number of other exclusive brands.

Their first essay in house marketing was in the promotion of Tifosi bikes. The success of this venture gave the company a tremendous boost, not least in enhancing the image of their other brands. The Tifosi bikes are fitted with 3T bars and stems, Vredestein tyres, Selcof headsets, Selle Italia saddles, Time forks, TA bottles and cages, Mavic rims and hubs. The raw frames are stocked in Belgium which is where they are painted, in one of the best paint shops in Europe. To begin with, the extended lead time from Campagnolo forced Chicken to fit Shimano groupsets, but before long, the Chicken brothers sounded out the illustrious Italian component-makers and from 2002 the Tifosi bikes – highly praised in the cycling press for performace and value – have been adorned with Campagnolo groupsets. The experience with Mavic helped in this. Not only did the Campagnolo components perform well, but the perceived excellence of the name – and the products – encouraged interest and purchase. As ever, Chicken and Sons stocked in depth, set fair prices and secured helathy business returns.

In 2004, Chicken added another estimable name to their portfolio, that of Cinelli, manufacturers of high-grades handlebars and stems, and in 2005 they promoted Transfil, a French family-run company making high quality carbon and regular stainless gear and brake cables and casings, with whom they had dealt on a lower key level for some seven years.

They continue to expand. For example, under the Tifosi brand they now offer two qualities of bike bag and, in 2005 they secured an exclusive distributorship for one of the best-known brand names in the world, Adidas. This is a singular success in what has become a pattern in the evolution of RJ Chicken: parting company with a number of suppliers who are still active, taking a step forward each time this was forced on them. In 2002, the UK-based EBC disc brake company assigned sole agency to RJC and KMC chain distributors,the largest manufacturer of chains in the world, assigned part agency for their products. Parting company with any manufacturer is a sad matter but change is an essential stimulus to renewed energy and enterprise.

Some things emphatically do not change: the companies with whom the Chickens work enjoy a close relationship with the human beings in the business, not simply with the order books and the fax machines. Some of the long-term associations survive: SKS pumps and mudguards remain a staple for the Chicken stock, as do the Pletscher (of Switzerland) kickstands and the French Velox rim tape.

As Robert put it to me, 'we are still in there, having learnt lessons and grown enormously in stature as a company. The Tour de France [2005] has just started and the winner may just come in on a Time bike. The future is healthy for us and, just imagine what it would mean for us, a Time win'.

Appendix

The physiology behind a fast sprint finish is primarily genetic. Sid, although he doesn't look quite the same now, had a very powerful build and youth on his side. He was genetically blessed with a reasonable percentage of fast twitch muscle fibres in his body, especially in the strong quadriceps group and the gluteals – the prime muscles used for sprinting on a bike. Take one look at the track riders of today and you see what I mean about bulk. They also do plenty of specific training to train the fast twitch muscle fibres to store glycogen – the stored form of glucose – sugar in its simplest form, and the only form that the body can use to create its own energy in the form of ATP – adenosine tri-phosphate.

Muscles create energy in three different ways:

1. Aerobically. Energy produced this way lasts longer without painful side effects. No matter what your sport it is important to have a good aerobic system – good heart, lung and circulatory system added to the ability to transfer and create energy with three essential ingredients – oxygen, free fatty acids and glucose, in the mitochondria, the little muscle factories around the muscle fibre cells. At the end of a long event, no matter how good your fast twitch muscles are, they would not be much good because without a decent aerobic system you would have used up all the stores of glycogen along the way. There would be nothing left for the finish and you would have been lucky to have got there anyway. So aerobic energy is vital for any performance.

2. Anaerobically, primarily by using fast twitch muscle fibres plus stored sugar in the form of glycogen. We do not work anaerobically much in general levels of work, but at a higher percentage of physical effort this method of producing energy is vital. Little sprints along the way, for example, deplete anaerobic stores. The waste product is lactic acid – painful – which will eventually clog the muscle and prevent if from being able to contract. Two minutes at 100% effort will use up all the glycogen that we can store.

3. In the final dash to the line, CP – creatine phosphate – which is stored in all muscle fibres, can be reconstituted into ATP very quickly indeed, but we have only around 10 seconds worth at 100% effort. At the end of the race for the sprint it is likely that all three systems are working flat out, so if you want to be a good sprinter the training done needs to focus on improving all three methods of energy production and efficiency. But ultimately, some people are born with sprinters legs and others are mountain climbers.

SOURCES
Bob Chicken, *Diaries,* S.O. Book 135, newspaper cuttings and personal records

BOOKS

Addison, Paul, *Now the War is Over* (Cape: BBC Publications 1985)

Alderson, Frederick, *Bicycling, a History* (David & Charles, 1972)

Arnold, Guy, *Britain Since 1945* (Cassell, 1995)

Asher, Michael, *Lawrence, the uncrowned king of Arabia* (Penguin, 1999)

Bowden, Gregory Houston, *The Story of the Raleigh cycle* (W.H. Allen, 1975)

Breckon, Michael (with Kitching, Ron), *A Wheel in Two Worlds* (Nottingham UK; MSS Handling, 1993)

Brera, Gianni, *The Giant and the File* (Campagnolo, 1993)

Durry, Jean, *L'EnCYCLOpédie* (Edita, 1982)

Graves, Robert, *Lawrence and the Arabs* (Jonathan Cape, 1927)

Greene, Jack, and Massignani, Alessandro, *The Naval War in the Mediterranean* (Rockville Center, NY; Sarpdeon, 1998)

Keegan, John, *Intelligence in War* (Hutchinson, 2003)

Laget, Serge, *La Saga du Tour de France* (Gallimard, 1991)

Lewin, Ronald, *Rommel as Military Commander* (Pen & Sword, 1968)

MacMillan, Margaret, *Peacemakers, six months that changed the world* (John Murray, 2001)

McGurn, James, *On Your Bicycle, an illustrated history of cycling* (John Murray, 1987)

Messenger, Chas, *Ride and be DAMNED* (Pedal Publishing, 1998)

Sutton, Richard, *Motor Mania* (Collins & Brown, 1996)

Vian, Sir Philip, *Action this Day* (Frederick Muller, 1960)

Watson, Roderick, and Gray, Martin, *The Penguin Book of the Bicycle* (Penguin, 1978)

Winton, John, *Cunningham, The greatest admiral since Nelson* John Murray, 1998)

Woodman, Richard, *Malta Convoys* (John Murray, 2000)

Rosen, Paul, *Framing Production* (MIT Press, 2002)

PERIODICALS
Cycle and Motor Cycle Trader
Cycle Trader
Cycling Weekly
International Cycle Sport
The Cyclist

Interviews and correspondence with Bob Chicken and his family, friends, industry figures, business colleagues, associates etc.

EDDY MERCKX

Belgian Eddy Merckx is universally acknowledged as the greatest cyclist that has ever lived. He began racing as a novice in 1961 and ended his career as a professional in 1977. During this period, Merckx won 525 races in all, 445 of them as a professional.

In his heydays, Merckx was virtually unbeatable and in the years 1970 to 1973, he won more than 50 races a season – unheard of today.

In 2004 he celebrated his 60th birthday and is still acknowledged as the biggest icon in the sport. He lives near Brussels and runs his own bicycle frame-building business while remaining very passionate about the sport he once dominated.

Here are just *some* of his principle wins.

Stage Races:

Tour de France(F)		1969; 1970; 1971; 1972; 1974.
Tour of Italy:	(I)	1968; 1970; 1972; 1973; 1974.
Tour of Spain:	(Sp)	1973.
Dauphine-Libere: (F)		1971.
Midi-Libre:	(F)	1971.
Paris-Nice:	(F)	1969; 1970; 1971.
Setmana Catalana: (Sp)		1975; 1976.
Tour of Catalunya: (Sp)		1968.
Tour of Sardinia: (I)		1968; 1971; 1973; 1976.
Tour of Switzerland: (Switz)		1974.
Tour of Belgium: (B)		1970; 1971.
Tour of Romandy: (Switz)		1969.
Paris-Luxembourg. (F-Lux)		1970.

Championships and one-day Classic races.

World road race champion:	1967; 1971; 1974.
Belgian road race champion:	1970.
Paris-Roubaix Classic: (F)	1968; 1970; 1973.
Milan-San Remo Classic: (I)	1966; 1967; 1969; 1971; 1972; 1975; 1976.
Tour of Lombardy Classic(I)	1971; 1972.
Liege-Bastogne-Liege(B)	1969; 1971; 1972; 1973; 1975.
Tour of Flanders Classic(B)	1969; 1875.
Paris-Brussels Classic:(B)	1973.
Fleche-Wallone Classic:(B)	1967; 1970; 1972.
Gent-Wevelgem Classic:(B)	1967; 1970; 1972.
Het Volk Classic:(B)	1971; 1973.
Henninger Turm Classic(G)	1971.
Amstel Gold Race Classic:(Hol)	1973;1975.